S0-AAE-714

UNSTOPPABLE ME

Toni Holt Kramer

First published by Dog Ear Publishing
4011 Vincennes Rd
Indianapolis, IN 46268
www.dogearpublishing.net

ISBN: 978-1-4575-5725-5

This book is printed on acid-free paper.

Printed in the United States of America

To my mother, Helen, who encouraged and pushed me
to succeed every day of her life.

To my husband, Bobby, whose love for both of us
made sure her wishes were fulfilled.

And to Donald Trump,
for inspiring me to create the TRUMPETTES USA.

A special thanks to my dear friend Ava Roosevelt,
author of "The Racing Heart", for her help with the editing of my book.

Dear Friend,

It has long been my thought that yesterdays don't have to make your tomorrows, that you just need a dream and the courage to go after it, and don't question what your inner voice whispers to you in the quiet of your day.

My reason to reach out to all of you is to share the amazing and unexpected highs of my incredible life as well as the earthshattering lows that threatened to bring me down. In doing so, my hope is that you will find a connection to your own lives.

I have always strived to make my dreams come true no matter how impossible they may have seemed. My mother was my rock. She played the role of both parents, and had an undefeatable desire to see me succeed.

Her mantra to me was always "If you think it, you can do it."

I have lived my entire life by that one sentence.

Toni

Toni at Mar a Lago, New Year's Eve, 2014.

CHAPTER ONE

Mar-a-Lago

Palm Beach, Florida. New Year's Eve 2014.

The party of the year was in full swing. The place: the Grand Ballroom at Donald Trump's world-famous Mar-a-Lago Club (not yet the Winter White House). The seventeen crystal chandeliers dripped from the gilded ornate ceiling like diamonds. The invited guests glided across the parquet dance floor in their Jimmy Choos and Louboutins. Gowns by Oscar, Carolina, Valentino, and Chanel rustled gently in the night air. Million-dollar jewels from the likes of Graff and Winston sparkled like stars. Champagne flowed like the Atlantic Ocean less than a hundred yards from the cream and gold-colored ballroom Trump had built after he purchased the fabulous seaside mansion, once the private residence of Marjorie Merriweather Post. The caviar was plentiful, as if Russian President Vladimir Putin had flown it to the party himself in his personal jet.

They don't call Palm Beach the home of the rich and famous for nothing.

The paparazzi snapped photos of the glamourous guests as they arrived. The lucky ones would find their photos on the pages of the Palm Beach Shiny Sheet the next morning, immortalized by the Queen Bee of Palm Beach society, columnist Shannon Donnelly. Celebrities like Rod Stewart, Jimmy Buffet, Serena Williams, Martha Stewart, Regis Philbin, Rudy Giuliani, and the former governor of New York, David Patterson, are often part of the dazzling New Year's Eve nightscape.

Nobody puts on a show like The Donald, whether it's at Mar-a-Lago or on his highly rated former TV series *Celebrity Apprentice*. The man is a perfectionist. He's a master at knowing how to entertain people. His very demeanor assured everyone that this was going to be an over-the-top night. Like every New Year's Eve at Mar-a-Lago.

Donald's beautiful, exotic-looking wife, Melania, reigned supreme as the empress of Mar-a-Lago. Born in Slovenia, the stunning former model and jewelry designer married Donald in a highly publicized wedding at The Episcopal Church of Bethesda-by-the-Sea in Palm Beach. The year was 2005, the culmination of a multi-year courtship. The event was made even more memorable when Melania walked down the aisle in a two-hundred-thousand-dollar Christian Dior wedding gown.

If you don't believe competition is at the top of every Palm Beach woman's playlist, think again. New Year's Eve brought out the heavy artillery. Diamonds, emeralds, rubies, and sapphires lit up the room like Fourth of July fireworks.

As for the men, they exercised their virility by doing their utmost to prove they were the richest or most powerful man in the room. In Palm Beach no one asks how you got there, nor is anyone going to tell you. But here's a hint: you can always judge a man by the jewelry his wife wears.

Palm Beach is truly a separate world unto itself. I'm happy to call it home for most of the year. The other months are spent at our home in Bel Air, California, just a breath away from the magnificent Bel Air Hotel. And our four-acre estate in Palm Springs, often referred to as a mini-Mar-a-Lago, except it stretches from mountain to mountain instead of sea to lake, like Donald Trump's historic landmark.

It took three years to build Mar-a-Lago, from 1924 to 1927. The 110,000 square-foot mansion has 126 rooms on seventeen prime Palm Beach acres. It was built by Marjorie Merriweather Post, who was married to E. F. Hutton, who founded the powerful stock brokerage in his name in 1904. Actress Dina Merrill was her daughter. When Mrs. Post passed away in 1973, she willed the estate to the United States government as a retreat for future American presidents and foreign dignitaries. It was said that she was a woman who always got what she wanted, and while it took a few years, her dream of Mar-a-Lago becoming the Winter White House would—in 2017—become a reality. A painting of her still hangs in the bar. Ironically, she looks across the room directly at a painting of Donald Trump. Donald, ever the deal maker, paid less than eight million dollars for the estate in 1985.

You don't need a calendar to know when it's spring in Palm Beach. All you need to do is look outside and see the huge car vans loading the

Donald Trump joins Toni and her husband Bobby at Mar a Lago.

Rolls-Royces, Bentleys, Mercedes, and Jaguars for the trip north to the summer homes of the winter residents. By April, most are relieved that the season has come to an end. Most everyone is tired of seeing one another at charity gala after charity gala, and their checkbooks are worn out from making donations.

Another sign the season is winding down is the Palm Beach Airport, where the private jets line up like a flock of birds preparing for the great migration. The most prominent one on the tarmac used to be a Boeing 757, bearing the bold letters TRUMP. In 2017, those bragging rights became the property of Air Force One.

Regardless of what's happening throughout the world, Palm Beach is the go-to destination for those seeking luxury and privacy. It's a four-square-mile island of breathtaking opulence that looks out at the Atlantic Ocean on one side—and the Intracoastal on the other, with three drawbridges that connect it to the rest of civilization. All that's missing are the dragons to guard the castles.

It was recently documented that there are thirty residents of Palm Beach with a net worth of 3.5 billion dollars or more, and that group includes Donald J. Trump. They say money equals power. If that's true, Palm Beach is the hard drive of the country.

Bizarre behavior is no stranger to Palm Beach. In the category of "truth is stranger than fiction," the social life is so important, it has been said that women have put their deceased husbands in the deep freeze until the season is over rather than miss a party. Yes, the beat goes on, at all costs.

For the record, I have the best neighbors. Dmitry Rybolovlev, the Russian billionaire, purchased a 33,000-square-foot waterfront mansion for one hundred million dollars in 2008. He bought the six-acre showplace from, you guessed it, Donald Trump. Dmitry's digs are right across the road from yours truly. The Russian fertilizer tycoon and majority owner of the Monaco Football Club is worth a resounding 7.3 billion dollars.

Dmitry was divorced a few years ago, and the settlement was splashed across headlines around the world. The agreement was consummated in Geneva, Switzerland. His ex, Elena (my mother's real name), reportedly walked away with a whopping four billion dollars. A judge reduced that to 604 million. Even though I flunked math as a kid, that still amounts to approximately twenty-three million dollars per year for every year of their twenty-six-year marriage. Just recently the estate was demolished, and the lots are being sold in the neighborhood of forty million each. Two have gone bye-bye, one more left. Imagine what they'll be worth with homes on them.

Next door to Dmitry is another waterfront special, this one owned by Nelson Peltz, the financial genius and founding partner of Trian Fund Management. Nelson is a frequent guest on CNBC and Fox Business. In addition to his oceanfront property, he owns a three-acre guest estate across the street that I can see from my second-floor bedroom. Like me, Nelson was born in Brooklyn, living proof that more than trees grow there.

Beth and Howard Stern, shock jock and popular TV personality, bought a fifty-million-dollar beachfront home just up the road from all of us. The stunning Beth is a cat-lover, and I know for a fact that anyone with a good cat story can get her attention.

Ava Roosevelt, a former countess and the widow of William Donner Roosevelt, President Franklin Delano Roosevelt's grandson, lives directly across the street from me. We became best friends two days after I moved in. The blonde, blue-eyed Polish beauty dropped her steamy new novel in my mailbox with a note, "Welcome to the neighborhood. Call me." And I did.

We are both driven women, and there isn't a day that goes by that we don't discuss our careers. Ava's thrilling novel, *The Racing Heart,* is a tale of sex and international intrigue set at the 24 Hours of Le Mans, the most prestigious auto race in the world. It wouldn't surprise me if at least some of the story is autobiographical, but I'm not going to say which part. She is now working on making it into a great TV series.

As New Year's Eve came to a close, my husband Bobby leaned close and kissed me. "Don't worry, my darling," he whispered. "The worst year of our lives is just seconds away from being over."

What Bobby was referring to was the stroke suffered by my young son David. I looked at Bobby and broke into a quiet version of an old Judy Garland song. "Forget your sorrows, c'mon get happy. We're headin' into a brand-new year. 2015 here we come!"

I caught a glimpse of Donald Trump out of the corner of my eye. Little did I know then he would be running for president six months later.

CHAPTER TWO

The Trumpettes USA

The desire to learn something new every day is what drives me to find the story within the story. After making my mark in Hollywood, I was looking for another challenge – another goal to achieve. Washington D.C., seemed like the logical next step. Much like Hollywood, Washington is a place where intrigue and corruption are commonplace, and politicians are no different than actors. Both are performers.

For most of my life, I wasn't the least bit interested in politics. I didn't know a leftist from a right-winger. Furthermore, I couldn't have cared less, but my non-political mindset changed drastically a few years ago. I looked around and suddenly realized what was happening to our country. With President Obama at the helm, I saw how things I took for granted were slowly disappearing. Things I never thought I would see were appearing at a rapid pace, and they weren't pretty. I began to pay more attention to what was going on in the world. The more I saw, the more disturbed I became. I knew I had to do something about it. At least I had to try.

Shortly after Bobby and I bought our home in Palm Beach, we joined The Mar-a-Lago Club. It was there I met Donald Trump. As I got to know him, I liked him more and more. I saw a man who was fearless, strong-willed, and kind. A businessman who understood how to make money, a no-nonsense leader with an obsession for detail and perfection. If I had to describe him with a single phrase, it would be: a winner.

Throughout my life I've had psychic visions, many of which have become reality. Because Donald and I were both born under the sign of Gemini, at times – as crazy as it sounds - I felt I could sense what he was thinking. I could feel his genuine love for our country. We Geminis are outgoing, gregarious, charming, and clearly motivated by our instincts. We have a lot of confidence in ourselves, and usually with good reason.

Before Donald announced his intention to run for office, my inner voice told me he was the only man who could return our country to greatness, the kind of person we desperately needed at a time when the values I grew up with were quickly becoming horribly distorted.

Donald saw how people's rights were gradually being eroded by the far left, led by George Soros and his socialist-minded allies hoping to turn the United States into a country dependent on welfare to exist. The result of that would be catastrophic and create a population with their hands out rather than looking for a hand up. Respect for others and ourselves was rapidly dissolving.

I could see it coming. And Donald J. Trump definitely saw it coming. Way before I did, I'm sure of that.

June 16, 2015 was my birthday. My husband Bobby and I were on a cruise in the Mediterranean with our friends Joe and Terry Ebert Mendozza. As I mentioned earlier, my son David had suffered a massive stroke from a drug overdose that not only left him paralyzed on one side, but legally blind. Bobby and I had spent the past year dealing with his health issues, and we booked the cruise in hopes of recharging our batteries.

At dinner that night aboard ship, we heard the news that Donald Trump had announced from Trump Plaza that he was running for president. I was so excited I forgot for the moment where we were, and shouted out loud, "This is the best birthday present I've ever had!" More than a few heads turned to see what was going on.

The following morning it was all Terry and I could talk about. What could we do to help Donald Trump get elected? That summer, Terry and I, along with Janet Levy and Suzi Goldsmith, tried to figure out what four women could do to bring awareness to Trump's campaign. After many, many glasses of iced tea, we decided to form a pro-Trump women's group. What we lacked was a name.

September 19, 2015. The four of us were in the lobby of the Hilton Hotel in Beverly Hills. "Let's call ourselves the Trumpettes," suggested Janet.

"Yes! The Trumpettes USA," I added.

We agreed unanimously. Our baby was born.

Founding Trumpettes

Toni with the founders of the Trumpettes. (left to right) Suzi Goldsmith, Toni, Terry Ebert Mendoza and Janet Levy. Beverly Hills, September 19, 2015.

Over the next year we worked hard to help get Donald Trump elected, but that effort was only the beginning. Our mission statement was to make people understand the kind of man Donald Trump was behind and beyond the headlines. We wanted to inform and appeal to not only the women who would vote for him, but to the women – and men – who might not vote for him.

Today, the Trumpettes are known all over the world, with tens of thousands of members. In the past twenty-four months, I've done over one-hundred-fifty television and print interviews with news and media outlets from around the world. Their thirst for insight into Donald Trump is unquenchable.

The virtual avalanche of press included the February 2016 issue of *Vanity Fair*, featuring a two-page spread of the Trumpettes in an article about Donald Trump and Palm Beach.

VANITY FAIR

FROM THE MAGAZINE

How Donald Trump Beat Palm Beach Society and Won the Fight for Mar-a-Lago

From the moment Donald Trump set eyes on Mar-a-Lago, the grand palace of old Palm Beach, he was on a collision course with one of the richest and most insular towns in America. Mark Seal chronicles how the president-elect created his "Winter White House" with brash ploys, lawsuits, and by turning Palm Beach's exclusivity against it.

by MARK SEAL

1/4/2017 How Donald Trump Beat Palm Beach Society and Won the Fight for Mar-a-Lago | Vanity Fair

To Trump's detractors, it was proof of ruthless bullying by him; to his supporters, a sign of strength. "Well, my God, the man is a born winner!" Toni Holt Kramer told me in her grand Palm Beach home. A former Hollywood reporter and the wife of retired car dealer Robert David "Bobby" Kramer, she is the bubbly blonde founder of the Trumpettes, Donald Trump's most die-hard fans. During the campaign the Trumpettes shouted their allegiance to their hero from sound trucks, and later in the halls of Mar-a-Lago, where they celebrated his victory. "Donald Trump will do whatever it takes to win!" Kramer enthusiastically told me. "People who succeed can't always be delicate debutantes!"

Other articles appeared in *Town & Country Magazine, Paris Match* and *The French Report* and I appeared on *French Presse TV.* The BBC filmed an epic documentary with me and my crew, and I was a featured guest on *Sept a' Huit,* France's version of *60 Minutes,* not once but three different times. A French filmmaker also did a documentary on the Trumpettes.

M 24 in Germany, Japan Tokyo Television Network, and Univision have all done interviews with us. I've been on *Good Morning Britain* and London's ITN several times. *Marie Claire Australia,* that country's number one magazine, spent two full days with us for a five-page layout.

Marie Claire

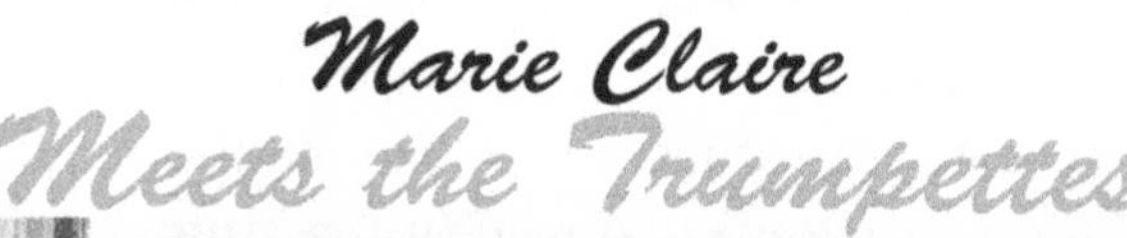

They're Trump's multi-millionaire neighbours who wear their hearts on their beauty pageant sashes

"I think Trump is sexy. He's dreamy. The corporate executive who's also kind" – Isabelle Robbins

AUSTRALIA

In the U.S., I've appeared on *Nightline* and *The Daily Show.*

bottom right Carol Connors, Toni, Rhonda Shear.
Just prior to the election and predicting Trump's win.

Every appearance and every interview has been an extraordinary and enlightening experience. Without question, the Trumpettes have become a movement. Each and every appearance generates more members, and more and more Trumpsters are joining our roster.

When I step back from the spotlight and ponder the positive response to the Trumpettes from countries that have no vote in our election, I come to one conclusion: they all have their hopes pinned on Donald Trump. Because many countries today are going through political upheaval that threatens their very sovereignty, they want to see if Trump's way can blunt the winds of change. If it can, they can emulate his style and right their own ship.

My big dream is that my passion and perseverance will inspire those who are just beginning their journey whatever it might be. Please don't feel that the only thing left on the horizon is the setting sun – your passion can take you anywhere you let it lead you.

Yes, I've come a long way from East 16th Street in Brooklyn, and believe me, I'm not done yet!

Toni filming for France's September Huit show, similar to "60 Minutes" in the U.S. L to R: Ambassador Robin Bernstein, Janet Levy, Terry Ebert Mendozza, Suzi Goldsmith, Toni.

CHAPTER THREE

Brooklyn

Brooklyn. Home of Coney Island. Home of the Dodgers. Home of Helen and Jack Kopelman, my parents.

Both my mother and father were born in America. My father was Jewish. My mother was half Jewish and Russian Orthodox. As a child we lived in the best apartment building in Brooklyn: Terrace Gardens, on East 16th Street and Avenue I. The building had a waterfall in front and an elderly doorman named Alfred who always wore a Navy captain's cap. Our apartment was on the top floor because my father believed that no one should live with someone walking over their heads.

My mother's real name was Elena, which is Russian, but everyone called her Helen. My father, on the other hand, had different names at different times depending on which bookmaker he was trying to dodge. Jack...John...Kopelman...King, they all worked at one time or another, and my name would change too.

My given name was Sandra Antoinette. The name Antoinette came from a novel my mother was reading when she was pregnant. Antoinette was the heroine, and her nickname was Toni. I've been Toni ever since my debut.

Extremely handsome and intense, my father was a charismatic man with dark brown eyes, jet-black hair, and a square jaw with a cleft in his chin. He was a dead ringer for the late matinee idol Victor Mature, known for playing Samson in the movie *Samson and Delilah*. In fact, people often mistook my father for the actor. He had the charm of Dean Martin and looked comfortable in an open dress shirt and tuxedo jacket. Mother always said he could walk into a room of five hundred strangers and within fifteen minutes everyone would cluster around, wanting to meet him. I guess I got that gene.

He had his own company, which sold aviation supplies from an office on Madison Avenue in New York. He did business with the biggest corporations. If nothing else, my father was a great salesman. People

Young Toni in Brooklyn.

would say he could sell the Brooklyn Bridge as it was falling into the water.

The truth is, it didn't matter what business he was in—his whole life was gambling. He was a character out of Damon Runyon. If there were two ice cubes, he would wager on which one would melt first. But nothing was more important than the horses and a hot crap game.

When I was six or seven years old, my father would take Mother and me to the racetrack, usually Belmont Park on Long Island. I was too young to be allowed in, so he would park the car by a little old-fashioned grocery just outside the track. Mother and I would sit in the car for hours while my father gambled his way through the afternoon. My treat from the market was always the same: a one-person pineapple pie in a little sack with the name printed on it. It was the highlight of my day and I looked forward to it, though I can't imagine how grueling those days must have been for my poor mother.

I have to admit, when times were good—meaning he won at the track or made eight the hard way—my father would always indulge me. He would take me shopping, to the big, beautiful children's store on Ave J in Brooklyn. He'd hoist me up on his shoulders and say, "C'mon, princess. Pick out everything you want; the sky's the limit." That memory remains with me to this day, and has influenced many of my expectations and relationships.

But the good times were often overshadowed by the bad ones. We were constantly in and out of hock. I could always tell which way the winds of my father's gambling were blowing by the presence of our silver tea service and Mother's mink coat. When things were down, they would disappear. When things were good, they reappeared. As a child, I didn't know it, but these were the telltale signs of a gambling addiction, and there is no doubt that is exactly what my father was—an addict. The mood swings, the borrowing of money, the selling of valuables; these are the same principal problems found in drug addiction or alcoholism. It is no different.

My childhood bedroom overlooked the BMT subway. I would sit at my window and watch the trains enter and leave the station on their way to or from New York City. The other corner window looked out toward Coney Island, a twenty-minute train ride from where we lived. It was a long way away, but I could still see the top of the Steeplechase. On Monday nights they would put on a display of fireworks I could see from my bedroom. I would watch the stream of flaming stars light up the sky and feel dazzled by the excitement and color of it all.

I loved Coney Island. It was the place to go, "the place where merriment was king." Every summer millions of people would visit the beach to sunbathe, jammed together on the sand like sardines in a can.

I remember we would walk up and down the boardwalk together and I would feel safe knowing my parents were on either side of me. They would take me to the carousel—the ride I loved most of all—and wait patiently as I rode around and around on the backs of those beautiful horses. There was a brass ring that I would always reach for as I circled around. It's funny to look back on my determination to grab at the brass ring. Even as a little girl, I always wanted more than I had.

Whenever we tired of pacing the boardwalk or riding the rides, we indulged in the Coney Island food scene. My parents ate hot dogs and fries from the famous Nathan's, and I had a chicken chow mein sandwich on a hamburger bun. Nothing will ever taste as good as that sandwich. I'm sure if I were to have one today, it would taste exactly like my memories of Coney Island.

I was an only child. I had friends but I was always sort of odd, and I never really formed close connections with my peers. For the most part, my life was in my bedroom. To me, the real world was never *my* real world—the real world for me was the one I created for myself.

The apple-green walls in my room were covered with countless photographs from movie magazines held in place with scotch tape. Mixed in with the pages torn from the fan magazines were black-and-white photos of movie stars. There wasn't an inch of wall space available for anything else.

My mother would help me write to the movie studios, telling them I was a big fan of this or that star, and the studios would always send back a personally autographed picture. God only knows if the stars themselves signed the photos, but the truth is, it didn't matter. To me, the photos and the signatures were real. They were my connection to my dream—an escape from the reality of my life and the constant arguments I would hear raging between my mother and father from the other side of my bedroom walls.

Late at night I would turn backward in my bed, raise my legs and cross my feet over the headboard, look around at the photographs, and make my plans for the future. I'd close my eyes and fantasize about being a movie star, about being rich and famous and driving around in a cream-colored Cadillac convertible.

My favorite movie stars were Rita Hayworth, Lana Turner, Gene Tierney, and Susan Hayward, but there was nobody more beautiful on the planet than Ava Gardner. There was something magical about her, and that's who I wanted to be.

I was eight years old when my parents split up. My father never said good-bye. I remember sitting at the breakfast table when my mother said to me, "Honey, your father won't be living with us anymore."

I didn't even react. I remember being outside myself for a moment and wondering, *Why aren't I crying?* I knew I should have been but I wasn't. It was as if at that very moment, my father had vanished into thin air—as if he had never existed. As the years passed I never heard from him. There was never a phone call, never a birthday card, a Christmas present...nothing.

People wonder if I harbor any anger toward my father. I always reply no. It's true his abandonment impacted my life, but being angry interfered with my dream. I couldn't turn back the clock, and dwelling on it ruined the present. I feel beyond lucky to have had the mother I did. Together we didn't need anyone else, least of all someone who thought he didn't need us.

I still feel pain knowing I missed out on something that other kids had—parents who were always there. Parents are the ones who give us the gift of existence, who come together to bring us into the world, and we are born thinking they will always be there to catch us when we fall. After eight years of seeing my father every day, he was suddenly gone—and that level of confusion at such a young age I'm certain created some lasting insecurity within me, although I didn't know it then.

My mother was the only safety net I ever needed. Over the years, however, there have been times I've connected with men I saw as a father figure—and one man in particular would try to ruin my life.

We never saw a penny in alimony or child support. After my father left, my mother could have gone to her family for financial help, especially to her sister Gertrude and her husband, who were very wealthy, but she chose not to. Instead, she got a job in New York City. Eventually, that one job turned into three. She worked morning, noon, and night plus the weekend to keep us going and never once complained.

The relationship my mother and I built was closer than close. We needed each other. She was my rock and together we faced the world. It comes as no surprise that my biggest fear growing up was that something would happen to her, that she would no longer be at my side to protect and love me.

I think every child is familiar with the feeling of deep dread associated with the idea of losing a parent. My own feelings of terror were amplified because my mother was all I had in the world. The idea that something horrible might happen to her petrified me to the core.

Every night at six o'clock I would stand at my bedroom window and search the corner of Avenue J and East 16th Street for my mother. Her routine was always the same: arrive at the Avenue J train station after work, walk to the market to pick up groceries, then walk up 16th Street to our apartment.

The instant I saw her, the tension disappeared and I silently thanked God for returning her home safely. I'd run to meet her at the door and forget the panic-stricken ordeal until the next night, when I'd be back at my window searching the skyline for my mother's familiar silhouette.

Despite my fears there was a certain sense of security about the sameness of her daily routine. The structure she provided helped to steady the world for me. I'm sure those years were no cakewalk for her, but she never once appeared to me as anything other than a pillar of strength.

* * * * *

I was ten when I got my first job. I went to work at Harnick's, a greeting card store on Avenue J. The girl who hired me could not have been more than twenty-five, and she knew I was young but it didn't really matter. Her name was Helen and she was the daughter of the owner. Helen was very beautiful and wore heavy, theatrical makeup. She had long, curly, dark auburn hair, graceful hands, and incredibly long red fingernails.

My job was to dust the greeting cards, and I can remember her showing me a special way to hold the feather duster. She would ever so gently pinch the handle between her thumb and forefinger so she wouldn't break her nails, and sweep the duster back and forth across the cards like she was ringing a bell. It took me a while to master the technique, but I finally got the hang of it. She let me work there during the week after school. I don't remember what I got paid, but whatever it was I felt like I was making a contribution to our lives.

Also on Avenue J, not too far from Harnick's, was a drugstore. I would go there every chance I had. A lady with a black pageboy hairstyle named Ann worked in the makeup department. She taught me how to apply "doe eyes" with a Maybelline eye pencil. It didn't matter to me if "doe eyes" were in fashion or not. Sometimes they were larger, sometimes smaller—sometimes black or dark brown—but always and forever doe eyes. She also showed me how to apply Max Factor pancake makeup, and together, we decided that tan rose was my color. Tan rose, a little rouge, a lot of mascara, and a splash of orange-red lipstick to complete the look. Ann would hold a mirror up so I could see our finished product…and the reflection I saw was a movie star!

As the years passed I went to high school in Brooklyn, but I couldn't have cared less about my courses, algebra and geometry in particular. And algebra and geometry wanted nothing to do with me. Oddly enough, when I got older, I became proficient at mathematics. As a teenager, I felt school was a waste of time. I wanted to be an actress—nothing else would do—and any time spent doing anything other than pursuing my dream was time poorly spent.

Over summer vacation my mother helped me get a job in New York City. I was fourteen by then, although I looked older, and I went to work as a receptionist for a company in Gramercy Park—not too far from where my mother worked. We were two working women and every day we would meet on our lunch breaks in the park and eat the sandwiches we had packed from home while chatting about our day. Unfortunately, the lights in the office gave me terrible headaches and I was forced to make a change.

As luck would have it, I went to work for a company called Sultana, where I sold hosiery from behind a counter. It gave me the opportunity to deal directly with people, something I loved, and I excelled at the job.

But money—or the lack of it—sometimes made it difficult for us to make ends meet. The pinch that we felt was personified for me one muggy afternoon when I decided to take a taxi from my job in the city to the subway so I wouldn't have to walk in the oppressive heat. My mother was ill that day and had stayed home.

When the taxi reached the station, I gave the driver a twenty-dollar bill to pay the fare. I was late and rushed into the station to catch my train, but as I was about to board, I suddenly realized that the driver had given me change for a five instead of a twenty. I was devastated. Twenty dollars was a lot of money in those days, enough to have taken the taxi all the way home to Brooklyn and then some. All I could think of was how many hours I had worked in order to get that twenty and how we could have used that money for other necessities. It was too late for me to correct the mistake—the taxi driver had already gone. I felt such a sinking feeling that I rushed to a pay phone to call my mother.

"I just did a terrible thing," I cried, and I told her what had happened. The heat and the rushing around had worked me into a tizzy, and tears welled up in my eyes. "I didn't look. I'm so sorry. I know we can't afford to lose this."

"Don't worry about it, honey," she said sweetly. "We're okay…and sometimes people do bad things."

There was no doubt in my mind that the cab driver knew exactly what he was doing, and I think that incident is why to this day I don't like to carry cash. Cash makes me nervous. I much prefer credit cards. I always say to people, "I'm like the Queen. I don't carry cash."

CHAPTER FOUR

The Copacabana

While still in high school, I saw an ad in the newspaper for the Copacabana nightclub. In a little box were the words: "Audition for showgirls." Despite the dance lessons I had taken, I wasn't a professional dancer by any stretch of imagination, nor did I really have any idea what a showgirl did. But if the Copa was good enough for all those great stars who performed there in the past, including Frank Sinatra and Tony Bennett, it was certainly good enough for me. The audition was scheduled for three o'clock the next afternoon. I circled the time and made plans to be there.

I debated telling my mother about the audition because I wasn't sure she would approve, but as partners in life, we had a pact: no matter what—even if it was the most terrible thing in the world—we'd never lie to each other. I'd spent the day planning how I would break the news to her that I was going to audition, but by the time we sat down for dinner that night, she knew that something was up.

"You're quieter than usual," she remarked. Dinner together was our time to chat and go over everything that had happened throughout the day, so my silence was completely out of character.

"There's an open audition for showgirls at the Copacabana tomorrow afternoon and I want to go." The words rushed together in a combination of anxiety and excitement.

I could tell from the look on her face that she was less than thrilled. She pursed her lips in silence. After what felt like ages—in truth it was more like seconds—she spoke.

"Well, if you want to see what it's like, go and do it."

That was all the blessing I needed.

The next day, I took the BMT from Brooklyn into New York and walked to the world-famous Copacabana on East 60th Street. I stood at the entrance to the club trying to work up the courage to go inside. Mind you, I was only fifteen years old at the time, I wouldn't be sixteen for another few months, and I was more than a little bit intimidated.

I glanced at my reflection in the window beside the door. I knew the importance of first impressions and I was determined to make a splash. I whipped out my Maybelline eye pencil, gave my "doe eyes" a quick touch-up, and smoothed out my outfit. I had channeled my mother that day when I got dressed, maybe in an attempt to harness some of her strength, and I was an absolute vision in pink. My skirt was tight at the waist with a big, full crinoline underneath it. My blouse was pink as well with puffed sleeves and a pointed Peter Pan collar. I took a breath and stepped inside.

The place was dark. The smell of stale cigarette smoke from the night before hung heavy in the air. I could barely see into the restaurant as my eyes adjusted from the light outside. I heard voices coming from the next floor down, so I followed their sound as my guide. I worked my way between the empty dinner tables and passed the bar, and walked down a short flight of stairs into the nightclub.

The smallish stage was brightly lit with the area surrounding it cloaked in total darkness. There must have been thirty to forty girls milling about on stage when I arrived. I was horrified to see that they were all wearing black net stockings and black leotards belted at the waist, with a sleeveless shirt tied in a knot around their tightly muscled abs. As I looked at their faces, I saw that each one was more gorgeous than the next. They all looked sophisticated and sexy, and there I was, standing in the corner, looking like Alice in Wonderland.

A couple of the girls snickered and tilted their heads in my direction as I made my way toward the stage. I was definitely out of my element, but instead of being frightened into a state of nervousness, I was even more determined to stand my ground. A gruff voice from the blackness ordered me to take my place on the stage, and I obeyed with confidence.

We were told to form single lines of five or six across. I joined a group of girls and we made a line near the center of the stage, but I didn't have a clue what to do next.

I must have looked lost because the pretty blonde on my right spoke to me out of the side of her mouth. "Hey, kid," she whispered in a tough, Irish voice. "Look to the front, stand up straight, and smile."

I did exactly as I was told. Throwing my shoulders back, I offered my very best smile and stood there in my pink Peter Pan outfit. Through the lights that were shining in our eyes, I could see the outline of a man with wavy hair and a weatherworn face seated at a table on the second ringside level in front of the stage. He was smoking a cigar and wearing a suit and tie, his shirt slightly opened at the collar. I watched as he slowly turned toward us, then thrust his arm toward the stage, his finger pointing directly at me like a dagger.

"You!" he growled. "I want you in the pink!"

I don't know who was more shocked—me or the other girls. I found out later that the man who singled me out was the boss himself, Jules Podell. I remembered reading somewhere that mob boss Frank Costello was one of the owners, and Podell, the man pointing his finger, was in charge of running the hotspot.

My excitement at being chosen was huge—but the elation I felt was quickly replaced by worry. The laws said you had to be eighteen in order to work in a place that sold alcohol, and I was three years shy. To me, this was nothing more than a small snafu; I would figure out how to make this Copacabana gig (and everything else in my life) work out to my advantage.

Nancy O'Malley came to my rescue. She was the blonde standing next to me at the audition, the one who told me to stand up straight and smile. Nancy was Tough with a capital T, but she had a beautiful face—a true diamond in the rough. She was also chosen by Mr. Podell, and after the audition, she took me across the street to The Hotel 19, where she had a room that couldn't have been much bigger than a closet. She introduced me to her boyfriend, a professional jockey. Nancy towered over him like the Empire State Building, but I felt at ease in their company.

Nancy had figured out right away that I wasn't old enough to have the job, probably because she had so many sisters and brothers. But Nancy had been around the track a few times and knew exactly what to do. We sat in her tiny room and she placed a comforting arm around my shoulders.

"Don't worry about it, kid," she said. "Get your birth certificate and I'll take care of the rest."

When I got home that night, my mother was eager to hear about what happened at the audition. I told her all the details: how my outfit was different, how Nancy had helped me, and finally (after building the suspense for her) how I had been chosen to be a Copa Girl.

"That's amazing, honey, but one thing—don't you have to be older than fifteen to work there?"

"Well, about that..." I said, hesitantly, "I'm going to need my birth certificate."

Mother showed an understandable amount of reservation. There were still a few months left of the school year. Insightful woman that she was, my mother knew I would put in even less effort with my classes if I somehow managed to trick the Copacabana into thinking I was older than I was. She held my birth certificate in her hand and I pleaded with her, giving my all to convince her to let me take the job.

"School just isn't important to me, Mom. Please let me do this; it's such a big chance."

I had never been more serious, and Mother could tell. She must have seen the drive in my eyes, and looking right back at her, I could tell the machine of her mind was clicking through all of those technicalities I was so good at skipping over.

"I'm definitely laying down some ground rules." She placed the birth certificate in my hand, and I could feel my heart fill with joy. I knew I had her backing to bail out of school for the time being.

Mother said we would see what happened with the job and leave the possibility open of enrolling in a private school in the city at the end of the summer. But she drew the line at allowing me to live in New York by myself. She decided we would keep our apartment in Brooklyn and rent a furnished, one-room studio at The Hotel 19, the same place Nancy O'Malley stayed.

The next day I brought my birth certificate to Nancy. A few days later it came back, and suddenly I was twenty. She didn't tell me how she did it, nor did I ask—I didn't need to know. Nancy helped me fill out the job application and get the rest of my paperwork in order. My level of excitement was positively through the roof, and I felt like I had found a job that would put me on the track to stardom, even though I was just a showgirl. Of course, the pay felt pretty good too—three hundred dollars a week was very decent money in those days. And I was one of the famous Copa Girls.

Copa Girl Toni (right) getting ready backstage.

Doug Cowdy, the choreographer, taught us some simple dance steps for the big production numbers. We would make our entrance at the rear of the club, then walk down the aisles between the tables and onto the small stage. There, we would parade across the footlights, make a few graceful arm gestures, and strike a pose or two between the dance steps. Our main goal, besides looking glamorous, was to be on target—to hit our spots when we were supposed to; otherwise, the number would be complete chaos. I'll admit we wore skimpy costumes, but they were beautifully designed: beige net stockings and elaborate headdresses that would have made Carmen Miranda proud.

Once I started performing, my mother laid down the rules. I would do the first show at the Copa at eight o'clock, and return immediately to The Hotel 19 when it was over. Then I would go back to the club for the second show at eleven and, again, come directly back to the hotel when we finished. It wasn't that Mother didn't trust me, but I was still a child in her eyes.

The hotel was a half block from the club at 60th and Madison. I remember that the window of our apartment looked directly at the Copa, and the instant Mom saw me leave the club, she would lean out the window and crook her finger at me to come back to the hotel. Funny, she would wait at the window for me the exact way I had waited for her as a child. The stress I put myself through waiting for Mom to come home from work was the same feeling she probably felt waiting for me to finish my shows. We both wanted nothing more in the world than to keep each other safe.

Working at the Copa was certainly better than going to school. And I loved living in New York. While it didn't take too much talent to be a showgirl, just the idea of being on stage, of being noticed and looked at, made me feel like somebody important.

Nancy O'Malley became a good friend, and she made sure nothing bad ever happened to me. She even taught me how to melt beeswax and use it on my eyelashes instead of mascara. She would place the wax in a spoon, hold a lit match underneath it, then dip the end of another match into the melted wax and apply it. The process made the most beautiful, thick eyelashes, and the wax easily came off at the end of the show. Nancy also taught me about shadowing my face and my nose to accentuate my best features. It was a fast-paced, electrifying time in my life, and I learned a lot about show business.

Unfortunately, three months later, my life as a showgirl came to an abrupt end.

It was June, a week away from my sixteenth birthday. A Friday night and the eleven o'clock show had just begun. On cue, I made my usual walk down the steps and across the stage when I heard voices from the crowd yelling, "Toni...Toni...hey, Toni!"

I squinted through the lights as I went through my routine and discovered, much to my horror, that the people calling my name were kids from my high school. Had I stayed in school I would have been a sophomore, but a lot of the people I knew and hung around with were seniors. They had come to the Copa after their Senior Prom. They made a huge commotion when they saw me, and it was all I could do to keep my composure, but the cat was out of the bag.

The stage manager came into the dressing room after the show and told me Mr. Podell wanted to see me. Nancy shot me a look and I promised not to say anything to get her in trouble. I took off my makeup, changed into my street clothes, and went up to Mr. Podell's office.

Mr. Podell was seated behind his desk, puffing a big cigar and scribbling notes in some kind of ledger. He didn't even look up when I entered. I stood silently in front of his desk, shifting nervously from one foot to the other, waiting for him to say something.

Finally, I couldn't stand the silence any longer, and the words just spilled out of my mouth. "You wanted to see me, Mr. Podell?"

He looked up, drilling a hole in me with his eyes.

"Toni, how old are you?" It was more of a demand than a question.

I took a deep breath and looked straight back at him. "You have my birth certificate, Mr. Podell."

There was a moment where I wasn't sure if he was going to shoot me or throw me out of his office on my head, but he remained calm. It was clear I was younger than I claimed, and nothing more needed to be said. My career as a showgirl at the Copacabana was officially over.

* * * * *

During my time at the Copa, I had overheard some of the girls talking about the Huntington Hartford Modeling Agency. After things had come to a head that June and Mr. Podell realized I was younger than my tampered birth certificate claimed, I needed to move on to the next thing, and fast, or else I'd have to go back to school and once again put my dreams on hold. More importantly, the Copacabana had lit a fire inside of me that needed constant fuel—if the world thought I could be a showgirl, I could certainly be a model. I called the agency and set up an appointment for myself.

Teenager Toni and her mother do some modeling.

I met with a woman there who said I had a beautiful face but didn't have the exact figure they required. I still had baby fat. She took the time to explain that models had to be very thin, not voluptuous, because the camera added weight. But she told me to get some photos taken, and if they liked them I could do beauty and lingerie modeling.

I had the photos taken, and the agency approved them. As a result, I graced the covers of lingerie catalogs during the next year.

If I learned anything about modeling, it was that it's excruciatingly boring.

CHAPTER FIVE

How Much Is That Doggie in the Window?

My mother and I decided to move permanently from Brooklyn to New York City. We leased a one-bedroom apartment at 136 West 58th Street, between 6th and 7th Avenues. It was one street from one of the best neighborhoods in the city, Central Park South. The Hotel Maurice was just across the street.

I was still working with the Huntington Hartford Modeling Agency and had gone through a period where I changed my name to Stephanie King. I didn't think the name Toni sounded right with my last name of King, so I opted for Stephanie. The name change did nothing for my modeling career, and I quickly switched back to Toni.

The agency booked me on a few jobs as well as a soap opera or two—but my career was pretty much at a standstill. I did manage to win the Miss Subway beauty contest, which led me to meet Robert Wagner, one of the contest's judges. He shook my hand when I was chosen the winner. We didn't know it then, but our paths would cross many more times throughout our lives.

Reflecting back on my life at sixteen always produces a sense of nostalgia, as I'm sure it does in any woman thinking of her teenage self. Sure, I cringe to think of some of the choices I made at that sweet, naïve age, but overall I feel a sense of pride in both the girl I was and the woman I was fast becoming. I was utterly tenacious. It seemed that no matter what life tossed my way, I was able to push forward, to keep going to the next thing. If one door closed, I was confident another would open. And at sixteen, I was more than willing to knock a few down if they didn't.

* * * * *

I went for an audition for a new Broadway musical written by Bob Merrill. If Google had existed in those days, I would have known that Bob was a famous songwriter. He had more hits than I can list, but among the songs he wrote were: "How Much Is That Doggie in the Window" for Patti Page, and "Mambo Italiano" for Rosemary Clooney. Both songs, along with so many others, were monster hits.

The audition was at the Shoreham Hotel on West 55th Street, between 5th and 6th Avenues. Bob had an apartment there that doubled as his office. A large-boned man with reddish hair and freckles, Bob had a slightly funny walk. He was considerably more than twice my age, but I still thought he was adorable.

When I arrived at the apartment for my audition, there was another man there with him. His name was Murray Kaufman, better known as Murray the K, the most popular and influential rock-and-roll impresario and disc jockey on New York radio. I definitely knew who *he* was—all the kids knew Murray the K. We listened to him all the time.

After the introductions, Bob handed me a sheet of lyrics and sat down at the piano to accompany me. It's important to note that when I was in school, Mrs. Greenway, who conducted our assemblies at PS 152, told me, "Never sing." She said, "You'll throw the entire auditorium off key." With that in mind, I confessed to Bob that I couldn't sing a note.

"But I could talk the song," I added.

Bob looked at me as though I had just arrived from some far-off galaxy. He patiently explained that what he had written was a musical—and I needed to sing. I guess he saw how unresponsive I was to his explanation because after a few minutes, he gave in and told me to go ahead and "talk it" if that's what I really wanted to do.

And so we began. Bob played the piano…and I talked. I did my best but it was pretty awful. Eventually, the two men could no longer contain themselves and they broke into hysterical laughter…and I did too. It was that ridiculous. I'm sure they thought I was so desirous of getting a job in show business that I would try anything, even auditioning for a musical when I had no musical talent. Of course, they were right.

"Don't worry," said Bob, as we wrapped up my audition. "Just leave us your phone number."

In other words, "Don't call us—we'll call you." Still, I liked Bob and I was pretty sure he liked me. And call he did, but it was obvious it wasn't my amazing singing talent he was interested in; he called to ask me out on a date.

I explained that my mother didn't allow me to date because of my age. Bob understood completely and solved the problem by taking both me *and* my mother to dinner. He took us to a very expensive restaurant and introduced me to the most delicious dessert I had ever tasted. It was called Coupe Marrone: a combination of vanilla ice cream, whipped cream, warm chestnuts, and a gooey sauce. It was fantastic.

Soon, the three of us were going to dinner on a regular basis. He told me one night that he composed his songs on a toy xylophone that he had bought at a local dime store for $1.98. After finding success, he graduated to one for $6.98, which I thought was kind of funny. In many ways we were truly an odd couple. Bob was so cynical and I was so young and innocent. I made him laugh. The three of us had some great times.

A year or so later, Bob came to our apartment. He was wearing a blue jacket, blue pants, and a gray vest, more formal than usual. "I'm going to Hollywood to make a movie," he said.

Before we could ask questions or offer congratulations, Bob addressed my mother. "I want Toni to come with me. I want Toni to marry me."

Mom's eyebrows nearly shot off her face. I stood next to her in my own state of shock. The three of us remained frozen for several seconds. It was as if someone had hit the pause button on their remote: three figures standing entirely still in excruciating silence.

Finally, I managed to say, "You'll have to excuse us for a second, Bob, I have to talk to Mom." I pulled her aside, and her concern quickly switched to relief as I told her I didn't want to marry Bob.

"I like him and enjoy being with him, but I can't *marry* him!" I whispered, somewhat frantic. I didn't want to hurt Bob's feelings, but just looking at him standing there in his blue suit, I could see how awkward the situation had become. Thankfully Mother took control. She grabbed my hand and we walked back to Bob.

"Bob, I am so flattered that you've taken to Toni so deeply, but you have to understand—Toni isn't even seventeen. She's much too young to be married. I just can't allow it."

"I understand," Bob said, his face forming a sad smile. We talked about his movie briefly, and after a few minutes, Bob said his good-byes and left. Mom's word was law, and no one was going to question it.

Even after we turned down his proposal, Bob and I remained friends. He went on to have an illustrious career, including writing the songs "People" and "Don't Rain on My Parade" for the musical *Funny Girl*, which put Barbra Streisand on the map.

Bob and I eventually lost track of one another, but the good times made me realize something about myself that up until then I hadn't given a thought to. It was the first time I noticed that I had a definite weakness (if not a need) for older men.

* * * * *

I was shopping at Neiman Marcus in Palm Beach a few years ago when I saw a woman in the most fabulous color lipstick. I had never seen the woman before and I questioned whether I should go over and ask her for the name. "Excuse me," I said. "Would you mind telling me the color of your lipstick?"

The woman smiled and pulled me over to the Yves St. Laurent counter and told the salesgirl to give me the same lipstick, plus a few other items. In a matter of seconds, she had taken over my entire makeup life.

As I finished at the makeup counter, I saw Ellen Graham. Years earlier Ellen had taken all my pictures when I first began my career in Hollywood. We hugged and caught up on old times before saying good-bye.

Because of all the interruptions I was really running late and hurriedly made my way to the front door. Just then I saw a woman with a magnificent, fluffed-up black poodle. Of course, I couldn't leave without complimenting the owner on her dog. The woman told me it was her service dog—and she couldn't get along without it. Thinking of my own poodles, I asked her where she got her dog groomed, and the conversation went on for another ten minutes.

By this time I was a full hour behind schedule, and I made a beeline for the exit to the street. As I neared the door I heard someone behind me call my name. "Toni...Toni Holt! Is that you?"

I turned around and saw a woman waving at me. I had no idea who she was. "I'm Suzanne Merrill," said the woman as she neared. The minute she said her name, I knew exactly who she was—Bob Merrill's widow, the same Bob Merrill who wanted to marry me when I was sixteen years old.

"My God! How did you know who I was?" I asked.

My past came rushing back to me with her answer.

"Years ago, just before Bob and I got married, you had a Celeb-A-Toy party at Alan Carr's estate." Alan, known for his flamboyant personality and colorful caftans, was the producer of *Grease*. "After Bob introduced me to you, I remember saying, 'Bob, what can you possibly see in me? Toni is the most beautiful thing I've ever seen in my life.'"

Toni with producer Alan Carr.

While I'm not prone to blushing, I could feel my cheeks flush when she said that. "And you still are," Suzanne continued. "I just knew it was you. Bob spoke about you all through our life. He was always interested in what you were doing. He told me you wrote a column and you did a TV show. He was so fond of you...and so fond of your mother."

Suzanne's face was suddenly masked in sadness. "You know, today is the fifteenth anniversary of Bob's death."

I was suddenly engulfed in goose bumps. I recalled reading that Bob had taken his own life with a pistol. He had been suffering from a lengthy depression due to a number of illnesses, and he didn't want to spend the end of his life in a wheelchair. At the time of his death Suzanne was quoted as saying, "Bob wanted to be the master of his own fate."

As I listened to Suzanne it became crystal clear why I was delayed leaving the store, and why I kept stopping and talking to people. I was *supposed* to meet Suzanne Merrill that day. It was meant to be.

"I wish Bob could know we met today," said Suzanne.

"Oh, he knows," I said. "Why do you think we're standing here together? He wanted us to meet again."

I'm absolutely convinced our meeting wasn't an accident. It's my belief that life is a series of seemingly unplanned events that lead you inescapably to your destiny.

CHAPTER SIX

Marjorie Morningstar

I was still a teenager when I met with Harry Mayer at the Warner Bros. offices on New York's West Side. He asked me to read for the lead in *Marjorie Morningstar,* based on the best-selling novel by Herman Wouk. I passed the reading and was one of five chosen to go to Hollywood to test for the part. I was the youngest of the group that included Ina Balin, Erin O'Brien, Phyllis Newman, and Andrea Martin.

Because my grandmother Regina had just died, Mother agreed to let me make the trip alone. With her blessings, I boarded an American Airlines plane and made my first trip to California along with the other girls.

I really hit it off with Ina Balin. She was a few years older than I and, like me, was born in Brooklyn. Ina had been working on Broadway and honing her acting skills, and still looking to land her first movie role.

Ironically, the last time I saw Ina we were also on a plane together. It was probably twenty-five years later and we were delighted to see each other. By then she was a single mom living in Connecticut with her three adopted Vietnamese children. The rumor was that at one point during her career, she had a major affair with John Wayne and a big-time romance with astronaut Pete Conrad, the third man to walk on the moon. Pete and his wife, Nancy, became good friends of mine many, many years later. Ina never married, and she died at the young age of fifty-two from pulmonary hypertension brought on by coronary heart disease.

When we arrived in California, we were brought to the Hollywood Knickerbocker Hotel. Each morning we were driven to Warner Bros. Studios to prepare for our screen tests. We were given scripts for the movie and allowed a few days to study our parts before the cameras actually rolled. During this time we were fitted for wardrobe and tested for makeup. Natalie Wood, who desperately wanted the part, would make an early morning walk around the makeup department to check out her competition.

Toni heads to Hollywood for screen test. (top to bottom) Andrea Martin, Phyllis Newman, Ina Balin, Toni, Erin O'Brien.

Toni (top right) along with the other four girls in the Warner Bros studio photo for the screen test.

I must admit I was a little intimidated. For starters, I was on the other side of the country in a place I'd never been, and I didn't have my mother at my side for moral support. And there was the fact that all the other girls had acting experience, while I had none. Oh, sure, I'd taken some acting classes and starred in a school play, but that hardly qualified me for stardom in Hollywood. In truth, though, it didn't seem terribly hard. I knew if I set my mind on being an actress, there was no question I would be an actress.

As the day of the test grew near, we were each teamed with an actor chosen by the studio. My partner was David Janssen, who was twenty-six or twenty-seven at the time (an old guy to me). We were having lunch one day and David asked me if I had an expense account. I told him yes, and he smiled. "Good. I'll have a drink." That was followed by another drink, then another. When the studio got the bill for our lunch, they must have thought I was an alcoholic. Though David basically drank his way through rehearsals, it never affected his work. He was always serious and genuinely tried to help me do the best screen test I could possibly do.

The day of the test arrived and Gordon Bau, the famous makeup artist under contract to Warner Bros., did my makeup. From there I went to wardrobe, then was escorted to the sound stage. David was waiting on the relatively barren set, and I remember taking note of the darkness. It was so completely black outside of the light on the sound stage that I felt like I was isolated in space, that this one patch of set was all that existed in the universe. I had expected to see the other girls, but they weren't there. I learned later that each test was done individually, and we all did the same scene so that the studio executives could compare our work.

The camera rolled and we did the scene a number of times. The director made sure the camera got shots of me from different angles to see how I looked and how I reacted. I didn't really feel nervous, although I didn't feel terribly inspired either. It was just the camera; there was no live audience there to pump me up. As we ran through the scene, I was reminded of my boredom with modeling, and I remember feeling a little disappointed that the reality of this part of Hollywood could be so bland.

Not surprisingly, I didn't get the part. In fact, none of us got the part. Natalie Wood did. Not only did she get the part, she later married my favorite movie star, Robert Wagner. Years after, we were all saddened when we learned of Natalie's unexpected drowning off the coast of Catalina Island in 1981. She was only forty-three.

On the surface, Warner Bros. claimed to be looking for a new face to play Marjorie Morningstar, but in truth the part was probably going to Natalie all along. I heard later that Gene Kelly, who eventually starred in the movie with Natalie Wood, had told Erin O'Brien she was too tall for the role. As for Phyllis Newman, who was driven to become important, she eventually married lyrist and composer Adolph Green. Years earlier Green wrote "Singing in the Rain" with Betty Comden. Together they had several major Broadway hits. Phyllis went on to have a wonderful career in the theatre as an actress and a singer.

* * * * *

My trip to Hollywood wasn't a total loss. Word of my test (or my looks) must have gotten out because I received a phone call from Max Arnow, casting director at Columbia Studios. He wanted to meet me.

Columbia was located on Gower, just off Sunset Boulevard. Unlike the glass domes and black towers of the studios today, Columbia was a three-story building that ran almost the entire length of the street. It housed the offices of the executives. Behind this administrative building was a row of old wooden bungalows where producers, directors, and stars had their production companies. If you followed a patchwork of stone walks, you would reach the back lot with the sound stages and make-believe streets, all of which were invisible to the outside world. The line between reality and fantasy was never more evident. I loved it!

At that point, interviews had become sort of my specialty. I was anxious to hear what Mr. Arnow had to say, but I never let my nerves get the best of me. Once I was inside his wood-paneled office, the deeply tanned Mr. Arnow explained to me that he was always on the lookout for someone with "star" quality. Sure, the ability to act was important, but the people who made it to the top in those days were more than just good actors and actresses—they had memorable personas. They had a face that could be identified by a name—and a name that could be identified by a face. The studios took great pride in their roster of talent, and

Toni's Warner Bros still from her screen test.

they did everything within their power to protect those images both on and off the screen.

Mr. Arnow told me he could make me into a star. To whet my appetite, he described a fantastic penthouse suite at the studio that was once occupied by Rita Hayworth. He told me the suite was now occupied by Kim Novak. Drawing a parallel to my own lack of experience, Mr. Arnow said that Kim Novak had very little training when she started out, and now she was one of the biggest movie stars in the business. He understood that I was a raw recruit, but he wanted to put me under contract and promised that the studio would pay me a salary and give me acting, singing, and dancing lessons—the entire star-making education. In addition, he took the time to explain how I would work closely with their hair and makeup people to create the proper look for me, plus meet with their public relations department to help shape my image.

"Understand, you won't be working for at least a couple of years," he cautioned. "You need to be trained. You need to learn your craft and you need to learn it well. We'll do whatever we can to help transform you into a movie star."

To say I was excited by the promise of stardom would be putting it mildly. I wanted to scream and yell and jump through the ceiling.

I told Mr. Arnow I was sure I could do it, but my mother wasn't with me. I couldn't make the decision without her. I phoned Mother the instant I got back to my hotel, sure she would be as excited as I at the incredible opportunity that awaited me. I could barely contain my enthusiasm as I told her about Max Arnow and how *Columbia* wanted to make *me* into a movie star.

"No, no, and no," said my mother. "You can do that when you're old enough to realize the commitment you are making."

I couldn't believe my ears. Surely, she had to be joking.

"If I don't do it now, I'll never get another opportunity like this again, not as long as I live!"

"Yes, you will," she insisted, her voice firm. "Come home now."

I begged her to reconsider. It made no sense. I was being offered this amazing contract, which was everything I'd ever dreamed of, and my mother—my best friend and closest confidant who knew just how much I wanted to be a star—was telling me no. I couldn't understand it.

"Mommy, please," I pleaded, "please can I stay? Please, please say yes. Come to LA, we'll do this together. This is the opportunity of a lifetime. They want me now because I'm young...and I can be trained... and they'll groom me and make me beautiful."

She listened and agreed it was a wonderful opportunity, but still she wouldn't give in. "You're just too young, and you're already beautiful. I don't want you to get into something you don't really understand. You have no idea what's out there. How do you know what those people are like? How happy do you think they are? It's a fantasy life. I can't give you permission to do something like that."

Her voice changed, and she spoke firmly. "Wait a few years, get a little older, gain a little more experience. If you want to make that decision then, fine. But as your mother, I will not let you do it now."

I was devastated. I was angry and confused. I understood the tone of fear in her voice when she thought of allowing me to get involved in something that might be bad for me, but I didn't understand how this opportunity could ever be bad, especially if she were with me. It was my dream come true, a fairy tale come to life, and my mother was ruining it.

Unfortunately, I had no one else to turn to, no one else to give me support. No sisters, no brothers...and no father. No one to change my mother's mind.

Being the good girl that I was, I listened to her and took the next plane home.

CHAPTER SEVEN

My Name Is Jack Garcia

Many years later I was having dinner in New York City at the Polonaise Restaurant with Shirley, a long-time family friend. Shirl was a tall, a statuesque brunette a number of years older than I. She had the beauty of Ava Gardner and the smile of Lena Horne. When she entered a room, all eyes turned her way. Shirl was irresistible to men, but didn't like to date. She liked being married and walked down the aisle too many times to count. She gave me lessons about life that you don't learn in high school or college. Shirl was like an older sister, and my mother considered her another daughter.

During dinner I noticed a man seated at the bar. My eyes were glued to his profile. I couldn't look away. Shirl took notice of my trance-like state and snapped her fingers to get my attention.

"Hello, earth to Toni," she teased. "Is there something wrong?"

"That's my father," I said, pointing to the man at the bar.

Shirl turned to get a closer look at him.

"How could you possibly know that man is your father?" she asked, a quizzical look blanketing her features. "You haven't seen your father since you were ...what? Seven...eight? How could you even begin to recognize him?"

There wasn't a doubt in my mind that the man at the bar was my father: dark eyes, jet-black hair and a dead ringer for actor Victor Mature. How many men look like that?

"I'm going to go talk to him."

"Wait a minute Toni," Shirl said, grabbing my wrist. She was concerned about the whole situation; even more, she seemed scared for me. "Say that man over there really is your dad. How can you expect him to recognize you? It's been years."

Shirl was right, and for a moment I hesitated. I wasn't the chubby little girl my father once knew. But there were too many unanswered questions I'd been living with for years, and I couldn't stand the thought

Toni with 'Auntie' Shirl at dinner in New York.

of adding another one to the list. I smiled at Shirl, squeezed her hand, and made my way to the bar.

The closer I got, the more certain I became that the man was my father. It was as though I had seen him yesterday, as though he had only just left. I felt small as I neared him, like I had been walking through a time warp that had shrunk me back down to the child I was when I last saw him.

I tapped him once on the shoulder. "Excuse me," I said. "Are you Jack King?"

He turned and looked at me but didn't answer. It was strange to be so close, to see his familiar eyes once again staring into mine. The illusion of stepping back through time disintegrated, and I could see that the years had taken a toll. He had wrinkles where his skin was once smooth, and his face didn't seem as perfect as the one I held so tightly in my memory. His gaze searched the features of my now grown-up face, but instead of giving me a dawning look of recognition, his brow furrowed. He turned back to his drink.

"You know who I am," I persisted. I pushed aside the stool between us, forcing myself next to him. "I'm your daughter."

"No," he responded gruffly. I couldn't have mistaken that voice for anyone else's in a million years. I knew I was right, but he persisted. "No, I don't know who you are. And Jack King isn't my name."

His voice lacked any emotion as he spoke, and he stared at his scotch as though willing the glass to shatter to distract from the uncomfortable situation playing out before him.

My body was made entirely of adrenaline at that moment, and I was determined not to let him off the hook.

"Okay, what *is* your name then?" I demanded.

"My name is Jack Garcia," he answered bluntly.

I kept my eyes on him. My father had a penchant for making up names—it was a trick he used to escape the troubles he ran into as a result of his gambling addiction. I used to think it was great fun when he pretended to be someone else, but now that I was older, now that I knew the truth, and now that it was me he was trying to escape, it seemed nothing short of cowardly. Jack Garcia was just another made-up persona. He didn't exist. The man in front of me was, without question, my father.

"Why are you lying to me?"

"I'm sorry," he said, turning to face me one last time. "You've made a mistake. I'm not who you think I am." He took a sip of his drink and repositioned himself so that he had his back to me. It was a clear dismissal. I was nothing more than a bothersome fly, and the conversation, if you could call it that, was over.

I was angry, hurt, and disappointed as I walked back to my table. The adrenaline coursing through my veins was dissipating. By the time I sat down across from Shirl, tears were running down my cheeks.

"Oh Toni, what happened?" Shirl asked tenderly.

I told her what he said. She tried to console me, but I knew I hadn't made a mistake. The more we spoke, the more infuriated I became. How could he not acknowledge me after all the pain he'd caused me and my mother? I had given up my childhood to help support my family. Instead of playing hopscotch and jump rope, I spent my afternoons dusting greeting cards at a shop on Avenue J in Brooklyn. I never asked my father for a single thing my entire life. Why couldn't he do me the one favor I had asked of him? Admit he was my father. The injustice was overwhelming. I couldn't let him get away with it!

My chair made a loud screech as I jumped back up. Keeping my eyes locked on my father's broad frame, I marched back to the bar.

The man who was most certainly my father must have heard me approaching because he was on his feet by the time I reached him. We stood face-to-face. My blood was boiling.

"I refuse to let you do this to me," I snapped. "Why do you deny me? I'm Toni. I'm your daughter." My voice cracked as I said the word "daughter," and my eyes burned once more with tears. "Don't you want to know me?"

His face seemed to crumple as I looked at him. A slight tremor was rattling his hand. After a long pause, he finally spoke.

"Yes, I'm your father. I know who you are."

For a few moments, it was as though a weight had been lifted from my shoulders. He had finally said the words I had wanted to hear from the moment I saw him. My persistence had been justified. It was a good feeling, but all too fleeting. This wasn't a movie moment—there was no grand reunion, no long overdue hugging or apologies spoken through tears. Damn the movies for making us think things might be resolved this way in our lives. They never are, and all that remained after my father's confession was stark reality.

I couldn't tell if he was happy to see me or embarrassed that I recognized him. The longer we stood there, the worse I felt. Sure, he had finally told the truth, but it hadn't solved a thing. It was all I could do to keep from crying.

"Don't you ever want to see me again?" I asked, urging him to say something, anything at all to fix the mess he had made.

"Yes, I do," he answered, but I could hear the lack of commitment in his voice. He had fed me cheap words, and though I didn't want to admit it, I knew I wasn't ever going to have a relationship with him. This was merely closure on a wound that had been open and bleeding for more than a decade.

I scribbled my phone number on a cocktail napkin. "If you ever want to see me again, call me," I said, handing it to him. I took a parting look at him and went back to Shirl, who quickly gathered her things and followed me out of the restaurant.

To my surprise, he actually called the next day. We talked for a while, and I told him how hard Mother had worked to make a life for us after he left—what a struggle it had been to keep our heads above water. But nothing, and I mean nothing, seemed to move him. That was the last time I ever spoke to him.

I found out later that he moved to Florida, which made sense because of all the racetracks there. He died twenty-five or thirty years later. I have no idea if he had a funeral or where he was buried. I didn't cry then, either.

I wonder what name they put on his headstone?

CHAPTER EIGHT

I Should Have Listened to Uncle Ben

Milton Holt was an executive with the Teamsters Union. He worked in labor relations and was friendly with Jimmy Hoffa, president of the union, as well as Alan Dorfman, another big union official out of Chicago. Hoffa and Dorfman were eventually murdered.

Over thirty years my senior, Milton was good-looking, average height, and had a rough edge to him. He always dressed in expensive clothes and looked impeccable, just like an actor in an old black-and-white gangster movie. I first met Milton when Auntie Shirl and I were having dinner at Gatsby's restaurant in New York. Milton stopped by to say hello to her. I must have made an impression because a few weeks later he called, and we went out on a date.

The very next day a package arrived at our apartment. Mother watched as I tore open the box, and inside was the most beautiful mink coat I had ever seen. I telephoned Milton to thank him, and told him my mother would not allow me to keep it. Milton simply responded by saying he didn't want me to be cold, and he would like to speak to my mother. No doubt it was the show of affection I had been lacking for my entire life—a concern for my well-being like a father would have for his daughter. I was smitten.

My uncle Ben, the richest uncle in our family, investigated Milton and didn't approve of him at all. He told me Milton was much too old for me and was definitely not the kind of person I should be dating. Uncle Ben was strangely adamant about the entire friendship, and he offered to send me to Bennington College if I stopped seeing Milton. But I wouldn't be dissuaded, and we continued to date.

Milton not only wooed me, he wooed my mother. He caught on quickly that my mother and I were a package deal. He would take us to dinner at the best restaurants, and once took us to see Edith Piaf—ringside seats, of course.

It was fun being with Milton, and in a way I was emulating Shirl, who liked Milton and his friends. It's easy to get blinded by the glamor of a well-dressed man who's kind to your mother, especially for a girl like me who had an emotional soft spot for older men.

After we dated for a couple of years, Milton finalized his divorce from his first wife, and we were married.

Initially, Milton was very good to me. He treated me like a fragile doll, dressing me up in fine clothes and showing me off to his friends. We moved into an apartment on the Upper East Side, near East End Avenue.

Because of Milton's job with the Teamsters, he knew a lot of people who lived "the life," like Johnny and Tommy Dioguardi, both well-known organized crime figures. Johnny, known by his peers as Johnny Dio, was instrumental in helping Jimmy Hoffa become president of the Teamsters.

On the outside, we put up a good show of a happy husband and wife, but our private life was very different than what friends saw. Within the confines of our home, and under Milton's reign of terror, I quickly became a prisoner. He placed all manner of restrictions on me. I wasn't to have opinions, make decisions, argue, or even speak. I didn't know how to write out a check because Milton would not let me have a checkbook. My job was to be the eye candy plastered to Milton's arm, and if I dared to defy him, I would be put through emotional hell.

As time wore on, the restrictions Milton placed on me spread outside of our home as well. We would go out to dinner and Milton would warn me never to speak for fear I would say something stupid or wrong. He'd say things like, "You are here only to be beautiful," and "It's not your place to be talking."

After a while, I began to believe him. I became very quiet and subservient. I realize now that Milton not only stole my voice but managed to convince me that I'd never had one in the first place. He made me dependent upon him for everything, and it reached a point where I would wake up each morning feeling more awful than I had the day before. I was a girl in my early twenties, kept docile and confused and stricken by what I thought was love. All I could do was obey. Obey and feel trapped.

When I look back on my relationship with Milton, I feel a deep sense of disgust. I was so full of hope when I met him that I never realized he was tearing away at my very core until it was almost too late. He'd assumed the position of power in our relationship, a fatherly figure that was, in many ways, just as selfish and uncaring as my father had been.

While I know I can't blame myself for the twisted way Milton treated me, part of me can't help but think that I let him do it. I let him convince me that I was nothing more than a beautiful face. I let him stamp out the spark in my personality and berate me until I was silent. A man can only dominate a woman if he keeps her insecure, and that's what I allowed Milton to do to me. I naively thought that being married meant sacrifice, and I sacrificed my sense of self until all that mattered to me was Milton's approval. But only for a short time.

It's easy to watch those movies or read those stories about women in abusive relationships and think, *How could she let that happen? I would never stand for it!* I'm not a weak person but when you're caught up in something, when you're convinced you've found a lifestyle you love or like—it's not so cut and dried.

Getting into a situation of emotional abuse is a gradual process. When I finally examined my life, I couldn't remember how I had gotten myself into the mess with Milton. All I knew was that I felt utterly helpless. I had to plot my out.

One night when Milton and I went to dinner with his friends, I spoke up and joined in the conversation. It started with one comment, and then another, and soon I was out and talking, engaged in what was happening in a way I hadn't been for what seemed like forever. I felt exhilarated. I had managed to contribute something other than my smile and passive nods of affirmation. I was certain Milton would be proud.

On the car ride back to our apartment, however, Milton drove in stony silence. As we pulled onto our street, he turned to me and said angrily, "Why did you do that tonight?"

"What do you mean?" I asked, genuinely confused.

His answer ripped my fragile moment of confidence to shreds. "You're not supposed to do that," he growled. "You're just supposed to sit there and be beautiful."

I was so upset I broke down and cried. I had spent so much time bottled up inside of myself that I finally reached a breaking point. My whole life changed right then and there.

Sometime later we moved from our apartment in New York to a house in Inglewood, New Jersey. By then we had two young sons, David and Adam. Our new home was on Next Day Hill Drive, an exclusive area where lots of celebrities lived. Tony Bennett lived across the street. It was a twenty-minute car ride into New York City over the George Washington Bridge. It was beautiful.

Everything about me was different, and the dynamics of our marriage had changed dramatically. I've learned over the years that I have the capacity to put up with a lot more than the average person, but when I turn…I turn, dangerously so. I cut my losses and never look back.

By then, it was like someone was shoving me to go somewhere. I just didn't care about Milton anymore. I was over him, and his reaction to me meant absolutely nothing. I knew subconsciously I was making a plan to get out from under our marriage, but it wasn't just about me. I had to think very carefully about David and Adam, particularly because I knew what it was like to grow up without a father.

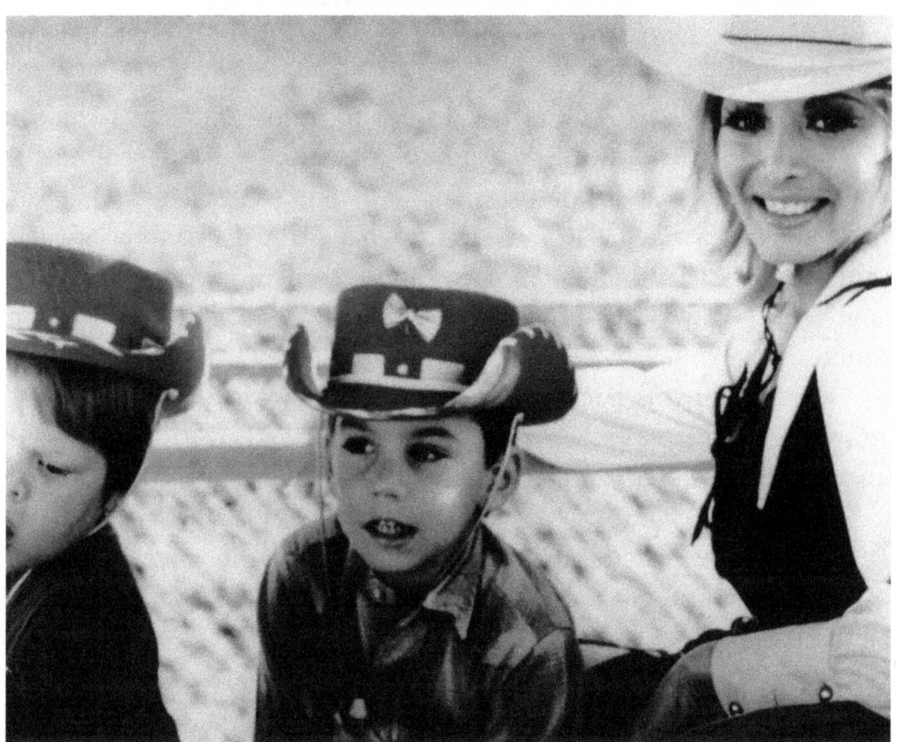

Toni with her sons Adam (left) and David.

CHAPTER NINE

The Lady in White

I credit Frank Sinatra with giving me the push that led me to Hollywood. And I give equal credit to my good friend Rock Hudson, whose kindness gave me the boost to put me on the map.

But before I tell you about Ol' Blue Eyes and my Rock—I mean that literally and figuratively—you need to meet the Lady in White.

I was living in Palm Springs at the time with my two boys. Milton and I were still married—sort of, and he commuted between New Jersey and the desert whenever it suited him. I was at a point in my life that I desperately wanted to find something useful to do, and being Milton's wife was definitely not one of them. The change of scenery was dictated not only by my desire to spend as much time as possible away from Milton, but my mother and her new husband, George Solon, had moved to Palm Springs a year earlier. They had opened a shop that sold gifts and rare books on the main drag, Palm Canyon, where Red Skelton was a frequent visitor.

Red was one of the biggest stars on television then, with a weekly show that was watched by tens of millions. Whenever Red would show up, Mother would lock the door, put the "closed" sign in the window, and pull down the shade. Red would lie down on the floor and spend hours and hours deciding which books to buy. He spent thousands and thousands of dollars buying volumes of gold-edged books.

From the time I was brought to Hollywood as a teenager to test for the starring role in *Marjorie Morningstar*, I was determined to find a place for myself in show business. My days in the desert were spent watching a lot of television, from game shows to news programs, interviews to entertainment specials. I weighed one possibility against the next until I saw someone who was successful at something I thought I could do. Her name was Rona Barrett.

Rona originally wrote Hollywood gossip for the Bell-McClure newspaper syndicate, and later tattled her tales on television. "Miss

Toni's mother, Helen, with her new husband, George Solon.

Rona," as she was known then, filmed and taped interviews with celebrities from movies, television, music, and politics. Hedda Hopper and Louella Parsons were the preeminent gossip columnists of the thirties, forties, and fifties, and Rona smartly filled the vacuum left by their demise.

The more I watched Rona, the more convinced I became that I could do what she did. With the personality I was developing and my natural ability to think on my feet, one of my best assets, I knew I could be a Hollywood news reporter. The term "news reporter" was important to me. I didn't want to dish dirt. Maybe it was my lifelong fascination with Hollywood movies and my admiration for the stars who were in them, but I wanted to tell their stories of success, not just air their dirty laundry.

Toni with Rona Barrett (center) and Ruta Lee, at a later time.

I knew I had potential, but as with everything in Hollywood, I knew I needed a gimmick.

For weeks, I played with all sorts of formats in search of a unique way to present celebrity news. The likes of *ET*, *Inside Edition*, and *TMZ*, which give instant snapshots of Hollywood life, didn't exist, so I needed to blaze my own trail. I had nowhere to draw inspiration from but my own mind, and I couldn't help but hear Mother's advice echo in my head: "If you think it, Toni, you can do it." I felt I could revolutionize Hollywood reporting and I was going to think up an idea that would allow me to do it. Another one of my traits: I always think big.

It eventually dawned on me that it wasn't the format of the show that needed to be unique—it was me. I set out to create a new persona for myself—a brand-new Toni Holt.

The first thing I did was to bleach my auburn hair an almost-white blonde. I was unsure at first at the starkness of the change. My hair stood out even more as a frame for my desert tan, but as it turned out, the choice was brilliant. Next, I gathered up all of my white clothes, added a bunch of new ones, and put together a variety of outfits that went with my concept. And voila! The Lady in White was born. As it happened, I already had a white Rolls-Royce, an older one but a Rolls nevertheless, to complete the picture. And what a picture it was.

I designed a simple set and found the perfect Victorian white wicker chair. The chair had a large round back that rose like latticework behind my head. The overall image was good, but I felt something was missing—an element that would make the concept really pop. I thought about it for days and finally realized I needed something to do with my hands while I spoke. I needed a prop of some sort—a piece of business that nobody else on television had. After discarding dozens of ideas, I finally came up with the solution: I bought a gorgeous white Persian kitten with the fluffiest fur I could find. I named the cat Gossip and decided that she would sit quietly in my lap while I spoke to the camera. At the end of every show I planned to look into the camera and say, "Now remember, it isn't nice to gossip." Then look down at my cat and add, with a twinkle in my eye, "Right, Gossip?" Sometimes she would even meow on cue. What a ham.

Toni as The Lady in White with her cat, Gossip. Photo by Ellen Graham.

The Lady in White was definitely my gimmick. All that was left to do was find a buyer.

* * * * *

In the spring of that year I took my idea, my cat, and my new persona to KMIR, the NBC affiliate station in Palm Springs. John Conte, the former film noir actor, was the president and general manager of the station. John and his wealthy Armenian wife, Sirpuhe, had started the station two years earlier and built it into the third largest station in the Coachella Valley.

John's broad smile showed off the whitest teeth I'd ever seen—I almost needed sunglasses—and his aqua blue eyes were mesmerizing.

He was very creative, innovative, and willing to take risks. I think his years spent in front of the camera provided him with a certain personality that set him apart once he finally stepped behind the scenes.

As we spoke, Sirpuhe played the audience, lolling on the sofa, soaking up every word I had to say. I proposed a five-minute segment that could fill a gap in the existing news hour. While the essence of my show would be celebrity gossip, I made it clear it wouldn't be a "kiss and tell" kind of show. Instead, I would focus on telling interesting stories and anecdotes about the movie stars I met at parties and sporting events in and around Palm Springs.

When I finally ran out of things to say, I sat quietly, waiting for their reaction. They shared a brief glance at one another, and Sirpuhe spoke.

"I love it."

The show was live twice a day. Eager to do the best job possible, I made damn sure I was always prepared before the camera started rolling. Prior to going on, I would rehearse in front of a mirror at home, reading the copy I'd written out loud to be sure I could say all I needed to say within my allotted five minutes. I would fret over my hair and makeup until I looked absolutely flawless, and I always made sure Gossip was in a pleasant disposition before filming. Even though I'd been on television before, this was the first time the camera was focused solely on me. It was completely nerve-racking but, at the same time, utterly exhilarating.

People do all kinds of crazy things to obtain a rush, like jumping out of airplanes or participating in extreme sports or even hard drugs and heavy drinking. For me, my rush comes from the camera. I couldn't get enough of it.

I worked with a veteran newsman on the set who graciously shared his experience with me and offered tips to make my show better. The whole thing worked perfectly, and my popularity gradually spread throughout the desert. Before long I became a well-known part of the very scene I was reporting on.

CHAPTER TEN

Ol' Blue Eyes

Ruby Dunes was *the* place to be on Friday nights in Palm Springs. That was the night they flew fresh lobsters in from Massachusetts. Irwin Rothstein, whom Sinatra had dubbed "Uncle Ruby," owned the restaurant. It was one of Sinatra's favorite hangouts, and he went there every Friday he was in town with his entourage.

Mother and I loved the Dunes and went there frequently. By this time my TV show had picked up steam and was gaining popularity. I was becoming somewhat of a local celebrity, and the Lady in White had turned into a full-time persona. For the first time in my adult life, I felt in touch with myself. I liked who I was, and who I was on the road to becoming.

I promoted my local fame with my light blonde hair, white outfits, and eating only white food in public. I kept my white Persian cat on my lap whenever I could. You get the picture. I wasn't gaudy—at least I didn't think so—and these eccentricities helped to pave my road into the spotlight.

I often spotted Sinatra at the Dunes on those Friday evenings, along with his friend Jack Daniels. He would nod in my direction and say hello in that smooth, velvety voice. That was about the extent of our interaction, although there were nights we actually had the table right next to his.

I was still very young, and Frank Sinatra was about the biggest star there was. The fact that he even acknowledged my very presence proved (as the hit Sinatra song suggests) "Fairy tales can come true, they can happen to you." To top it off, Frank was not only good-looking but he was extremely generous. Hundred-dollar tips for the waitresses were par for the course.

One night, Mother and I were having dinner when Sinatra entered without his usual gang. It was just Frank and Danny Schwartz, one of his best friends. We spotted him but didn't think anything of it until our usual waitress came over to our table.

CELEBRITY INTERVIEWS - FASHION - SPORTS - MOVIES - THE SOCIAL SCENE - TRAVEL

PALM SPRINGS STAR®

California's Premier Arts and Entertainment Magazine

DECEMBER 1997 $4.00

HAPPY BIRTHDAY FRANK

COVER STORY PAGE 10

INSIDE: HARRISON FORD AND THE ENVIRONMENTAL MEDIA AWARDS

TIGER WOODS AT THE SKINS GAME PLUS: PRESIDENT GERALD FORD AND GUIDE DOGS OF THE DESERT

DIANE KEATON AT THE TEDDY BEAR BALL THE GETTY CENTER

Palm Springs salutes Frank on his birthday.

"Excuse me, Toni," she said quietly, "Mr. Sinatra would like to see you." She nodded toward his unmistakable figure at the end of the bar.

I looked back and forth between my mother and the waitress, contemplating my next move. "Frank Sinatra wants to see *me?*" I asked.

"She'll be right there," Mother interjected, always Mama Rose from *Gypsy* giving her daughter a push. I watched as the waitress hurried back to Sinatra to relay the message.

Mother looked at me and I took a few deep breaths. While I felt comfortable interviewing celebrities, this command performance had caught me off-guard.

"Guess I'll be right back," I said, smiling nervously. She gave me a nod, and I made my way across the restaurant to see The Man.

With Frank, there was no beating around the bush. "We're watchin' you, kid," Sinatra said, and introduced me to Danny Schwartz. Frank's eyes were piercing blue, and I was unable to look away from him as he spoke. "You're good enough to make it in LA. Get out of here, kid, go to work there."

The room was dark or Frank and Danny would have noticed me blush. Actually, it didn't matter how dark the room was—the stars in my eyes at that moment could have lit up the room.

"Thank you, Mr. Sinatra," I managed to say. I kick myself now for not thinking of a clever one-liner to really make an impression, but the curse of moments like these is that we often think of the perfect thing to say or do only after the moment is gone. Before I could say anything else, Sinatra turned back to his drink and his friend. The conversation was over.

I don't think my feet even touched the floor as I made my way back to tell Mother what Frank had said.

* * * * *

I'd have been a fool not to take Sinatra's advice to heart, so I furiously began making phone calls. One led to another and thanks to some friends, I was set to audition for a job at KTLA, the local TV station in Los Angeles owned by the most famous movie cowboy of yesterday, Gene Autry.

Luck and perseverance guided me to the interview itself, but neither would be able to save me from the audition. It was absolutely terrible! After working so hard to create the Lady in White, where I was comfortable, I realized I had to go back to being just Toni Holt, a regular, real person whose segment had to fit within a news program format. My glamour shtick was stripped away entirely. No more fabulous outfits or exotic makeup, and certainly no more pussycat. These physical things had given me the power to believe in myself as the Lady in White, but for KTLA, I had to leave them behind.

It seems silly to think that simply removing the clothes and makeup from my routine would upset my entire ability to report, but it did. When you spend time working at something, really diving into it full-steam ahead, the results of such a stripping away were devastating. Without the Lady in White I had no identity, no structure within which to orient myself as a person, let alone a reporter, and I was completely unsettled during the audition. And worse yet, I looked positively awful. To make matters even more difficult, they had me read from a teleprompter, which I hated to do more than anything in the world.

Needless to say, I didn't get the job. Not right away.

In the days that followed my horrific experience with KTLA, I was launched into crisis. I couldn't stop replaying the interview and audition in my head, analyzing every little bit of where I had gone wrong. I was worried that I would have to rely on the Lady in White forever, that I'd never be good enough to get a job as just me.

Thankfully, my overthinking didn't last long. A few weeks later I received a phone call from KTLA. They decided to hire me despite my dreadful audition. The phone call was the positive reinforcement that I would be more than fine without the Lady in White, although I would have to work at it.

I was set to do a five-minute segment on the six and ten PM news. It reminded me of my time as an inexperienced teenager dancing at the Copacabana in New York. Only this time Mother wouldn't be hanging out of the apartment window across Madison Avenue, keeping an eagle eye on my every move. No, I was on my own for sure, but totally lacking direction.

One thing I did understand was how to get attention and build a buzz about myself. Now that I had the job, I knew I needed to get my name out there. After all, that's what Hollywood is all about. Noise, promotion, and publicity. Self-praise does not stink in La La Land.

First order of business was to change my look. The Lady in White had to vanish. I needed a fresh face for this new chapter of my life. I was introduced to a famous hairdresser by the name of Jimie Morrisey, who had a shop on the Sunset Strip. Jimie set to work changing me from blonde to a bronze color, ala Sophia Loren. He created a Gibson Girl hairstyle, which allowed me to go back to my more flattering doe-eye makeup. The new hairstyle gave me an aura of sophistication, and having a real artist like Jimie change my image provided a much-needed boost.

I needed to cause a stir to build suspense for my on-air debut. A few phone calls and a couple of weeks later, a giant billboard went up on the famed Sunset Strip.

Stretched across the picture were the words: "Move over, Rona, here comes Toni..."

CHAPTER ELEVEN

Gene Kelly and Gregory Peck

The new gig at KTLA only added to the whirlwind of changes occurring in my life. We rented Jose Iturbi's house on star-studded Rodeo Drive. Iturbi was a famous Spanish orchestra conductor, pianist, and movie personality.

A few days after we moved in, there was a jarring earthquake. It frightened the hell out of me. It was as though some giant had picked up the planet and shook it like a maraca. The ground beneath my feet moved so violently, I ran to find the children a safe place.

Once everything stopped shaking, there was a knock on my front door. I steadied myself and opened it. There stood Gene Kelly.

It was a total MGM musical moment, a scene cut from a Hollywood movie interjected into my life. He leaned against the door jamb in the quintessential Gene Kelly pose: one leg crossed over the other, one hand behind his head—the picture of calm, cool, and collected. I'm not sure if it was because of Kelly or the earthquake, but I nearly fainted.

"You must have been scared to death," he said with genuine concern. "I know you just moved in. Are you okay?"

"We survived," I responded, trying to maintain a casual air about the entire ordeal, including the shock of seeing Gene Kelly at my front door. He smiled at the remark, a smile I'd only seen on the big screen. "It's so nice of you to check up on us," I said.

"Isn't that what neighbors are for?" he replied, hooking a thumb to the house two doors down where he lived.

Truth be known, it took me a lot longer to recover from the sight of Gene Kelly than it did to calm down after the quake.

* * * * *

The Academy Awards show was rapidly approaching, and I desperately wanted to go to enhance my KTLA segments. I flashed back to my days as a kid in Brooklyn and the posters of movie stars pasted to the walls of my apple-green bedroom.

Despite my growing reputation as a Hollywood reporter, I was still relatively new and unknown. As a consequence, KTLA did not send me to the Academy Awards with a camera crew. Nor did a ticket to the event arrive in my mailbox as I had hoped it would. But I wanted to go, and when my mind is set on something, I find a way to make it happen.

Gregory Peck was president of the Screen Actors Guild. I called and asked the switchboard to please connect me with his office.

"Who's calling?" asked the operator.

"Toni Holt," I confidently replied.

"And may I ask what this is about?" the girl questioned.

"I just need to talk with Mr. Peck," I responded. "I have a TV show on KTLA where I report celebrity news, and I need to ask him a question."

A beat passed before the girl answered. "Mr. Peck isn't in right now. Can anyone else help you?" I could tell this wasn't going to be as simple as I naively thought it would be.

"Oh no, thank you," I said sweetly, but forcefully. "I need to speak to Mr. Peck."

The girl asked for my phone number, saying she would pass the message on. I didn't have an office at the time, so I gave her my home number.

That evening the phone rang and my mother, who was visiting, answered it. "Hello?"

"Is Ms. Holt there?" the man on the other end asked.

"Who's calling?"

"This is Gregory Peck," he replied. I could hear his familiar voice come through the phone.

"Oh, sure," Mother replied, rolling her eyes at me. "And I'm Betty Grable. Now who is this?"

"Mother, it's really him," I whispered, frantically waving my arms.

"It is?" she said, her eyes widening.

I nodded and tugged her wrist until she handed me the phone.

"Mr. Peck, thank you so much for calling me back. My mother was just kidding," I said apologetically. "I really have a favor to ask you..."

"I'm listening," he said, an element of apprehension clearly audible in his voice.

"I'm new in town and I've just started a television show on KTLA. I don't know if you've seen it…but it would mean so much to me if I could go to the Academy Awards, so I just wanted to give you a call to see if that would be at all possible."

My mother stood a few feet away listening to the conversation, staring at me in disbelief.

There was a brief silence on the phone and I added quickly, "And also to the Governor's Ball after the ceremony. And I'll only be one person, Mr. Peck. I'm not asking for two tickets…just me alone."

I must have gotten to him because Peck let out a laugh and said, "Yes, of course."

I thanked him profusely and hung up. Looking back, I shake my head in amazement at my audacity. It came from a good place, though. I've always been a driven woman, but it still astonishes me that I thought it was totally natural to call up Gregory Peck and ask for a ticket to the Academy Awards. The sense of brazenness we experience when we are young and naïve is absolutely mind-boggling, but without it, we would never experience some of the things we have in our lives. And guess what? I'm still doing it today.

Lo and behold, tickets to the Awards and the Ball arrived a few days later, and the events more than lived up to my expectations. At the Governor's Ball, I spotted my benefactor across the room. I walked up to Gregory Peck and introduced myself, and told him how grateful I was for his kindness. He smiled graciously and we chatted for a few moments. Our encounter was brief, but I doubt I will ever forget what a true gentleman he was, a to-the-core nice guy who took a chance on an ambitious stranger and sent me a ticket to the one place I'd always dreamed of going.

It seemed as though my life was finally in bloom.

* * * * *

Other than my days as the Lady in White, I had very little experience reporting news and gossip. Nor had I spent that much time

Toni interviews Gregory Peck.

Toni with Gregory Peck

in front of the camera. I boldly jumped headfirst into a pool and learned how to swim as I went along, something I would repeat the rest of my life.

Every day was a learning experience, and being on-screen made me come alive. In the same way a mirror helps us to see what we look like on the outside, knowing that people were watching me became a way for me to connect to myself on the inside.

I poured myself into my career. I was on fire. My thirst for fame and recognition was unquenchable. Once I established a foothold in Hollywood, I knew I had to keep reaching, stretching my arms out to grab hold of success just as I had as a child for that brass ring on the Coney Island merry-go-round.

At the same time, I was anxious and impatient. I'd been on KTLA for barely twenty minutes and found myself disappointed that I wasn't yet a household name. But instead of getting bogged down by my impossible goals, I became even more motivated to take Hollywood by storm.

I was a busy young woman, and my hard work started to pay off. I was hired to do a celebrity-profile column for the *Hollywood Citizen News*. Between my TV show and the newspaper column, I suddenly had access to just about anyone I wanted to interview. My first in-depth newspaper interview was called, "At Home with Gene Kelly."

Toni interviews Gene Kelly at his Beverly Hills home.

I don't think Miss Rona was ready to move over just yet, but she had to at least be peeking over her shoulder.

I was constantly scheming new ways to gain exposure, to reach the top of my game. One day, the thought occurred that I needed to somehow get on national television. Mother's advice once more crawled to the forefront of my mind: "If you can think it, you can do it." My God, how far that advice has taken me.

Dick Cavett was the star of a hugely successful talk show on ABC, a run that started in 1968 and lasted until 1974. Cavett, never afraid of controversy, was extremely bright and witty, and often sparred with his guests about taboo subjects like war and politics, topics usually off-limits for other talk shows. Perhaps the most famous on-air confrontation erupted between future senator, presidential candidate, and Secretary of State, John Kerry, and fellow Vietnam vet John O'Neill. Kerry, who served honorably in Vietnam, was dead set against the war, while O'Neill vehemently defended the actions of our government. It was classic TV at its genuine best.

I found it most impressive that Cavett rose from joke writer for Jack Paar, one of television's first late night icons, to having his own show in prime time before going head-to-head with Carson in the late night time slot. It was a rise to the top that I both envied and appreciated.

I started calling the Dick Cavett Show office in New York every few days, and I always said a variation of the same speech: "Hello, my name is Toni Holt. You don't know me yet—but you will. I have a billboard on the Sunset Strip and a new show on KTLA, and I'm going to be really, really famous. I know I'm going to be a big star, and you should have me on your program because it will do a lot for your ratings—not to mention a lot for me. I'll come on and you'll have yourself an unforgettable show...I promise, I promise." I must admit, I didn't have a clue what I would do.

I can't tell you how long this went on. And their polite response, like my pitch, was always the same: "When we have a spot where we think we can use you, we'll call you."

I knew this meant they weren't interested, but I kept calling anyway—and for some strange reason, they kept taking my calls. They never once said they were "out to lunch" or that they were too busy to talk.

Every single time I phoned the office, they took my call and I went through my whole routine again and again. I began to think it was a question of who would fold first. Would I give up or would they would give in?

One thing was certain, I wasn't giving up.

CHAPTER TWELVE

Rock Hudson

My TV show was gaining popularity, and my face was becoming more and more known around town.

Attending Hollywood parties was an unspoken requirement of my job as a gossip reporter. I got to brush shoulders with many of the A-listers, and my innately social personality was right at home at the various events I was invited to. At one such party, I was introduced to a Southern gentleman named Tom Clark, who happened to be Rock Hudson's press agent. Tom offered me the opportunity to interview Rock as a result of our chance meeting. I wasted no time setting up a lunch date at the legendary Polo Lounge at the Beverly Hills Hotel, my new favorite hangout.

Toni with Rock Hudson, the first day they met.

At the time, Rock was starring in a hit TV series, *McMillan & Wife,* alongside Susan St. James. Prior to that TV gig, Rock was a major romantic idol on the big screen. His films with Doris Day were some of the most popular and profitable movies of their time. Though he wasn't particularly known for his acting, Rock's enormous appeal and magnetic persona made him a giant star from the 1950s through the 1980s.

Rock's celebrity came about in an era when people went to the movies to be entertained, far different from today. The movie-going public is vastly critical now. People see a movie and write homespun reviews on the Internet, presenting their opinions to the general public as though they possess a PhD in film studies.

During Rock Hudson's time, "going out to the movies" was a source of pure fun. People went to see the likes of Rock Hudson, Tony Curtis, Gary Cooper, Cary Grant, Jack Lemon, and Marlon Brando—not only because they were great actors, but because they were popular personalities first and foremost. No matter how good or bad they were in a part—you always knew who they were. That's the mark of a real star. Actors of this era were gifted with personalities that could smash icebergs.

Rock Hudson and his peers were titans. They were gods and goddesses, and the studios nurtured them and protected them like found gold. Back then the studios were run by passionate dictators—powerful, decisive men who loved movies and the bottom line with equal fervor. They were feared and respected at the same time. Each studio had a list of contract players they moved around like chess pieces, placing them in movie after movie in an effort to create stars. And boy, did they. The six major studios each made as many as fifty movies a year then, not like today where maybe they greenlight ten.

Similar to the differences between movies then and now, celebrity gossip in those days was also wildly different. Today rumors about celebs are "tweeted" or "instagrammed" around the world, spreading like wildfire in seconds. No subject is considered off-limits or too personal. The rush to be the first one with the story—true or not—often creates inaccurate reporting.

We live in a much different society these days. A measure of basic respect for the privacy of celebrities as human beings has been entirely lost to the digital age. Hacking into private emails and personal cell phones has become as common as walking your dog.

In days past, the general public knew only so much about movie stars as studio executives and press agents would be willing to share. Close control was the name of the game, and what people read in movie magazines about their favorite actors and actresses was actually carefully choreographed and often fairy tales. Things would be written and revised, edited and dispensed in a way that aimed to hide any embarrassing or career-changing truths.

The fact that Rock Hudson was a homosexual was a closely guarded secret. The studio even had him married to squash any rumors that he was gay. It wasn't until Rock was diagnosed with HIV in June of 1984 that the public had any inkling of his personal life.

When I think back on that time, I'm reminded of Rock's role on the hugely popular TV series *Dynasty*. He appeared in the show from December 1984 to April 1985, and he played Linda Evans' love interest. It was widely reported that he was having trouble memorizing his lines, and his speech had deteriorated to the point that he was forced to use cue-cards. The storyline included a romantic kiss with Evans that created a huge stir when the public learned that Rock had AIDS. Ironically, his tragic death from AIDS brought public awareness to the horrible disease and helped to raise much-needed money in an effort to find a cure.

Rock was still safely concealed in the closet when I interviewed him that day at the Polo Lounge. The interview went so well that a few days later Tom Clark invited me to Rock's home for a dinner party. I was thrilled.

Rock lived in an area off Coldwater Canyon known as the Crests because of the street names: Lindacrest, Ridgecrest, Readcrest, and so on. His was a beautifully landscaped home positioned high on a hilltop. I was greeted by Tom and Rock, both of whom made me feel very welcome. I noticed immediately that there were only eight others there, all personal friends of Rock's. No one, other than our gracious host, was a movie star, and it quickly became obvious that this was an intimate affair. I was overwhelmed with a deep sense of honor to have been included on the short list. After a while we sat down to dinner, with Rock at the head of the table and yours truly seated directly to his right, the seat of honor.

Conversation flowed over the delicious meal. After we finished Rock asked if I'd like a tour of the house. He guided me around, pointing out various meaningful possessions that he cherished. He took me into his bedroom, where I couldn't help but notice the huge framed black-and-white photograph that hung above his headboard. It was easily four feet square. The image was a very recognizable male movie star.

I didn't understand the implication of the photo at the time, and I certainly didn't connect the dots, but I could feel Rock watching my face for a reaction. I continued to look around the room, doing my best not to show any emotion one way or another. Rock never said anything about the photo, and neither did I, and in that one brief moment of silence, a bond of everlasting trust formed between us.

Back at the studio the next morning, I spoke about my dinner at Rock's, but I left out the detail about the photo above his bed. A day or so after the show aired, I received a call from Tom Clark. We shared the kind of charming greeting found only between new friends before he got down to the reason for his call.

"Listen, Toni," he said, "Rock wants you to have his private phone number. Keep it with you, and if you ever need him, he'll be there for you." The smile dancing across my face as I jotted down the number could have been seen all the way back to Brooklyn. I thanked Tom and hung up, wondering how it was that I made such a lasting impression on this incredible movie star.

I realized that my on-air silence about the photo had gained Rock's respect and loyalty as a friend. As I said, when I first began reporting as the Lady in White, I wasn't trying to dish low-down dirt or throw kindling on a bonfire of rumors. I preferred to leave that to others.

A dear friend and mentor of mine, John Anderson, a real estate tycoon who built much of Century City and Westwood in LA, abbreviated it most succinctly: "DTRT. Do The Right Thing." For me, that covers it all.

Rock's enormous career as a movie star didn't exempt him from the right to personal privacy, and in return for an action I considered respectful, he rewarded me with a loyal friendship.

(left to right) John Anderson, Marion Anderson, Toni, Erica Brunson.

* * * * *

My incessant badgering of *The Dick Cavett Show* finally paid off. During my routine phone call to his office one morning, the woman on the other end of the line gave in.

"Well," she said, exhaling the heaviest sigh I've ever heard, "... Okay. We'll have you on."

I was incredulous. After months of racking up my phone bill and vowing to continue my calls until the day I died, the moment arrived when I finally succeeded.

"You'll have to pay for your own airfare and accommodations..." the woman continued brusquely. I squealed out an excited "yes" before she even finished. I don't know if they agreed to put me on because of the growing success of my show, or if I had simply worn them down with my persistence. Truthfully, it didn't really matter. I was going to be on national television.

When the blinding sparkle of finally being given the go-ahead from the show's producers had faded down to a more normal glimmer, I began to fret about specifics. Namely, what was I going to wear? As I searched my closet I felt a growing concern that I had nothing appropriate. This was the real deal—I had to look perfect. At the advice of a friend, I made a call to publicist Lee Anderson. Lee's business savvy was matched by an impeccable taste in clothes, so I was told.

"Lee, would you do me a big favor?" I asked. "I'm doing *The Dick Cavett Show* in New York, and I don't have a clue what to wear. Would you please help me?"

"Oh, my dear," she immediately responded, her affected English accent making her sound like an old-world fairy godmother. "Don't fret. We'll go shopping and fetch you something flawless."

She took me to the Elizabeth Arden dress shop on Rodeo Drive in Beverly Hills. She picked out two dresses. One with a voluminous black taffeta skirt that was tight at the waist and featured a big white collar, and another that was a pale turquoise sheath. The black dress struck me as very New York, so I bought it on the spot. It wasn't until after the show that I realized my dress bore an uncanny resemblance to the black-and-white uniforms worn by the waitresses at Schrafft's, a once-famous ice cream parlor in New York City. Instead of finding a dress to show off my cute little figure on national television, I had effectively clad myself in a penguin suit that made me look like an overweight waitress. My God, there was enough fabric in that dress to cover a Rose Parade float.

As it turned out, my outfit choice didn't matter at all. What happened on the show was far more important than that expensive and silly black dress.

CHAPTER THIRTEEN

The Dick Cavett Show

The week of my appearance arrived in a flash. I was all set to leave for New York, but before hopping on the plane, I needed to make one more phone call.

Jack Scott was one of the top executives at Ideal Publishing, which included *Photoplay* magazine amongst its vast stable of titles. Photoplay was well-known in the industry for its artwork and in-depth profiles of celebrities as well as for carrying columns by notable Hollywood legends such as Hedda Hopper, Louella Parsons, Walter Winchell, and Dorothy Kilgallen.

For someone in my line of work, it was an absolute coup to have a column in *Photoplay*. Jack Scott had no idea who I was and certainly had no interest in giving me space in this mega-magazine, founded way back in 1911.

I got him on the phone and told him about my upcoming appearance on *The Dick Cavett Show*. My plan was to convince him to watch my segment and see what I was all about. In my mind he would swoon over my talent and call me unremittingly until I agreed to write for *Photoplay*. Despite my unrealistic goal, the phone conversation went well. He agreed to watch the show and meet with me the following day. Everything was in place.

The day of the show, I was ecstatic. The sense of joy I felt over the realization of my dream to be on national television was so filling, room for nerves and anxiety simply didn't exist. I put on my black waitress dress, quadruple-checked my appearance, and headed over to the studio.

As I stood in the wings waiting for my turn to sit on the couch, I could see and hear everything that was going on. Cavett's first guest was actor Victor Buono, a heavyset man who reminded me of Sidney Greenstreet or Raymond Burr. At one point Cavett asked Buono what he thought about gossip. I was a little surprised by the question, since I wasn't due to join the panel until later in the show. But Cavett, the consummate professional, was obviously setting up the theme. I took it as a compliment. Unfortunately, Buono's answer did nothing to spark conversation.

"Gossip? Oh, I don't know. I don't have anything to do with that."

I was a little miffed at his cop-out answer, but I could understand his response. Victor Buono was the last person on earth anyone would ever gossip about. I think the only thing Buono was interested in outside of acting and Shakespeare was a refrigerator.

The next guest was Tony Randall, the quirky and erudite actor who starred in a number of movies with Rock Hudson and Doris Day. He also played fussy Felix to Jack Klugman's messy Oscar in the TV version of Neil Simon's hit, *The Odd Couple*.

I had seen Randall on enough talk shows to know that he was never short on opinions and loved to stir the pot with outrageous observations. I winced from the dark outskirts of the stage as I heard Cavett pose the same question about gossip to Randall.

"I think it's a sleazy profession," replied Randall. No sooner had the words left his mouth than a chill ran up my spine. I'd been too excited to really feel nervous about the show, but in that single moment I became petrified.

"Why would anyone choose that profession," Cavett bellowed.

Randall took the bait. "I don't know," he said venomously, crossing his arms and leaning back. "I mean, it doesn't take any talent to do something like that. It's just a terrible job. What kind of person would do something as dreadful and vulgar as spreading rumors about people they don't even know?"

My entire body stiffened as I listened. The elation I felt at my success in getting on the show was being torn out from under me with each and every word Randall spoke. I looked out into the studio audience, but instead of seeing a sea of happy faces I would use to energize my performance, I perceived a crowd of onlookers anxiously awaiting my crucifixion. Cavett and Randall were digging my grave, and the moment I stepped on stage, I'd be finished.

It was then the connection between Randall and Rock Hudson flashed through my mind. I spotted a pay phone on the wall, and borrowing some change from a stagehand, I rushed over to it. My trembling fingers furiously dialed Rock's private number, which I had committed to memory.

When I heard Rock's voice, I almost broke down in tears. Words tumbled out of my mouth, garbled by panic.

"Rock, this is Toni Holt. I'm really, really in trouble."

"Whoa, Toni, calm down. What is it, what's wrong?"

"I'm going to be on *The Dick Cavett Show* in about two minutes. I'm backstage now waiting to go on…and Tony Randall is on the couch… and he's preparing to kill me."

My voice caught at the end and I could feel my eyes welling up with tears. I was being set up for humiliation on national television. To make matters worse, I knew Jack Scott would be watching. He was about to see me fail at the hands of Tony Randall, and I'd never get the column in *Photoplay*. The fear of screwing up this potentially momentous move in my career caused me to imagine every negative outcome possible. It was a mental landslide.

"Toni," Rock said, snapping me back to reality. "Slow down. Breathe. You're not making any sense."

Heeding his advice, I took a deep breath. Then another. I could feel the tears fade from my eyes with each breath, and I started to explain the situation again. "Cavett and Randall are on stage talking about gossip… and Randall is saying that there's no decency in the profession…that you have to be a real sleazeball to report on that kind of thing. Rock, I'm about to go out there and get positively slaughtered."

A few seconds passed. I could almost hear the gears of his mind whirring.

"Okay, listen to me," Rock said. His voice was firm and steady, refueling me with confidence as he spoke. "When you go out there… *think timing*. Don't open your mouth until you can't hear a sound from the audience. There's a publicist named John Springer that works for Tony. All you need to know is that Tony pays him twenty-five hundred a month to represent him. Your line is this—and remember, deliver it at the right time. You say, 'Mr. Randall, if you think gossip columnists are so awful, why do you pay John Springer twenty-five hundred dollars a month? Do you do it to keep your name in—or out—of the news?'"

"Oh, Rock, thank you, thank you, thank you."

He wished me good luck and we hung up just in time for the commercial break. Rock's words had pulled me back together in a moment of crisis, and as I walked away from the pay phone, I felt armed for battle.

I was ushered onto the stage between commercials, and before I knew it, we were on air. Cavett introduced me and asked a few innocuous questions, and then let me have it right between the eyes.

"Why would a pretty girl like you choose such a sleazy profession like gossip?" he said with a smile.

The audience cheered his question.

"I certainly don't look at it that way," I retorted, smiling sweetly back.

Even before I finished my answer, the audience started to boo me. At that point, Randall, who had been sitting next to me in silence, jumped into the conversation.

"What a terrible way to make a living," he said, shaking his head in disdain.

"Why exactly is it so terrible? I think getting news about famous people out to the public is a good thing," I responded quickly, playing solid defense.

The audience was not my friend, however, and the back-and-forth only got worse from there. Whatever Cavett and Randall said was applauded—whatever I said was roundly booed. It was like I was the ball at a Ping-Pong match, getting swatted from one side of the net to the other between Cavett and Randall. It was difficult, but I remained patient, waiting for the perfect lull in conversation to drop the bomb Rock had armed me with.

The audience finally fell silent and I immediately perked up. This was it. My time.

"Mr. Randall, can you tell me something?" I asked in a loud, cool voice. I stared straight at him, my doe eyes parted all wide and innocent. "If you absolutely hate gossip—and you hate gossip columnists as much as you say you do—why do you pay two thousand five hundred dollars a month to John Springer, one of the finest public relations men in the country?"

I paused just long enough to see the blood drain from Randall's face before I swung the hammer. "Is it to keep your name *out* of the news...or *in* it?"

The sound of cheering radiated from the audience. Randall squirmed in his seat and cleared his throat repeatedly. He opened his mouth to respond, but his answer came out as arrogant and indignant.

"Why, to keep my name *out* of the news, of course," he scoffed.

I had gotten my rise out of him, and the audience didn't buy his answer for a single second. A shower of boos rained down from the dark seats surrounding the stage.

Filled with confidence, I turned my gaze to the show's host. "And Mr. Cavett, respectfully, sir…if you didn't get people to tell you gossip every night when you sit here with them—stories they couldn't hear anywhere else—I don't think your show would be as successful as it is."

The audience cheered and applauded even more, and I could see that Cavett loved it. His nightly goal of controversy had been achieved, and I saw the corners of his mouth go up in a faint smile.

At the commercial break Cavett summoned his producer and told him to hold the next guest, Ernest Hemingway's widow, Mary Hemingway.

"Tell her we'll pay her—and have her back another night."

They cut her spot and kept me on for the rest of the show. At the end, they brought Mary Hemingway out onto the stage, sat her down on the couch, and apologized for not having her on.

She threw back her head and laughed. "My dear, I feel like a piece of dry Rye Crisp after a banquet dinner." I could have kissed her.

The next morning I had my meeting with Jack Scott at Ideal. As promised, he had watched me on the Cavett show and said he was impressed with my show-stealing stunt. Based on what he saw, he would be willing to give me a column, but in one of their lesser magazines—not *Photoplay*.

When he made the offer, I smiled, but shook my head. "No, thank you," I said. "I can't start in a lesser magazine. I've loved *Photoplay* all my life, and that's what I want."

His eyes went wide and his eyebrows arched upward at my audacity. "But my dear," he replied, "you've never written for *any* magazine—how can you ask to start at the top?"

"Why not, Mr. Scott? You saw what I did on the Cavett show, and you were obviously impressed or I wouldn't be sitting here today. I want *Photoplay*."

Jack sat there looking at me like I was off my rocker, but I returned his stare so that he knew I was dead serious. After several moments of deliberation, he nodded and extended his hand.

"*Photoplay* it is."

Toni gets Photoplay Magazine, a dream come true!

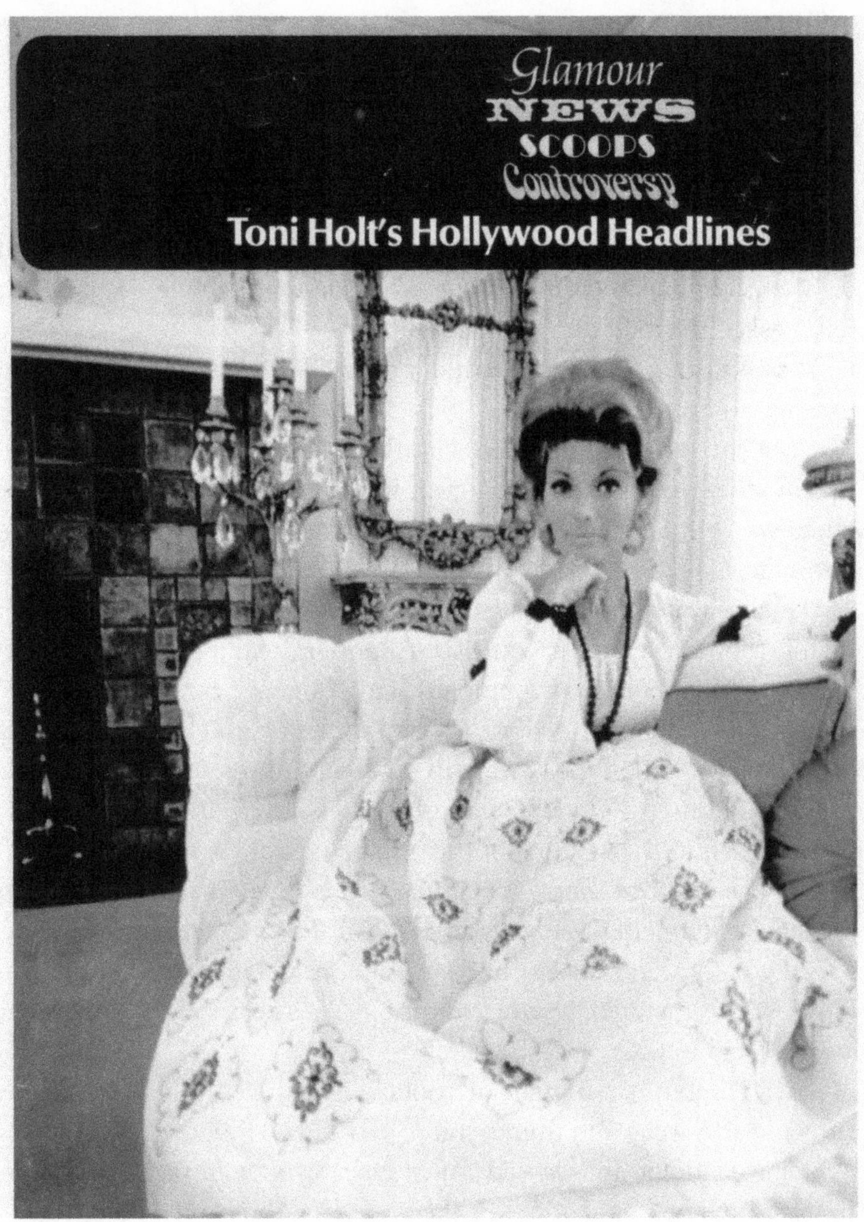

Toni's Hollywood Headlines

CHAPTER FOURTEEN

Howard Hughes

I was getting ready to go to work at KHJ—the Los Angeles TV station that stole me away from KTLA, when my phone rang. "Is this Toni Holt?" asked the man on the other end.

"Who's calling?" I asked. I didn't get many phone calls early in the morning, so I was on guard.

"My name is Robert Maheu. I work for Howard Hughes."

My doe eyes popped open even wider. I had no idea who Robert Maheu was, but I certainly knew Howard Hughes. Everyone knew of the billionaire.

Hughes was an industrialist, an engineer, an aviator, a filmmaker, a philanthropist, a genius, a womanizer...and more than a little eccentric. He formed Hughes Aircraft Company and designed the "Spruce Goose," a gigantic aircraft intended to transport troops and supplies during WWII. It barely got off the ground in an infamous test flight that lasted a minute and went no more than a mile.

I've been told that some of the original designs for the Goose were done poolside at my estate in Palm Springs in the 1930s, some sixty years before I bought it. Hughes acquired Trans World Airlines and later merged it with American Airlines. He was considered by many to be one of the wealthiest men in the country. So yes, I certainly knew who Howard Hughes was.

"Mr. Hughes is a big fan of yours," Maheu went on. "He watches your show every day and thinks you're very talented."

I stayed silent and waited for Maheu to offer more information. After all, anyone could identify themselves without any proof, and I wasn't about to be played for a sucker. I thought it best to wait and listen.

"Mr. Hughes wants to give you a scoop that will make you famous around the world," Maheu said.

Ah yes, this was it. The bait!

It wasn't that long ago that I put up my billboard with the quote "Move over, Rona, here comes Toni," and I always wondered whether I'd eventually fall into someone's crosshairs because of that stunt. For all I knew, Rona—or someone else—hired this guy to play with my brain, to test my mettle as a reporter. I could almost hear them conspiring: "We'll fix that little bitch. We'll make her look like a fool. We'll feed her some phony info, she'll put it on television, and she'll be finished. Bim, bam, boom…just like that!"

Well, I may have been inexperienced, but I wasn't stupid—or so I thought. I wasn't about to let some phony-baloney get the best of me.

"What's the story?" I asked.

"You can announce to the world tomorrow that Mr. Hughes is going to leave Las Vegas to live in the Bahamas."

Everyone knew Howard Hughes had been holed up like a recluse at the Desert Inn Hotel for the past four years. A couple of years earlier, he had refused to vacate the room he was staying in, and retaliated by buying the entire hotel. Now, that's style.

Did Robert Maheu, if he was Robert Maheu, really expect me to believe that Hughes was set to move out with no warning, no fanfare, nothing? There wasn't a more far-fetched story around for me to be fed.

"Thank you so very much for the tip." I hung up thinking, *You want me to report that? No way!*

Needless to say, I didn't go on the air with the story.

Biiiiig mistake! A couple of days later, I glanced at a newspaper and saw the headline plastered across the front page in bold font and block letters:

"HOWARD HUGHES LEAVES LAS VEGAS TO LIVE IN BAHAMAS"

I was shocked. I couldn't believe the man who called me had been the real deal. I felt foolish and stupid for even thinking the tip was a setup. I spent the day imagining what could have happened had I taken the risk and run the story. For once, I hadn't done my homework.

If I'd just made a few phone calls I would have known that Robert Maheu was Howard Hughes' chief aide, the same man who engineered the deals for Hughes' gigantic business empire. The same man who was a confidant to President John F. Kennedy and his brother Bobby. Legend has it that Maheu never once met Hughes face-to-face in all the years he worked for him. Fascinating.

In that infernal light of hindsight, I realized I could have easily circumvented the situation's whole potential for sabotage by reporting the conversation exactly as it happened. I could have said something like this: "I just got a phone call from a man who *claimed* he worked for Howard Hughes. He told me Mr. Hughes was leaving Las Vegas for the Bahamas. I don't know if it's true…I'm just reporting the phone call. We'll have to wait and see." I was truly kicking myself. I'll never know what the story would have done for my career at the time had I chosen to air it.

A few months later, I got a second chance. I once again received a phone call, this time from a man who identified himself as Howard Hughes' pilot.

"Well, you didn't use the first tip Mr. Hughes gave you, but here's another one." The pilot went on to say that he was flying Hughes from the Bahamas to a hospital in Houston.

This time I used it. It was 100 percent on the money. Sadly, Hughes didn't make it to the hospital. He died on the plane during the flight. I felt so badly that he didn't live long enough to know that I actually used his tip.

To say that Hughes was odd would be putting it mildly. One explanation is that he suffered from obsessive-compulsive disorder. It's been reported that he was obsessed with the size of peas. He used a special fork to separate the peas according to size. In his later years, the rumor going around was that Hughes was fixated on germs and would only drink orange juice freshly squeezed in front of him, and that he wore Kleenex boxes on his feet instead of shoes. One thing was certain, his mood swings and erratic behavior were legendary.

At the time of his death, the man who years earlier had set world airspeed records weighed an anemic ninety pounds, and his hair, beard, fingernails, and toenails were excessively long. While his kidneys were damaged and there was reported evidence of drug use, his brain was perfectly normal. I can only imagine how he must have suffered. That was April 1976.

Despite his penchant for secrecy, it was well-known that Mr. Hughes had a passion for pretty ladies. It's rumored he bedded his way through Hollywood during the thirties, forties, and fifties. His dance card overflowed with some of Hollywood's brightest stars, including actresses Rita Hayworth, Lana Turner, and the sultry Creole, Faith Domergue, another Gemini who shares my birth day (not my year).

But there was one special lady in his life, Ava Gardner. Their friendship lasted off and on for some twenty years, but Ava claimed she was never in love with him. In her autobiography, Ava described Hughes as being "...painfully shy, completely enigmatic and more eccentric than anyone I had ever met."

Kathryn Grayson, a star of the great MGM musicals, once told me that Hughes sent an entire Mariachi band to her Brentwood home one night to serenade her under her bedroom window like a scene from a movie. Grayson said she'd never even been out with him when it happened.

A tribute to the man is that the Howard Hughes Corporation remains a public company, and even today, HHC trades very well on the New York Stock Exchange.

I never met the man in person, but from everything I've read and heard, there will never be another Howard Hughes.

CHAPTER FIFTEEN

Playgirl Magazine

It was early 1973 and *Playgirl* magazine had set a launch date of June for their first issue. Their goal was to attract women readers the same way *Playboy* attracted men.

Cosmopolitan had just struck gold with their Burt Reynolds centerfold. He was totally naked, which the women went wild for, but you didn't see anything of importance. Regardless, the idea was brilliant and the issue sold hundreds of thousands of copies. *Playgirl* planned to go after the female demographic in a similar way, and they put together an A-team of professional photographers and smart writers to make sure it would be a slick, classy magazine. In short, the idea stood to make millions.

I met with Doug Lambert, the man with the golden idea who started the magazine. He was tall, lean, with dark, piercing eyes and even darker hair that he combed straight back with a slight pompadour-like mound in front. He wore a suit and tie, and had a nice way about him. His expensive clothes and well-appointed office couldn't quite camouflage the basic purpose of the magazine: to sell flesh.

During our meeting he explained that they were looking for someone to front the launch, someone who could represent the magazine in an elegant, attention-getting way. They needed a person who could speak well to audiences, who could be entertaining and lively, and who didn't need to rely on a script: my forte. I sat across from him, mentally checking off each of the requirements. When he was done listing them, I told him they had found exactly the right person.

Doug assured me they were going to do their centerfolds in a tasteful way with class and dignity. He made it clear that I would not be involved in selecting the centerfold firsthand or I wouldn't have taken the assignment. My job was simply to tour the country, as well as Europe, and promote the magazine in a way that garnered as much publicity as possible. How I chose to do that was pretty much up to me.

I hit New York, Chicago, Paris, London, and a slew of other major cities across the globe. Using my wit and charisma, I stirred the press into a frenzy over *Playgirl*. My quick mouth seemed to carry me miles in those days.

I've always been that way—the overachiever with a big heart. Constantly striving for perfection has led me to a load of insecurities and stress over the years, and criticism is rougher to take when you're this kind of person, but with the *Playgirl* job, I felt confident. I knew what could sell the idea to the public.

My concept was remarkably simple: wherever I went I would name the person I'd most like to see in the centerfold. I picked only the most famous people from any one city or country, and the more outrageous I made my suggestions, the more press I would receive. By throwing out a recognizable name as a potential centerfold, I gave the public a real reason to be interested in the magazine. After all, who would care about *Playgirl* if we only showcased Joe Smith from nowhere? Who cared about what Joe Smith looked like naked, except maybe Mrs. Smith? What's more, I was a true natural in front of a crowd. I instinctively knew how to build suspense and keep my audience squirming in anticipation of what male celebrity I might nominate next.

That's not to say that *Playgirl* didn't do their part as well. The magazine's public relations machine must have worked overtime because whenever I stepped off a plane, it was like a movie star arriving. Reporters and paparazzi were waiting for me. Flashbulbs popped as television and newspaper reporters fired questions. I was becoming a celebrity in my own right.

Playgirl took me everywhere and allowed me to meet countless VIPs. On a stop in London, I interviewed John Wayne and told him that he would make a real hero's center spread.

"I'll do it..." he replied, talking to me as though I were his favorite horse, "...if you pose nude beside me." A big grin spread across his face and I giggled. That exchange, complete with a picture of the two of us, was picked up for the front page of the *London Daily Mirror* the very next day. Nice work, Toni.

Later on, at a press conference, I expanded my list of centerfold nominees to include Richard Burton and Lord Anthony Snowden, the

Daily Mirror

EUROPE'S BIGGEST DAILY SALE

4p Saturday, January 19, 1974 No. 21,773

THE STRIP TEASERS

MANHUNTING Miss Toni Holt meets her match in big John Wayne. Miss Holt, who is looking for nude beef-cake for her male pin-up magazine, met Wayne at his London hotel yesterday. She thought he would make a "yummy" centre spread. Big John, 66, outstripped her by replying: "I'll do it, if you'll pose nude beside me."

Toni interviews John Wayne in London

husband of Princess Margaret, Queen Elizabeth's younger sister. That one really put the press in a tizzy. As the words left my mouth, I could hear audible gasps throughout the audience. At first I thought I had made a faulty move. The magnificent bouquet of yellow roses that arrived for me at the Dorchester Hotel the next day dispelled my doubts. They were from Lord Snowden himself, and included a card in his handwriting that read, "Dear Miss Holt. Thank you for including me on your illustrious list, although I have yet to hear from the Queen. Yours truly, Lord Anthony Snowden."

Toni gets flowers from Lord Snowden.

But these highlights run utterly pale in comparison to what happened when I travelled to Paris.

Toni in Paris for Playgirl Magazine.

Picture a ballroom in a hotel set up for a press conference—row after row of chairs all facing a large platform, a special stage built just for me. The ballroom was immense and it was absolutely alive with reporters. The anticipation of stepping up to the microphone was exhilarating. People were jammed together, including the entire French press corps, all eagerly waiting to hear me speak.

When it was time for the press conference to start, hundreds of pairs of eyes followed my every move as I made my way to the center of the stage. The buzz of the reporters became a hush. I explained how *Playgirl* would revolutionize the world, about how important it was to

Toni has fun in Paris.

engage major personalities that were known around the globe to be centerfolds. "After all, men look forward to looking at centerfolds—why shouldn't women?"

I went on to explain how the magazine would accomplish its somewhat lustful task with utmost elegance and taste. I barely made it to the end of my speech before members of the press started shouting. They couldn't wait to find out who I wanted from France and why.

I held up my hands for quiet, and a hush came over the crowd. I felt like Eleanor of Aquitaine, the former Queen of France. I milked the silence for a few seconds, then gave them my first choice.

"My most desirable person here in Paris is...Aristotle Onassis."

Needless to say, the mention of Mr. Onassis's name drew more than a few overwhelming "oohs" and "aahs" from the crowd.

"Why Onassis?" yelled one reporter.

"Because I think he's brilliant." I looked around the room. "Powerful." I scanned the room again. "And mysterious. And to me a man with all those assets is very sexy. I think he has a great sense of humor, and he truly understands how to get where he's going."

You could hear a pin drop in the ballroom as the reporters leaned forward with inquisitive looks, anxious to hear what I had to say next. There was no doubt I had them in the palm of my hand, and I purposely kept my voice soft and low as I told them the story.

"A friend of mine met Mr. Onassis when he first came to Paris. They used to go to a restaurant on the Left Bank where all the *right people* went to dine." My voice began to build. "Mr. Onassis didn't have much money at the time, but he looked terrific in a suit and tie. It was like he was born in the finest custom-made, pinstriped suit money could buy. Everything was always perfect about him. He went on to explain to my friend, 'If you want to be successful and important, it doesn't matter where you live. You can live in a one-room apartment over a garage, but to look important you must always dress in the most expensive clothes and shoes, and be seen having a drink in the finest restaurants, even if you can't afford to dine there.'"

The press loved my tale. I closed my reason for wanting him in *Playgirl* by saying, "Besides being brilliant and impeccably dressed, when Mr.

Onassis stands on his bank books, he is six-foot-four and overwhelmingly gorgeous...and he doesn't need that pinstriped suit."

The line brought thunderous laughter and applause, and a lot of head nodding as only the French can do. At that moment I felt like more than just a guest in their country. I felt like one of them. Some would disagree, but when you embrace the French—they embrace you back.

CHAPTER SIXTEEN

Aristotle Onassis

Two public relations men who worked for the European division of *Playgirl* took me to the world-famous nightclub Chez Regine, on the Rue de Ponthieu. I'd certainly heard about it, but I'd never been there.

Regine Zylberberg, a holocaust survivor, opened the restaurant-bar in 1957, and it quickly became world renowned for the rich and famous who enjoyed her incredible hospitality. From Sinatra to Maria Callas, Audrey Hepburn to Charlie Chaplin, they all came. It was the place to go and the place to be seen. While every tourist could go to the Eiffel Tower, few could get into Regine's, let alone get a good table.

I was truly excited to be going there. Just walking into the club took my breath away. The décor was 1930s Paris. Dark furniture. Muted colors. Mirrors on the walls. Crystal everywhere. It was a long way from the sound of the BMT subway whistling in my ear.

Shortly after we arrived, the PR people introduced me to Regine herself, the captain of the biggest society ship in Paris. The first thing I noticed about her was the laughter in her voice when she said "bonsoir." She was dressed flawlessly, all the way down to her high heel shoes. Her hair was a burnished red and she wore it full and curly, down to her shoulders. She was a tad on the short side, but to me she was a giant. Most of all, she was incredibly charming. Regine was known as the Nightlife Goddess, and it was easy to see why.

"Come, cheri, walk with me," she said. "I will introduce you around."

She took my hand and led me through the club. I felt a smile from ear to ear as we maneuvered through the crush of socialites and celebrities who seemed to fill every corner of the room. I don't think I'd ever seen so many gorgeous people in one place. While I thought I looked fairly chic that evening, the more people I met, the more I felt I had come up considerably short on the fashion scale. Every woman was dressed to the nines. Each one looked as if she should have been on the cover of French *Vogue*. Even the most unattractive woman there was able to create a fashion illusion that made her appear beautiful. I was convinced then and there that French women are without question the most elegant women in the world. They understand fashion far better than anyone else. To say that if you "dress well, you look well" was never more true than that night.

As for the French men in the restaurant, they weren't so bad, either. Every man looked handsome, powerful, and rich. When I was introduced to them, an eyebrow would lift in response. But only one. They all had suntans in the middle of winter. I imagined it was because they skied in Staad or flew to the Bahamas for a week. It was amazing.

Finally we arrived at a table of eight at the far end of the club. The guests were immersed in an animated conversation, which stopped the instant they saw Regine. My gaze went immediately to a slender, dark-haired woman seated at the far end of the table. My mouth went dry and my heart started beating really fast. It was Jacqueline Kennedy Onassis. She glanced quickly in my direction, then looked away and resumed her conversation as if dismissing me. Regine said something to them in French that I couldn't understand, and they all chuckled politely. I always loved the language, and it was at that moment I made a promise to myself to learn how to speak it.

"This is Toni Holt, my friend from America," Regine said simply, pulling me close. Then she gestured to the man sitting nearest to me. "This is Mr. Onassis."

I was well aware that my name and face had been splashed all over Paris for the last forty-eight hours, so I assumed everyone knew who I was and why I was there. With all the press I had received, it was hard to miss me. Nothing much was said after the introductions, and I felt like little more than a blip on Mr. Onassis's radar.

I was giddy and giggly when I returned to my table. I told my two chaperones about everyone I had met. I had never had so much fun. We ordered dinner and drank champagne. A short while later Regine came over and said, "Toni, Monsieur Onassis has invited you to join his table."

I looked to my dinner companions for help, hoping they would know the right thing to say—but they offered no help at all. They were obviously as stunned as I was. After what seemed like an eternity, I replied.

"Regine, thank you so much, but it wouldn't be appropriate for me to do that. We really have business to discuss."

I gestured to the PR men, and they nodded their heads in agreement like cartoon characters. Regine did not look happy but she retained her incredible charm. "Cheri, nobody turns down Mr. Onassis," she said quietly, although the reprimand in her tone was apparent.

Fear and panic swept through my very core. Had I done something terribly wrong? Was I about to be kicked out into the streets of Paris? Almost pleading, I looked at Regine and said, "I'm not turning him down. It's just not a comfortable situation for me."

Regine's response was silence. I felt doomed. I needed to say something more and fast. I couldn't believe the words that spilled out next. "If Mr. Onassis would like to join *our* table, I'd be delighted."

Regine turned as cold as the night air. Her warmth and charm suddenly evaporated. "*Vraiment*?" (Really?) she uttered as if I had insulted the entire country of France. Then she pursed her lips together and, as only the French can do, blew air through the narrow opening to create a sound something like "...pffffff." There is no English translation for this, but the sound says it all. It's just pure exasperation. It's saying, "You're insane; you're out of your mind! And you have an inflated opinion of yourself!" When you're this frustrated, all you can say is... "pffffffff!"

"Monsieur Onassis will never do that," Regine added in a haughty way as she quickly turned and walked off.

I felt like I had committed a terrible sin and would never be allowed back inside the club. Ever. Not only that, I thought for certain I had done something that would reflect badly on the magazine. Besides, the former First Lady of the United States—and now Mrs. Onassis—was sitting right there, albeit a good distance from her new husband. I just knew it wasn't the right thing for me to do. In addition, I didn't know for sure if he was aware of what I had said about him at the press conference, which would have put me in an even more awkward position. I had several reasons for not joining him. Primarily, I was petrified.

Two minutes later, lo and behold, there was Mr. Onassis standing at my table.

"I understand I have been invited to join you," he said politely.

I still get chills when I think about it. It was an "omigod" moment. What do you say to a man like him? What was I going to talk about? Seeing him up close and personal gave me a firsthand sense of his strength and power. He wasn't a tall man by any means, but his head was like a kingdom by itself.

I invited him to sit down. The two PR men pushed closer together, and Mr. Onassis sat next to me. "Ton-e…" he began. The "i" in my name had magically become an "e."

Without a doubt there is something very romantic about being called "Ton-e" by someone with a European accent. There's an underlying affection to the sound of the name that didn't exist before.

"Ton-e," he went on. "I am very flattered by all the things you said about me."

A-ha, I thought, feeling the blood rush to my face. He *did* know about the press conference.

"Well, Mr. Onassis, I think you're quite incredible. You're an amazing success story. And it's a privilege to meet you in person."

The two men I was with couldn't believe what was happening, and they pretended to carry on a conversation between themselves, desperately trying to be invisible. The music and the conversation in the restaurant were loud, but I clearly heard what Mr. Onassis said next. He leaned close and spoke in a soft, intimate voice. "I would like to invite you to fly with me to California tomorrow."

The bold invitation sent shock waves through my entire body. I felt my knees bang together under the table, and I quickly replayed his words in my mind to make sure I had heard him correctly. I tried not to respond in an accusing manner, but the words just flew out of my mouth.

"You're married," I said.

"I know," he responded simply. "But I am inviting you to join me. I want you to come with me to California." This was a man who was totally sure of himself, sure of what he wanted. And *I* was what he wanted.

There was a part of me that felt like this was happening to someone else, and another part that knew exactly what was going on. Was I tempted? Are you kidding? Who wouldn't be? But it was clear he had made an assessment of me based on what he had read, what he saw, and what I had said about him.

In my secret moment of reality, what I really wanted to say to him was "How could *you,* Mr. Onassis, a married man—married to the most beautiful and envied woman in the world—invite *me* to come away with *you*? You don't even know me. You don't know anything about me. For all I know, I could go away with you, and an hour later you could be so disenchanted you would drop me in the Atlantic without a life jacket.'

I glanced at my associates to see if they had heard what Mr. Onassis had said. If they had, they didn't let on. I was definitely on my own.

I gathered my thoughts, returned to reality, and gave him my answer. "I'd love to," I said. "I really would, Mr. Onassis. But there are a few problems. You see, I'm working. I'm here doing my job. And in California I have a television show. I'm not free to fly around the world. And quite honestly, I'm just bourgeois enough to say I couldn't imagine flying with you having Jacqueline Kennedy as your wife."

His answer was short and to the point. "You don't have to worry about your work anymore. I will take care of you."

I was so startled I almost slid to the floor. Not only did he want me to go away with him, he wanted me to be his mistress. And this was all in one minute! Yet, there was nothing crude or sleazy about his offer. It was all very elegant and proper, if something so improper could be proper. The European culture for many of the wealthy is—and always has been—that the wife is the Madonna, and the other women are entertainment. I don't know if I knew it then, but it kind of made me feel how insecure a woman could be, being married to someone like Onassis.

"Oh, Mr. Onassis," I said. "I thank you with all my heart. But I have a mother, two children, and—"

He stopped me before I could say anything more, hushing me with a wave of his hand. My reluctance was unmistakable. "Ton-e, if you change your mind...please let me know." He slipped a card into my hand and looked into my eyes, "I do hope you change your mind."

My heart was beating so fast I could feel it in my throat, but I was not about to change my mind. "Thank you very much," I said, barely able to get the words out. "I will never forget you."

He slid his hand from mine. "I have to go back to my table now." Without another word, he got to his feet and walked back to his wife and friends.

I did not know this story at the time, but the rumor was that Onassis believed his marriage to Jackie had come with the Kennedy luck, most of it bad. He confided to a dear friend that his luck went south from the moment Jackie entered his life, and it never got better. When I think back on that night at Regine's, it's entirely possible Onassis knew that he had to get away from Jackie, and in his own fantasy—by chance or fate—was hoping I was the woman to change his luck.

I never saw him again in person. And I never forgot him.

The other rumor going around Paris was that when he married Jackie, he was still in love with his constant companion, the opera singer Maria Callas, and he died still in love with her. Many believed that Onassis married Jackie mainly because he wanted a step up in society, and that she wanted to get away from all the tragedies of the Kennedy clan.

While you can't say that Aristotle Onassis was a handsome man, it wasn't about being handsome—it was about power. My moment with Onassis made me realize that when a man can buy whatever he wants—he wants whatever he can buy, and he doesn't let a little thing like hurting someone's feelings or being married get in his way.

It made me recall a 1964 cover of *Town & Country* magazine. The headline beside a photo of Aristotle Onassis read: "WHAT ONASSIS WANTS ONASSIS GETS."

For some women, power is the most seductive trait in a man. This is especially so for someone like me who was deprived of a real father/daughter relationship. I think that's why I was always attracted to older men, strong men, at least as I envisioned them.

Of course, things didn't always work out the way I thought they would.

Incredibly, within a few months of our meeting, Aristotle Onassis was dead. Only sixty-nine years old.

CHAPTER SEVENTEEN

Frank Sinatra and Ava Gardner

My show on KHJ was a solid hit. Periodically, I arranged trips to Palm Springs to take a break from the daily stress. I missed the desert community that I'd come to call home and I found it comforting.

I had been gallivanting around town for a few days when I bumped into Frank Sinatra. It was a brief encounter, echoing our first meeting at Ruby Dunes restaurant. He told me he was proud of what I had accomplished since my days as the Lady in White. As we parted ways, he said to me, "Toni, I'm going to have my PR man Jim Mahoney give you a call."

My phone rang a few days later. It was Jim Mahoney, just as Sinatra had promised.

"Mr. Sinatra asked me to reach out to you," he said, all business. "Can we have lunch?"

Can we have lunch? I would have brought a three-course meal to his office if he wanted me to. We met a few hours later at the Brown Derby, one of the great Hollywood landmarks of yesterday.

As a play on its name, the restaurant was shaped like a derby hat and the walls were lined with caricatures of movie stars. The maître d' guided me to a table in the back corner of the dining room where Mahoney was seated. We made our in-person introductions while reviewing the menu. The Brown Derby was known as the site where the famous Cobb salad was created in 1937. We decided to order them in honor of history.

We chatted pleasantly about a number of things while we waited for our food to arrive; then Mahoney steered the conversation back to business.

"Mr. Sinatra thought you would like to make a prediction," he said simply.

"A...prediction?" I asked, a little confused.

"Yes," Mahoney continued, ever the professional. "Mr. Sinatra suggests you might want to predict on your show that he's going to retire."

"Frank Sinatra is giving *me* the inside scoop?" I asked, needing to be sure I had heard him correctly. Mahoney confirmed the message with a nod of his head. "Well, when should I run the story?" I asked.

"As soon as you want," came the reply.

As the information sunk in, I realized that the news itself—that Sinatra was retiring—was more shocking than the offer I was given to report it.

That same day I wrote it into my column—and that night I released the news on my KHJ TV show. "Watch the news," I said, "because I'm predicting right here, right now that Ol' Blue Eyes is going to retire." I went on and on about his records and his movies, providing background for the story, and I finished by saying, "No matter what, he'll never leave us, even if he's home cooking pasta in Palm Springs."

A couple of days later, Frank Sinatra announced his retirement. Since my show was only a local show—and not on one of the networks—I didn't get as much play on it as I would have hoped, but the entire thing sure sent my stock soaring, and I had my superstar friend to thank for that.

It just goes to show how people who play even the smallest role in your life can change everything for you. I never spent much time with Frank, but he was one of my guardian angels. He had popped up in my life to give me the push I needed to go to LA, and now he was back to give my career another push forward.

* * * * *

I had added a syndicated TV show to my routine which took me to London to conduct interviews. I called my show *Toni Holt in Hollywood.* While in London a friend invited me to dinner at the very chic White Elephant restaurant on Curson Street. The restaurant was right around the corner from the Dorchester Hotel, where I was staying, and I positively loved the atmosphere and charm of the place.

We arrived at about 6:30, and because of the early hour, the long, narrow dining room was all but empty. There were only two other people having dinner—two women I barely took notice of as we were escorted to the table directly beside them. As I slid onto the red banquette against the mirrored wall, I got a good look at the woman who would be sitting next to me. It was Ava Gardner, former wife of Frank Sinatra, and one of my childhood idols.

She looked even more gorgeous in person than she ever did on the screen or in any of the photographs that hung on my wall when I was a kid. Her hair looked beautiful, her makeup perfect. There was definitely something about her in person that film could never quite capture. And there she was, in the flesh, sitting right beside me.

I'm sure I let out a little gasp of surprise at the initial shock of seeing her, but ultimately I managed to control myself and offer a shy smile. I didn't know whether to laugh with joy or ask for her autograph. It was one of those moments that seem far too coincidental to be real, a moment that makes you question whether there is someone out there planning your every move.

What are the chances that Ava Gardner would happen to be in the exact same restaurant—at the exact same time—and on the exact same day? My gambler father would have said that the odds weren't very good, and for once, I would have agreed with him. I wondered why she was there so early. After all, dinner in London is seldom before 8:30. Was it because she didn't really want to be seen?

She smiled back at me, a smile so lovely and genuine that it immediately put me at ease. To this day, I remember exactly what she was wearing: an exquisite, form-fitting black wool dress with a high neck and long sleeves. Over one shoulder was a long black fox stole that she left in place while she ate. I tried not to stare but it was impossible to pull my eyes away.

As I settled into the banquette, I could feel her turn to me.

"Excuse me, but aren't you Toni Holt?"

I couldn't believe she had spoken to me, let alone known my name! All I could muster was a simple "Why, yes, I am."

"Oh, I'm so familiar with you," she continued.

"How come?" I asked, eager beyond words.

"My sister Beatrice lives in Los Angeles and I often visit her. She never misses your television show—she just loves you. And I've become a fan as well."

"I...I don't know what to say. I just think you're the most beautiful, wonderful person I've ever seen." I was so nervous all I could think of doing was to compliment her.

Ava laughed that flirty laugh of hers and issued a warm and friendly "Thank you." She said she was going to tell her sister she'd met me, and that her sister would be very excited. I wanted to ask Ava for an interview, but I didn't dare. I recalled seeing her picture in the London papers a few days earlier—she was wearing a cap and sunglasses, and walking her dogs in the park by the Barkley Hotel. Something about that photo told me that Ava Gardner wanted to be left alone, so I didn't intrude on her privacy. Sometimes a moment has to remain that—a moment.

When she and her friend had finished dining and got up to leave, I wanted to grab her and give her a hug because she was so nice, but I resisted the urge. As I watched her walk out of the dining room, I caught sight of her high-heeled black suede pumps and the black suede dinner bag she was carrying. I remember thinking, *No matter what, I'm going to get an outfit just like that.*

When I returned to California, at the top of my must-do list was a note to find a black, tight-fitting wool dress. I finally found one, and bought a pair of black suede pumps to go with it. Then I bought a long black fox stole. Whenever I put on that outfit—and I put it on often—I knew I looked fabulous. Ava Gardner had inspired me that night. She dressed me and taught me so much, just from the one brief exchange we had in that restaurant.

I was devastated when I learned that Ava had a stroke in 1989 and was partially bedridden. They say Frank Sinatra paid for some of her medical expenses, and though I don't know whether that bit of gossip is true, it sure makes sense. Even though Ava could afford her own expenses, Sinatra did pay for a medically staffed private plane to take her back to the U.S. to see more doctors. I know that many people have said Sinatra never got over his love for Ava, even after their marriage ended in 1957. After seeing her that night at the White Elephant, I can truly understand why. To me she was a goddess.

On January 25, 1990, Ava Livinia Gardner died of pneumonia at her home in Westminster, England, outside London. She was sixty-seven. I wept. For the first time in my life I experienced the crushing feeling of losing a childhood idol. I felt a bit of light go out of the world that day, but in my heart I know that Ava's beauty will never die—not as long as there are TV channels like AMC, TCM, and TNT to refresh our memories with movies of a time when movie stars were real movie stars.

Ava was buried in a pink dress (just like my mother) in her hometown of Smithfield, North Carolina, in 1990.

Before Frank married Ava in 1951, he was married to Nancy Barbato. They had three children together: Nancy, Frank Jr. and Tina. Despite his reputation with the ladies, Frank must have liked being married, as he wed Mia Farrow in 1966, although the marriage only lasted a couple of years.

But the good times continued to roll for Frank, and eight years later he married his close friend Barbara Marx, former wife of Zeppo Marx, one of the famous Marx Brothers. Barbara and Frank had homes across the golf course from each other at Tamarisk Country Club in Rancho Mirage. There were jokes at the time that Barbara was planning to dig a tunnel under the fairway to Frank's house.

Tunnel or no tunnel, the dream she confided in me a few years earlier came true when she married Frank on July 11, 1976. They remained married the rest of their lives. Barbara passed away in July of 2017, nineteen years after Frank. They are buried side-by-side at Desert memorial Park in Cathedral City, California.

Barbara, a former model and show girl, left quite a legacy as she and Frank founded the Barbara Sinatra Children's Center at Eisenhower Medical Center in Rancho Mirage. The non-profit facility provides therapy to young victims of physical, sexual and emotional abuse.

If you visit Palm Springs you can see Barbara's golden star on the Palm Springs Walk of Stars. And while you're there, take a peek at mine, too.

Above: The Sinatras Engagement - 1976

Below: Frank and Barbara Sinatra's Wedding July 11, 1976

Photo Credit: Springer/ Corbis-Bettmann

Page 19

Frank marries Barbara Marx.

Barbara and Frank Sinatra, the happy couple.

Frank & Barbara Sinatra

Fans can send messages to Frank and Barbara via the Internet:

www.sinatracenter.com

The Barbara Sinatra Children's Web Site will provide you with information regarding the Sinatra's philanthropic activities and showcases the latest Sinatra activities including the Tenth Annual Frank Sinatra Celebrity Invitational Golf Tournament February 5 through 7, The Sinatra Celebrity Cook Book, recipes and much more.

Frank and Barbara, later years in Palm Springs.

CHAPTER EIGHTEEN

Glenn Ford and Rita Hayworth

Glenn Ford was one of my first interviews for *Photoplay* magazine. He was a movie star in the most classical sense, and I was lucky to land the interview. In 1958, he topped the list of box office champions for his performance in Frank Capra's *Pocketful of Miracles.*

Richard Gully, Glenn's press agent, was the original Dapper Dan. English and elegant, Gully knew everyone. For some reason he also knew who *I* was. He contacted me out of the blue to ask if I wanted to meet with his famous client. The meeting was set at Glenn's house behind the Beverly Hills Hotel, right next door to Rita Hayworth. It didn't get any better than that.

I knew I had to ask all the right questions or the interview would be a disaster. I asked everyone I knew about the famous actor. I squeezed information about Glenn out of anyone and everyone who crossed my path. By the day of our meeting, I felt relatively well-informed.

That morning, I took pains to look as attractive as I could. My fashion style was inspired by Raquel Welch following an interview I did with her a few days prior. I dressed in a long, off-white, lace cotton dress with high-heeled, ankle-high boots. Convinced I looked as fetching as Raquel, I rang the bell and Glenn himself opened the door.

"I'm so happy to meet you," he said with a dazzling smile. We went into the living room and he sat down in what I came to learn was his favorite club chair. The leather was worn and crackled, a testament to how often he sat there. I sat across from him on a small sofa.

Because of my research I knew Glenn had a reputation for being tight-fisted with a buck. I noticed that while the house was furnished nicely enough, the clothes he wore were not what one would regard as up to date or stylish. They looked lived in and comfy. My guess was that he was the kind of man who couldn't care less about what was fashionable. As I got to know him over the years, I saw him wearing the same checkered sport jacket time after time.

We launched full-steam into the interview. I sensed he was enjoying himself, although at times his answers were a little guarded. The years of Hollywood socializing taught me a little trick to help get people to open up. If I sensed a conversation was drowning, I would ask the person I was interviewing if they ever had a psychic experience. The question is simple enough, and people really respond to it—especially if the answer is yes.

As the interview progressed, I found myself wanting more answers. "Do you think you ever lived before?" I asked.

His answer was animated, "Oh, yes! I lived before…in Scotland."

Glenn told me that his friend Uri Geller, the spoon-bending Israeli mentalist, assured him that he was once a soldier who had been stabbed in the chest with a sword and buried in Scotland. "I traveled to Scotland and found my grave from another life."

To prove his story, he opened his shirt and showed me a scar on his chest that he was born with. He said the scar came from the sword. He added that when he was in a hypnotic trance, he could play the piano like a professional. Any other time, he assured me, he couldn't play a single note.

Part of what I like to do when I interview stars is to walk through their homes with them. You gather a lot of information about a person this way, and that helps provide insight as to who they are and what is important to them. As we toured the house, Glenn told me about his yearly trips to Canada and how he loved spending quiet time fishing for salmon. I could sense how he looked forward to those trips—to getting away from the hustle and bustle of Hollywood.

Glenn pointed out his vast collection of autographs hanging on the walls. The scribbled names ranged across genres, from politics to entertainment to sports, and spanned decades. The impressive collection had to be worth an absolute fortune, and it obviously meant a lot to him. I'm guessing that's what Glenn spent his money on.

By the time we finished the interview, my audiotapes were full. I made a habit out of using a tape recorder because I had to be absolutely accurate for my column. Ever the gentleman, Glenn walked my handful of tapes and me to my car, and we said our good-byes. I can't explain

Glenn Ford shows Toni his autograph collection.

why, but as I looked back at his home in the rearview mirror, I had a hunch we were destined to become good friends.

My intuition proved right, as it often has over the course of my life. Over the ensuing years, Glenn invited me to dinner or cocktails, and I could always expect to receive a salmon from his annual Canadian fishing trip. I occasionally called him with a question or two about a particular celebrity, and he was always helpful and eager to talk to me.

There was a rumor around Hollywood for years that Glenn had a drinking problem, but I never saw any evidence of it. At the same time, I've learned that some of the best drinkers are private drinkers, so I can't make the call one way or another. I always thought Glenn was a perfect match for his neighbor, Rita Hayworth, and wondered why they never hooked up. After all, they sizzled as the romantic duo in *Gilda*. Check it out on TCM or AMC.

Glenn called me often over the next few years, including an unexpected invite to his wedding to Cynthia Hayward, his current girlfriend.

Cynthia was a model and an actress. She was thirty years younger than Glenn, who was sixty-two when they got married. Glenn was meticulously slow and cautious about everything he did, so I'm sure he gave his impending marriage a lot of thought, four years to be exact. He was not the luckiest guy when it came to being married. Glenn walked down the aisle four times. His first wife was Eleanor Powell, the extraordinary dancer from the great movie musicals of the 1930s and '40s.

I had met Cynthia several months earlier. She was living with Glenn at the time, although they had separate bedrooms. He had a gorgeous master suite on one floor of the house, and she kept an equally beautiful bedroom on the lower floor. I found that to be a revealing peek into the private life of Glenn Ford. Clearly he didn't want anyone too close to him. I had no idea why, but it did make me think.

Cynthia was pleasant in a standoffish way. She supposedly came from an upper-class family, but didn't like to discuss it. If I asked her a question, she declined to answer in a very ladylike manner, claiming she wasn't in the habit of talking about herself.

The wedding was set for 11:00 a.m. on Saturday, September 10, 1977. When I arrived I saw that the press had already surrounded the house. Reporters, photographers, and TV cameras were everywhere. A few of the guys knew me, and as I walked up the driveway, one of them shouted, "Toni, no...no, you can't go up there."

I called right back, "Oh, yes I can! I'm an invited guest."

I have to admit it made me feel good as I walked to the front door knowing I'd caused a stir among my peers. I could almost hear them talking, wondering how I came to be invited to the wedding. In fact, I was the *only* member of the press to be invited!

Inside, it was a night at the Oscars, only it was eleven o'clock in the morning. Stars, stars, and more stars, everywhere I looked: John Wayne, Frank Sinatra, Jimmy Stewart, the mayor of Los Angeles, Tom Bradley... oh, and little old me, Toni Holt. Seriously though, every face was a veritable legend. If you could have frozen the room and taken a picture, it would have made an incredible poster. Oh, if only I had an iPhone then.

I immediately dove in and made my rounds. To those I didn't know, I introduced myself. It was like dying and going to heaven for me, only better. I'm sure I had a glass or two of champagne, I don't really remember. I was so overwhelmed and excited, I could have done anything. And I did get a big hello and a grin from Frank Sinatra.

The wedding was held in the garden, followed by a sumptuous sit-down luncheon. It was over by two-thirty in the afternoon. I drove back home and passed out on the bed, exhausted from socializing.

* * * * *

While doing my Hollywood segment on *Good Morning LA*, I was overjoyed to see that Rita Hayworth, another of my childhood idols, was booked to come on. I marked the day on my calendar, and looked forward to it like a child on Christmas morning.

On the day of the interview, Rita arrived at eight o'clock to take her seat in the makeup chair. It was early, yet she seemed kind of unbalanced in a way. I knew that she had a reputation for drinking, but I couldn't tell for sure if she was drunk or not. I prayed that she wasn't. I recalled how Glenn Ford, Rita's next-door neighbor, had told me in strictest confidence that Rita used to go out in her garden when the moon was full and bay at it. How strange is that?

Unfortunately, time had not been kind to Rita Hayworth. Yes, she still looked lovely in the floor-length emerald-green and white print shift dress she wore, but the unhappiness in her life was evident on her face. The gorgeous red tresses that were once her trademark had been chopped off. Instead, her strawberry blonde hair was cropped short, just above her shoulders. When Rita joined me on the set for the interview, she didn't just sit down in the chair next to me—she collapsed into it, and she seemed to have trouble putting her thoughts together as we talked. Luckily for me, there were a few other celebrities on the panel that morning, so the pressure to keep the conversation flowing wasn't overwhelming.

Thinking back on the interview—and Rita herself—it was entirely possible and probably more likely that she was more affected by the onset of Alzheimer's, which eventually took her life, than she was from alcohol.

CHAPTER NINETEEN

Dean Martin

I'd been in the mix of the celebrity crowd long enough that most of the stars knew who I was. I had developed a reputation for delivering gossip with a fun, humorous style. My careful avoidance of all things disparaging gave me an edge when it came to getting stars to trust me. I wasn't white bread, but I had the natural ability to take the edge off even the ugliest gossip. Celebs would call me directly with items, knowing a story was about to drop and hoping my light-hearted spin would help to ease the sting. I took each call as a sign that all my hard work and sacrifice were paying off.

At the same time I couldn't rely only on the stars themselves to feed me stories. Every star had a press agent, and I made it a part of my daily routine to call as many as possible to see if they had any scoops to give me.

I understood it was a game. For instance, if they gave me a "hot story," I would air a lesser story for them. Or, they might give me news on something and ask me to sit on it for a few days until things solidified. I might get clued in about a celebrity divorce, and be asked to wait until a wife served her husband with the papers before broadcasting the news to the world. I always obliged. Press agents and I needed each other. Quid pro quo was the nature of the beast.

I quickly realized that celebrities and press agents weren't the only ones with stories to tell. I learned to tap other resources: hotel doormen, car parkers, waiters, a maître d' at the hottest restaurant, even bathroom attendants. Everyone with something to spill was a potential source of information.

I was living in a house on Roxbury Drive then, probably the most famous street in Beverly Hills. It was positively studded with stars. Milton paid somewhere in the neighborhood of a hundred and seventy-five thousand dollars for the house—quite a pretty penny at that time. A recently divorced and remarried Lucille Ball and her new hubby, comedian Gary

PATTY DUKE TELLS HOW LUCILLE BALL DEFEATED HER
"Desi has deserted me! All I have is his baby..."

PHOTOPLAY

SEPT. 50¢

Dean Ma
Sin

ANDY WARNS
He's
but

th
Heart

RNS
INS!

s!

HAPPENINGS
Toni Holt

WE WONDER: One of our most exclusive Beverly Hills bistros played host the other night to none other than Senator Ted Kennedy and long-time friend, Angie Dickinson—Burt Bacharach's wife. Apparently, Burt couldn't leave the family nest that night, because they dined without him. Their conversation appeared so

board was Claudine Longet, who Kirk dropped off in Paris for a visit with her mother and sister. All of which proves, it pays to have rich friends!

HOSTILE DUO: Raquel Welch's estranged hubby, Patrick Curtis, is carrying a king-size chip on his shoulder. He's been very uncooperative with the press, and even punched a photographer who tried to take his picture. Well, perhaps after all these years with Raquel, some "cool the press" tricks have rubbed off on him.

CAMERA SHY: And another one who doesn't like to see the bulbs flash is Candice Bergen, which surprises us because she herself is an accomplished photographer. Of course, the reason for her display of temperament could be that she doesn't like her secret dates with Lou Adler to be recorded on film . . . And believe me, they have been having plenty of them.

Toni's Photoplay column with Frank Sinatra and Dean Martin.

Morton, were our neighbors, along with Jimmy Stewart and his wife, Gloria. Rosemary Clooney lived down the street, next door to Ira Gershwin's widow. Freddie Fields and Polly Bergen lived a few houses away, as did singer Joni James, who had a number of chart-topping hits.

Life on Roxbury Drive seemed to settle right in on me. The youngest kid on the block, I could hardly leave the house without running into a well-known actor or actress. I suddenly found myself living among the very people I was reporting on.

It has always been my experience that fame and money breed elaborate eccentricities among people. For example, just down the street from us lived Agnes Moorehead, the award-winning character actress who had played Endora in the long-running television show *Bewitched*. Her house had previously been owned by Zsa Zsa Gabor.

Agnes threw a "girls only" dinner party for me shortly after we moved in so I could meet all the gals on the street. She gave me a tour of her amazing home, which included a room on the lower level that was decorated exactly like the Moulin Rouge in Paris. It even had black-and-white checkered floor tiles, bistro tables, and emerald-green décor. It was a Hollywood set right there at home.

My house was the perfect size for entertaining. I started throwing parties, which I found not only pleasurable, but also helpful in giving me instant access to celebs I would ultimately interview. It was a time of fierce networking for me. People would come over with their friends, who would bring along *their* friends, and before I knew it, my house on Roxbury Drive had become a social destination.

The night Lawrence Harvey stopped by sums the whole thing up for me. The actor swept through the front doorway with his favorite bottle of white wine clasped under his arm, and wearing a cape that he promptly slid from his shoulders with a flourish. With all eyes riveted on him, he greeted the guests, shouting, "Fuck you, everybody!"

Ah, the weirdness of Hollywood. It was grand.

Sometimes a tip would come from an old friend, like my dear pal Duny Cashin. Duny was a flamboyant and wonderfully entertaining bisexual. He was said to be the one-time boyfriend of Hal King, the famed makeup artist at Warner Bros. King did Lucille Ball's makeup, and he was known as the master of the mini-facelift. He would accomplish this feat by putting a star's hair in teeny-tiny braids and pulling it back really tight around their hairline. It was almost impossible to detect, but I'm sure it led to some heavy-duty headaches.

Duny wasn't famous like Hal King, but he did have the grandest style. He was a character out of a Noel Coward play. He had a wry sense of humor and loved to dress in a tuxedo, a long black cape, and patent leather shoes. Duny had many eccentricities, but he also had many friends. One of them was the king of Morocco. Every year Duny went to the king's palace for weeks on end. When he wasn't visiting royalty, he kept a beautiful apartment in LA that he decorated in Moroccan chic.

It was the Fourth of July weekend when Duny phoned. I knew he was working for Max Factor Jr. at the time, and he was at Max's house in Malibu for the holiday weekend. It was nearly midnight and he could barely contain his excitement.

"I've got a *big* scoop for you," he said, his words rushing together in a fever.

"Well, go on, spill it."

"There was a gunshot at Cathy and Dean Martin's house tonight."

I was suddenly wide awake. I knew Duny would never feed me false information. Still, I was skeptical. "Are you sure? Maybe it was fireworks..."

"No, Toni," he assured me, his voice edged with grave certainty. "It didn't happen until *after* the fireworks display..."

Dean had met Cathy Hawn when she was working as a young receptionist at Gene Shacove's Beauty Salon in Beverly Hills. Only months after his shocking divorce from long-time wife Jeanne, Dean and Cathy got married. They had a house in Malibu, just down the road from Max Factor.

Adding to the credibility of the story was Duny's Rolodex of connections—the man knew everyone. He even knew the Malibu sheriff, which meant if a shot really had been fired at the Martin estate, Duny would be able to find out about it.

"A big black limo came and picked up Cathy, and from what I could find out, Dean went to a hospital near Century City. I think he had a gunshot wound in his hand. My guess is, that limo was there to whisk Cathy out of town," Duny reported breathlessly.

"You're a gem, Duny. I love you," I said, and placed the phone back in its cradle. My hand lingered on the receiver as I contemplated what I had just been told. If what Duny said was true, this story would be absolutely huge.

I racked my brain for any connections I had to Dean Martin, any possible sources who might be able to confirm Duny's tip. Though I had chauffeured Dean around the golf course at Chuck Connor's golf tournament in Palm Springs and had seen him around in many other places, our conversations were more light and breezy than serious.

I did know his ex-wife Jeanne, however. She was a beautiful, sweet woman, and I took an immediate liking to her the first time we met. I soon learned that most people felt the same way. I remember the ice-blue sunglasses she always wore captivated me. Dean and Jeanne seemed like the most loving, perfect couple. That's why the news of their divorce sent shockwaves throughout the Hollywood community.

I grabbed the phone again. The earpiece was still warm from my conversation with Duny—as if the phone itself knew what a hot story this was—and I set to work making calls.

Given the late hour, and the fact that it was a holiday weekend, I didn't make much progress. I tried the hospital, but of course, they weren't allowed to tell me anything. Just when I was about to call it quits, I remembered I had the number for Mort Viner, Dean's agent. If anyone knew anything it would be Mort, but I didn't have the audacity to call him so late into the night. Instead, I set his number aside and told myself I'd call first thing in the morning. I got into bed and lay there thinking about Cathy and Dean and obsessing over what could have happened that night in their Malibu home.

I awoke to the sun streaming through my window. I launched myself out of bed, rushed over to the phone, and quickly punched in Mort Viner's number.

The phone rang four times before Mort's gruff voice finally answered.

"This is Mort," he said. Maybe I was just imagining it, but he sounded like a man who hadn't gotten much sleep, a man who maybe spent the night in the hospital by the side of his long-time friend and employer.

"Mort, this is Toni Holt. I'm sorry to bother you so early, but I heard that Dean had an accident last night..." I paused briefly to see if he would fill in the gap, but the line stayed silent. I continued, "I was wondering if you wanted to elaborate on it because I'm going to use it on my show today. I don't want to say anything hurtful—I just want to make sure I have all the facts."

"I have nothing to say," Mort responded.

Admittedly, I felt dejected. I was lucky enough to have been given this big tip, but my follow-ups had gotten me nowhere. Mort's contribution of information would have given my report major credibility, but it was clear he wasn't going to speak about what happened.

I dressed for work, weighing the pros and cons of going with the story. Ultimately, I decided to run with it, even though I knew the risk of running an uncorroborated story. At the same time, I knew Duny's word was good. I simply had to trust my source.

My TV segment that morning was only three minutes long, so I didn't have a lot of time to elaborate. As soon as the red light on the camera blinked on, I was off and running with the story:

"Well, I hear there were big fireworks last night in Malibu—not just in the air but at the home of Cathy and Dean Martin. The newlyweds apparently had some kind of spat—and according to my source at the airlines (yep, gotta have 'em everywhere), Cathy was quietly shipped off to Hawaii on a United Airlines flight to cool down. Meanwhile, Dean was supposedly rushed to the emergency room. It seems that while making a sandwich for himself, he decided to use a gun to slice the salami." I paused and smiled into the camera as I wrapped it up. "Dean, next time you want to make a midnight snack, please use a knife instead of a gun." I chuckled to lighten the impact.

The next night at around six thirty, I was between shows and went to PIPS, a private club on Robertson Boulevard. I walked in and sitting at the bar right in front of me was none other than Dean Martin. I did a double-take when I saw him and immediately wanted to back out the front door. I had no idea if he had heard about my report or how he would react, but most importantly—I didn't want a confrontation.

I veered away from the bar and almost made it into the restaurant when I heard, "Hey, Toni...hi!" My stomach dropped to my feet. I turned and saw Dean waving me over to the bar with a big smile.

"Come on over!" he shouted. I had no choice but to oblige. He patted the bar stool next to him. "What are you drinking?" he asked.

"Ginger ale, please," I said, prepared for the worst.

Dean caught the bartender's eye and ordered me a ginger ale. He turned back, laughing as he spoke.

"Mort called and told me to watch your show."

I might as well pack it in now, I thought, because Dean Martin was probably going to make sure my career was over right then and there.

"That was the funniest thing you've ever done," he said, while slapping the bar and laughing. "Seriously, Toni, that was hysterical!"

I took a deep breath and laughed right along with him. People were always saying that Dean had the best sense of humor, and now I was seeing it firsthand. Despite my airing his story, Dean never said one bad word to me. Come on, how can you not like a guy like that?

Unfortunately, Dean's mask of comedy was replaced by a mask of tragedy in 1987 when his son Dino was killed in a plane crash. They said Dean was never quite the same after the crash, and I believe that.

I often went to Hamburger Hamlet restaurant on Sunset for Sunday dinner with my friend Ruta Lee. Dean was usually there, sitting alone at a table for two near the bar—always the same table for two. It was sad to see a star of Dean's magnitude—and a great guy to boot—sitting by himself nursing a drink. Sometimes Mort Viner would join him for a while, then drive him home, but he never entertained any company. The knee-slapping, laughing Dean was gone.

One night, Ruta and I decided to cheer him up and went over to his table.

"Hi, Dean. It's Toni and Ruta," I said. He looked up as if wrapped in some sort of hazy veil and muttered a soft "hi." We tried to joke with him, anything to bring a smile to his face. "Hey, good-lookin'. What are you doin' out alone?"

He laughed, but you could tell it wasn't real. It was absolutely heart-wrenching.

Despite his depression, Dean was always polite, warm, and friendly. He just seemed to be stuck in someone else's body. A month might go by and I would go back to the Hamlet for Sunday dinner, and there would be Dean, seated at the same table, still alone. The other six nights of the week were spent at his favorite Italian restaurant in Beverly Hills, sitting alone most of the time.

A heavy smoker, Dean was diagnosed with lung cancer in 1993 and died two years later on December 25, 1995, with his beautiful ex-wife Jeanne at his side. A sad Christmas for all. The lights on the Las Vegas Strip were dimmed in his honor.

To this day I still smile with a loving heart when I think of him.

CHAPTER TWENTY

The Gabor Clan

I knew the entire Gabor clan well. So I was shocked when I noticed a small article buried in the back pages of the newspaper announcing the death of Francesca Hilton, daughter of Zsa Zsa Gabor and the late hotel magnate Conrad Hilton. Francesca died of an apparent stroke/heart attack at the age of sixty-seven. By any measure, she lived a difficult life.

Francesca was the only child born to any of the Gabor sisters. Unfortunately, she didn't inherit the Gabor beauty nor did she share the kind of fame enjoyed by the rest of the family. When her father died, his estate was valued at about two hundred million. He left Francesca a mere one hundred thousand dollars. Francesca challenged the will, but lost.

Over the years, Francesca tried to earn a living as an actress and a stand-up comedian, but any real success eluded her. Her publicist and longtime friend, Ed Lozzi, told me Francesca had been evicted from her apartment and was living in her car in North Hollywood. Suffering from heart issues, she was in and out of Cedars Hospital for about ten days prior to her passing from a massive heart attack on January 6, 2015.

While life may have treated her harshly, she didn't fare any better in death. Her funeral was delayed several weeks for an alleged autopsy, after which her friends and the Hilton family gave her a grand send-off that was attended by nearly 300 people. Francesca was cremated and her ashes interred at the Westwood Memorial Park Cemetery, near her aunt Eva Gabor. Westwood Memorial is also the resting place of Marilyn Monroe and Natalie Wood.

As for the rest of the Gabor clan, the ride was totally different.

When I first arrived in Palm Springs in my early twenties, the desert community was chic and magical. It was more like a village than a city. When you went to a party, you always saw the same faces. Everyone knew everyone else, and all with extremely illustrious backgrounds.

Except for me, of course.

I was the baby of the group and had much to learn. Thankfully, everyone in Palm Springs seemed more than willing to take me under their wing. They educated and sophisticated me. I soaked up everything like a sponge.

At some point in my whirlwind of activity, I was introduced to Jolie Gabor, the matriarch of the Gabor clan. Within moments of meeting she said to me in her inimitable Hungarian accent, "Dahling, you remind me so much of my own. You are definitely my fourth daughter."

Me? A Gabor? Ha! I was positively thrilled.

Jolie and I became good friends. She was married to Count Edmund de Szigethy, many years her junior. They had a beautiful house on a hilltop that overlooked the entire desert. Edmund left much of his money behind when he left Hungary, but he didn't leave his style and grace behind. He was totally devoted to and madly in love with Jolie. Every morning he made sure Jolie went for her swim and took all her vitamins. Edmund was a great cook as well. They lovingly called me "Tonica."

Jolie once told me: "Dahling, remember…it doesn't matter vhich vun of you has the money, as long as vun of you does."

Mama Gabor was the mother of Magda, Eva, and Zsa Zsa, all absolutely beautiful, and all actresses. They were a handful, and Mama raised them in a spectacular manner. I would bet that her bedtime stories were not your typical fairy tales.

Magda was the oldest, a stunning redhead who was fluent in five languages. In a cruel turn of the universe, she was the victim of a stroke or a bad fall—perhaps both, depending on whom you talk to. As a result, she only had the use of one arm and could only say a single word, "beau-ti-ful." She would repeat the word over and over as if it were a sentence, but her smile and enthusiasm filled the void left behind by her inability to communicate.

Through it all, she never lost the art of applying her makeup. At ten in the morning—any day of the week—she was earthshakingly beautiful.

Magda was married six times, most notably to suave British actor George Sanders. It was said that Zsa Zsa arranged the marriage. Sanders agreed to it because he was broke and Magda needed someone to look after her. It was a good arrangement for both, and the couple lived in

Toni with Jolie and Magda Gabor

Magda's house in Palm Springs, which was decorated primarily in red, her favorite color.

I recall getting a very strange phone call from Francesca when Magda passed away. She said there was no money to bury her aunt, and asked if I could help. Knowing the Gabors, I found the story difficult to believe, if not entirely absurd. I politely suggested she contact her family.

Eva, the youngest sister, was only married five times—an amateur, by family standards. She was the most likable of the clan and best known for her role in the TV series *Green Acres* with Eddie Albert, and the movie *Gigi* with Louis Jordan. Prior to her death she had a lengthy relationship with Merv Griffin, although they never married. Merv was so generous and kind, and showered Eva with the most extravagant jewelry. I adored him, and so did Nancy Regan. Merv was a frequent visitor at Nancy's dinner parties.

In a bizarre twist of fate, Eva had a tragic accident in Mexico while visiting her former stepdaughter. When Merv received the news, he sent a private plane to bring her back to Los Angeles for treatment at Mt. Sinai Hospital. Unfortunately, it proved too late. Eva succumbed in the hospital from respiratory failure and pneumonia on July 4, 1995. The man she was dating at the time—who I knew—had begged her not to make that fatal trip to Mexico. He wanted to take her someplace else. Had Eva listened, she might be alive today.

Toni with Merv Griffin

Eva made a big deal about her Catholicism, shutting down rumors that the family was Jewish. Eva's funeral was held at Good Shepherd Church in Beverly Hills. Her best friend, actress Suzanne Pleshette, Bob Newhart's co-star in the popular TV series *The Bob Newhart Show*, gave a stirring eulogy. I can still hear Suzanne saying in her distinctively deep voice, "Now that Eva is gone, it will no longer be a Technicolor world, just black and white." I recall sitting in the church and getting goose bumps when Suzanne spoke. It struck me as a beautiful compliment given from one woman to another.

Eva was buried at Westwood Village Memorial Park Cemetery, a short distance from her TV husband, Eddie Albert. Ironically, it would be her longest "marriage."

Zsa Zsa, Miss Hungary of 1936, was the most famous of the Gabor sisters. She was married nine times, including to George Sanders, about fifteen years before Magda married him. Among her husbands was Conrad Hilton, the handsome heir to the Hilton Hotel chain fortune and the father of Francesca.

At the time of her death on December 18, 2016, just two months shy of her 100th birthday, Zsa Zsa was still married to Frederic Prinz von Anhalt. They had been married for thirty years. Sadly, Zsa Zsa spent her final five years on life support. Her funeral service was held at the same Good Shepherd Church in Beverly Hills as her sister Eva. Zsa Zsa's ashes were destined to join the rest of the Gabor clan at Westwood Memorial, but there are some who say they never got there.

Toni with Zsa Zsa.

Looking back on my memories with the Gabors, I would definitely count Mama Gabor as one of my Professors of Life. If I had to pick my favorite lesson, the one that stuck with me the most through the years, it was her emphasis on always looking your best.

"Dahling, you never get up in the morning without putting on your makeup. Don't worry about your hair—you can always wrap a towel around it. But the makeup, dahling. That's vhat's important. Vhen the postman rings, you must look beautiful, even to him." Now that's star thinking.

To this day, Jolie's advice has influenced me. I truly believe that when you look good, you feel good. There's a reason they say to put on a nice outfit if you're feeling down—it's a reverse psychology that works wonders on the mood. Past the age of forty—certainly over fifty—there is no woman in the world who is going to look stunningly fabulous without makeup. It's a fact of life.

Which reminds me of the time Jolie fell and broke her arm. Edmund called and asked me to come to the hospital as soon as possible. When I got there I quickly learned that the emergency had nothing to do with Jolie's broken arm—she simply needed me to put on her makeup so she would look beautiful for the doctors and nurses.

Another time, Jolie and I were walking along Madison Avenue and she was complaining about having to wear flats instead of the high, high heels she always wore. Despite being in her nineties at the time, Jolie felt flat shoes didn't show off her fabulous legs—and believe me, she had fabulous legs.

Having the same addiction to high heels, I understood completely.

* * * * *

My abysmal existence with my husband Milton didn't improve with time, although my life in Palm Springs lifted me out of my prison of misery. Milton and I still had a house in New Jersey, and he would often remain there for business while I stayed in Palm Springs or Beverly Hills. It created a welcome space between us.

After a brief vacation in Paris taught me a lot about cooking and entertaining, I couldn't wait to throw a dinner party at our New Jersey home.

While in Paris I'd become particularly taken by a dessert called "Le Snob." It was a combination of melted dark chocolate poured over ladyfingers and topped with fresh crème that was simply out of this world. When the waiter brought it to the table, he poured brandy over it and lit it on fire. It was absolutely delicious and appropriately showy for my dinner party.

Jolie Gabor was the first person I invited. She owned an incredible faux jewelry shop on Madison Avenue in New York at the time. I received an unexpected phone call from her the morning of the party.

"Dahling, Zsa Zsa is going to be in New York tonight. Please tell me it would be all right for her and her tall, gorgeous Texan to come to dinner?"

"Of course," I said. "I'd love to have them."

After I spent the day stressing about every detail, the time finally came for my guests to arrive. Mama Gabor and her husband, Edmund, came with Zsa Zsa and her six-foot-four escort, who looked like Gary Cooper. The other four guests were friends of mine, all in the entertainment business.

The dinner conversation was lively. I felt vibrant and charismatic in their presence. It was a far cry from the dinner parties I attended with Milton in years prior where I would sit in stony silence, too afraid to offer what Milton regarded as stupid input. By this time, Milton had backed off and I was determined to shine. I suppose in a strange way he enjoyed my celebrity and all that went with it. He was the ultimate user.

Because I didn't want to spend the night in the kitchen, my help was in charge of serving and clearing the table. I learned in Europe that when clearing the table, it's not proper to leave a place setting empty, so I filled some small crystal bowls with water and floated rose petals from my garden in them to make the table look pretty. After the dinner plates were removed, a fingerbowl of water and rose petals was placed in front of each guest.

Jolie was impressed. "Dahling, you are so imaginative," she said. "You are just vun of a kind. Only you vould think of something so creative!"

I smiled at the compliment. A moment later my jaw dropped as Jolie took her spoon and dipped it in the water, scooping up a rose petal and sipping it down like it was soup. Everyone's eyes immediately turned to me as if to say, "Are we really supposed to do that?"

Imagine all the thoughts that raced through my mind in that moment as Jolie continued to sip away at the fingerbowl of rose petals. I was torn between the feeling that I might crawl inside myself and die, and the urge to laugh uncontrollably. As my guests eyed me expectantly, I recalled how they served sherbets and ices in Europe between courses.

Without missing a beat I cooed, "This is just a little touch of something to cleanse your palate. Like an intermezzo. Dessert is coming shortly."

With that, I picked up my spoon and went fishing for a rose petal just like Jolie. Taking my lead, every person at the table had a rose petal or two. It was hysterical. The truth never came out, and the dessert that followed was the smash hit I hoped it would be.

Over the years we were friends, Jolie provided me with a tremendous sense of self. She would never tell anyone how old she was, and the records of her date of birth vary. Some say she was born in 1894, which would have made her 102 when she died on April 1, 1997. Others said she was 106. Really, what difference do a couple of years make when you're a hundred?

The fabulous Gabors were one of the most glamorous families ever to grace the Hollywood scene.

CHAPTER TWENTY-ONE

So Long, Milton!

I was shopping at Bonwit Teller in Beverly Hills. My loathsome husband, Milton, had adopted the annoying custom of dressing like he was twenty, and while waiting for me by the entrance, he tried to pick up a young girl. He told her he was very important and married to the star Toni Holt. Not only was he trying to pick up a girl—he was using me as bait. Talk about nerve.

The girl wasn't interested. How did I know? As it turned out, the girl's mother was a friend of *my* mother, and she called her immediately. My mother called me and told me what happened. That was all I needed to hear. I told Milton he was the "creep of creeps" and kicked him out of the house on the spot. The only reason I stayed married was because of my boys.

It didn't take me long to learn that Milton had mortgaged our Roxbury house up to the gills, including a second mortgage I knew nothing about. He was way behind on the payments, but since I didn't write the checks, I had no idea what was going on. It was exactly the way Milton wanted it. Thinking back, he never gave me reason to believe him, so shame on me for trusting him. Ladies, are you paying attention?

The less I knew, the fewer questions I could ask. It was all about control, and Milton had controlled me right into the arms of debt. All of the money from my career was gone, siphoned away or spent by Milton. We were going to lose the house on Roxbury Drive, and there was absolutely nothing I could do about it.

The day came when the bank foreclosed on the house—and I foreclosed on Milton. My divorce lawyer was recommended by neighbor Pamela Mason, although I wasn't quite sure whose side he was on. By the time we got to court, Milton had found five different people to testify that he owed them hundreds and hundreds of thousands of dollars—and therefore he couldn't afford to pay me back the money I was owed. Because of their testimony and not the best legal counsel, the court awarded me a pittance, plus minimal child support.

As part of the settlement, Milton promised to pay a small amount every month to assist with the children. In the court's eyes, all was settled. But as any woman who has gone through a rough divorce with a deadbeat like Milton knows, the reality of it is not always as smoothly ironed out as the courts believe. Time and time again Milton managed to short me a month's child support, continuing in his great tradition of being consistently immoral. I needed the financial support, but I was so exhausted with the situation that I wished he would evaporate into thin air.

A shocking coincidence unfolded from the whole debacle. Within a year's time of the court case, each and every one of the five men who testified on Milton's behalf was dead. They ranged in age from forty to seventy. It was shocking. They lied for Milton, and apparently their bad karma came back to them tenfold. But that quickly? And *all* of them?

With help from my mother and her husband, George, I moved to an apartment in Beverly Hills with my children, David and Adam.

During the time my marriage was falling apart, I was doing a series of five-minute segments called "Toni Holt in Hollywood." The series was in syndication around the country, but thanks to Milton—I never saw a dime. He'd arranged for the money to come to him and stay with him. He never allowed me to have a checking or savings account throughout our marriage, so I was totally in the dark about our financials. Call me naïve—although stupid would have been more on the mark—I actually believed what he told me, that he was saving the money for me. Later, I learned that Milton kept two sets of books: one for himself, and one for everybody else.

He did give me some beautiful jewelry at one time, an emerald and diamond bracelet and a five-karat diamond ring. Not long afterward, he told me he was in terrible financial trouble and asked if I would loan him the jewelry. I did. I never saw it again.

Milton possessed absolutely no character whatsoever. However, my marriage to him taught me the importance of looking out for myself in the future. It was a lesson learned the hard way, but it's always the hardest lessons that stick with us. The only excuse I can render is that I was still very, very young. Case closed.

I was working at KHJ, a local TV station in LA, and my entertainment segments aired twice a day. That, combined with my column in

Photoplay, meant I was bringing in a modest income. Making ends meet proved extremely difficult, but thankfully, Mother and George were there to lend a hand when necessary.

But life wasn't done throwing hardballs at my family just yet. We'd been living in an apartment in Beverly Hills for just a few months when, sadly, George took ill and died. Mother moved in with me and the children.

In an attempt to bring in some extra cash, I began to work around the clock. There wasn't a day that went by that wasn't scheduled to the brim with interviews, lunches, or social gatherings. I had to stay on the scene, more determined than ever to turn my name into a household word.

I could tell that my absence was impacting my children. My son David specifically seemed to bear the brunt of it. He would constantly beg me to stay home, tugging at the bottom of my dress as I rushed about the house getting ready to go somewhere. It broke my heart. "But Grandma's here," I would tell him.

I tried to explain that if I didn't work, I wouldn't get paid and we wouldn't have the things we needed. "I don't care," David would say. "I just want you to stay home with me."

It's now clear to me how my divorce from Milton and the shift in living situation created a lot of insecurity for my children. I was so busy, so intent on making it in my business that I was blind to the sense of abandonment they were obviously feeling. When I think of my life's biggest regret, I picture David's face, looking up at me as he pleaded with me to stay with him.

The fact that I didn't spend as much time as I should have with my children saddens me. But being poor was something I simply couldn't allow to happen to my family or me. I had made my decision.

I traded my family time for my career and financial security.

CHAPTER TWENTY-TWO

The Silver Rolls-Royce

Everyone in Hollywood knew my mother, Helen. We were inseparable. If you saw me—you saw my mother. We were a team, a support system for each other.

Mother wasn't tall, maybe five-four at most, but she had a certain regal manner about her that gave people the impression she was taller than she really was. Maybe it was because of the turbans she liked to wear. She had a beautiful face reminiscent of Lana Turner. Her eyes were green and she was blessed with a Grecian nose and high cheekbones.

She absolutely adored Ann Southern, who starred in a television series decades earlier, *My Favorite Secretary*. Mother would emulate Southern's style by wearing black or navy-blue dresses with big white collars. As the years progressed, Mother changed her style and wore mostly pink. We called her the "Pink Queen."

My friends referred to Mother as Bird Dog, a moniker she earned for her uncanny ability to find out information. Google didn't exist in those days, but Mother could find out anything. I swear she could have worked for the CIA.

Mother taught me to take risks. She made me understand that you have to create the opportunity for something to come your way. You have to give God and Fate a chance to work together. She would say, "If you sit in your bathtub all day, good fortune will never find you."

She never spent a lot of time on herself, but she always looked great, no matter the occasion. In a lot of ways she was a very serious person. After all, she carried a world's worth of weight on her shoulders. She had a job. Her job was me.

After my divorce from Milton cost me my house, my car, and just about everything else, she came to me one day with fire blazing in her eyes.

Toni and her mother, Helen.

"Toni, listen to me. You need a car. You had a Rolls-Royce, and I won't let you drive anything less. Get dressed and look your best."

"Where are we going?"

"We're going to the Rolls-Royce dealer, of course."

I couldn't help but laugh. "We don't have the kind of money to buy a Rolls-Royce."

"You'll see," Mother replied.

So together we walked to the showroom of Charles Schmidt Rolls-Royce. It was only three blocks from our apartment, across the street from the Beverly Wilshire Hotel.

We stopped in front and looked through the windows at the expensive cars sitting on the shiny showroom floor. With our hands cupped around our eyes and faces pressed against the glass, we could see a blue Rolls and a silver Bentley, the paint gleaming like diamonds in the sunlight. Mother took me by the arm and marched me inside.

We must have looked pretty sharp because the entrance door to the showroom had barely closed when a salesman came up to us.

"May I help you, ladies?"

I've always trusted my mother's judgment, but at this point I was ready to do anything I could to spare us the humiliation that undoubtedly awaited us as she attempted to purchase a Rolls-Royce with no money. I was all set to respond, "No, thank you. We're just looking," when Mother's voice rang through the showroom.

"We'd like to see the owner, please." Her voice had the commanding presence of Rosalind Russell in *Auntie Mame*.

The salesman tried to throw up a roadblock, but she wouldn't yield. "The owner, please," she repeated.

The salesman disappeared into the back offices, and a minute later, a tall man with a happy face and sandy blond hair emerged. His eyes seemed kind and his smile sincere.

"I'm Charlie Schmidt," he said. "You wanted to see me?"

Mother introduced herself, then turned to me. "This is my daughter, Toni Holt. She's about to become very famous. Until recently she had a Rolls-Royce, but because of a temporary problem we're having, she was unable to keep it."

Charlie Schmidt nodded as if he really cared. "I'm sorry to hear that."

Mother plowed on with incredible calm. "We're here to give you the opportunity to become her sponsor in a way. And this is going to be very, very good for you."

Charlie smiled. "Really? Tell me more."

I couldn't tell if Charlie was genuinely intrigued or if he thought the situation was an elaborate prank. Mother linked her arm through mine and said, "Toni is very honorable. I'm asking that you lease her a car. We're not asking for a new one—and we don't have a down payment, but let us lease a Rolls-Royce, and I give you my word within a year or so we'll be back here, and she'll *buy* a new one from you."

I remember thinking that if there was a hole in the floor, I would have crawled into it and lay down forever. I made eye contact with Charlie, who miraculously appeared to actually be weighing the proposal in his head. I looked away and a moment later I heard Charlie laugh.

"Okay. Fine. You can have a Rolls. Not a new one," he cautioned, "but a used one."

Mother impulsively gave Charlie a hug. "Thank you. You won't be sorry. Oh, one other thing. Would you mind not starting the payments right away?"

Part of me was waiting for her to ask for a share of his dealership, but she didn't.

Charlie laughed again, this time with honest admiration for her audacity. "How long would you like?"

"Oh, just a few months. I promise we'll never miss a payment. You have my word."

Charlie and my mother shook hands on the agreement. A few minutes later we filled out the necessary paperwork, and drove out of the dealership in a silver Rolls-Royce.

As promised, I never missed a payment.

* * * * *

In moments of great despair, it is often the help of our friends that gives us the strength to get back on our feet. Elaine Young was one such friend.

My apartment on Charleville was simply too small for my mother, the kids, and me, so we needed another place to live. Elaine was the premier real estate broker in Beverly Hills at the time, a girl after my own heart. She was a self-made woman with great flair who had succeeded in creating a buzz about herself, crafting an image that would take her to the top of her profession. She was a fixture in Beverly Hills, driving around in a Mercedes convertible, her blonde hair blowing in the breeze. Her custom license plate read: 7ELAINE.

Thanks to Elaine, I was able to rent a house on Doheny Drive, a few blocks below Sunset Boulevard. It was just perfect for us, and everything seemed to be back on track. Perfect until I discovered that Milton was stalking me.

It started one night when I heard a strange rustling in the bushes outside my house. I assumed it was an animal, but the noise persisted. I ran to get my mother, and arm in arm we walked outside to see what was causing the ruckus. We couldn't find anything, but the incident gave me a feeling of dread that I couldn't quite shake.

The next night I was near the living room window when a face popped up outside the glass. I screamed. It was Milton. He disappeared into the darkness while I sat inside, clutching my heart, trying to restart it. My sense of security was suddenly gone.

I became paranoid, double-checking the locks on the doors and keeping my drapes pulled closed. I probably should have called the police, but it seemed pointless. It would mean tons of paperwork and no real protection.

It got so bad that Milton, once a high-powered executive with the Teamsters, actually went to my boss at KHJ and told him if he didn't fire me, they might have to deal with the consequences. A few days later they let me go.

I was beyond despair. I had my mother and two children depending on me and I was afraid to leave the house. I had no job. And almost no income.

I was back to square one.

CHAPTER TWENTY-THREE

The Hitman

At a point of desperation and trying to figure out what to do next, I received an unexpected phone call. A man with a gravelly voice spoke through the line.

"A very close friend of yours asked me to call."

"Who is this?" I asked, confused and impatient. I had thin skin in those days, and I wasn't looking for any more trouble than I already had on my plate.

"We understand you're having a lot of problems with your ex-husband," the unfamiliar voice continued, ignoring my question. The mention of Milton made my blood run cold. If the call was about Milton, it couldn't be good.

"Listen," the voice pressed on, "we'd rather not talk about this on the phone... We're sending you a ticket to fly to New York, with a return ticket back to LA the same day. There will be a car and driver waiting for you at the airport. We will talk to you in person."

He hung up. I sat there for a minute trying to digest what I just heard. The caller said he'd been tipped off to my troubles by a "close friend." Who could that be? What was this all about?

What people generally see in me is great strength. At the same time, I've always been a little fragile emotionally. Carrying on each day knowing that Milton was out there, hell-bent on ruining me, wore me down to a nervous wreck. The phone call came at a time when I was completely lost—out to sea without any sense of how to get back to shore. As bizarre as the story was, something in my gut was telling me to pay close attention.

I asked Mother what I should do. Always the strong one, she said simply, "You go, of course."

So I did.

The plane ticket appeared just as the man on the phone had promised. I arrived in New York two days later. There was a driver with a sign that read "Toni Holt" waiting for me at the gate at JFK.

As we drove from the airport into the city, I asked the driver where we were going, but he wouldn't say. He just told me to sit back and enjoy the ride. He turned up the music to stifle any further conversation, and we drove the rest of the way in silence.

It was late afternoon when the car came to a stop in front of a little restaurant/bar on West 46th Street, between Seventh and Eighth Avenues, in the heart of the Theatre District.

The light from the street cast shadows across the restaurant, and it took a moment for my eyes to adjust to the dusky interior. It was then I saw the most gorgeous man I'd ever seen in my life step out of the gloom and walk toward me. I'll never forget what he looked like: well over six feet tall and wearing an elegant, navy-blue pinstriped suit with a crisp, freshly laundered striped shirt and a tastefully conservative navy tie. He had dark hair, flashing brown eyes, and an olive complexion. He was every woman's fantasy, more handsome than a movie star, but the image went to hell in a hand basket the minute he opened his mouth.

"We're glad yer here," he said with a tough Brooklyn accent.

He introduced himself as John and gestured to the bar across the way. "Sit down."

It was more like a command than an invitation. I hoisted myself onto the bar stool next to him. An aging bartender stood quietly in the shadows polishing glasses. As I glanced around I realized that aside from the bartender and the two of us, the place was deserted. The whole situation made me nervous, and I began to feel like I was starring in a B movie.

"Wouldja like somethin' to drink?" John asked.

I'm sure John wasn't his name, and the last thing I wanted to do was drink something that might cloud my judgment. "No, thank you. I don't drink," I responded.

"Have a soda."

Again, it was more of a command than a friendly suggestion. I ordered a ginger ale. John didn't order anything. The bartender slid the drink onto the bar and made a hasty retreat. John waited until the bartender disappeared completely into the darkness, then spoke.

"We understand yer havin' a real tough time...that yer ex is makin' yer life miserable."

"Yes, he is," I said tentatively. I was very uneasy, but something about John's eyes told me I was safe. "It's not right," I continued, my voice getting steadier as I spoke. "I've worked really hard to get where I am…and I have two children…and my mother to worry about."

"Well, we want you to know you won't have to worry about him anymore. We're gonna take care of him. We don't like his actions… you're not supposed to treat a lady like that."

I could feel my heart thumping. I desperately wanted to ask who "we" referred to, but I decided I better keep my mouth shut and listen.

"Don't worry about him," John continued. "He's not gonna be a problem to you anymore."

"But…what does that mean?" I asked timidly. A part of me didn't want to know the answer, and a part of me already knew it. I had seen my fair share of gangster movies—I knew how these things played out. What I didn't know was how I had gotten thrust into the middle of a real-life hit man scenario.

"You don't need to know. Just go back to California and know that yer problem isn't gonna exist anymore."

John's brown eyes never left mine. There was no doubt he was serious. Fear flooded my body.

"But…but wait…what are you going to do?" I asked, trying to control my voice. This wasn't just a movie—this was real life. John and whomever he worked for or with weren't playing around.

"He's just not gonna be around anymore. That's all you have to know."

I suddenly found myself pleading for Milton's life. "No, please… please, you can't do that. You can't do that. Yes, I hate him…but you can't do that."

"Why not? We're tryin' to help you." John seemed hurt, almost insulted that I wouldn't want the job to be carried out. I started to cry.

"Because…because I can't be responsible for something like that. I couldn't live with myself…you don't understand. Please, please…I beg you. Don't kill him. Don't kill him."

Looking at my small, sobbing frame, John finally seemed to grasp that though I wished Milton would disappear, I could never be responsible for his death.

"Fine," John said. "But when you get back to California, one thing I'll promise you—he'll never bother you again. Don't worry about it. You're free to fly."

When he took me back outside to the car, I asked again who told him to call me.

"A good friend, a really good friend," he answered. "We can't tell you who. Just know that it was a very good friend of yours."

Nothing more was said. I got into the car, and the driver took me to the airport, again in silence. I always wondered why John allowed me to see his face, but I figured he wasn't the hit man—just the connection. Who knew the real truth? Certainly not me. To this day, I still don't understand why they brought me to New York for the meeting.

I got home to LA late that night and told my mother what happened. She had a lot of opinions about who might have set up the meeting, but we never actually found out who it was so I never could say 'thank you'. Whatever John and his associates did, believe me when I say I never had another problem with Milton again. It was like a cage of invisible bars had gone up to protect me. There was nobody in my way anymore.

Seemingly overnight, everything fell back into place.

CHAPTER TWENTY-FOUR

The Seance

A few years or so later, I began having premonitions. These glimpses into the future became a big part of my life.

It was Friday and I was with my mother at a dressmaker when I had a psychic premonition about my ex-husband. I suddenly felt overcome with a sense of dread.

"Mother," I said, grabbing her arm. "I have this really strong feeling that Milton's going to die."

"Does it have anything to do with your visit to New York?" she asked.

"I don't know, I can't explain it. I just know he's going to die. It's a real feeling. I'm terrified."

Ever the practical one, Mother urged me to call Milton right away. "You don't need any money from him now, but he never gave any insurance to the children or provided for their education like he promised. You need to address this immediately."

So I called him.

"Milton, you have to take care of something," I said, wanting to be as clear as possible. "I want nothing for myself...I'm fine financially, but you've been a real rat. You haven't taken care of the children as you promised. You must call your insurance person and take care of their education because I don't know what's going to happen to me in the future. You have to do this now."

He could sense the strangeness in my voice. "Why? What's the sudden urgency?"

"Because...I believe you're going to die."

There was a long silence before he responded, "What makes you think that?"

"I just have this really strong premonition."

My voice was so grave that I think I truly frightened him. Hell, I had frightened myself! I didn't know how to explain how I knew what I knew, but I guess I conveyed my certainty because Milton agreed to call his insurance company first thing on Monday morning.

Mother and I left the dressmaker and drove the two hours to Palm Springs. I had a deal to tape a series of one-minute segments called "Toni's Tips" for a Latin American station. It was a different format from my regular TV show. The segments would not be about show business, but rather everyday tips on life for women. We always felt it was more relaxing to work in the desert than in LA, and the plan was to rehearse the tips there—then drive back to LA early Monday morning to tape them.

The weekend away served a dual purpose. Being back in the desert I had called home when I first came to California helped unravel the knot in my stomach over Milton. My feeling of dread faded. I absorbed myself in writing and the rehearsals.

Back in Hollywood on Monday, during a break at the studio where we were taping, I called my answering service to see if there were any messages. Those were the days when real people took messages rather than answering machines. The girl at my service told me a Mr. Winston had called, and said it was urgent that I call him back as soon as possible.

I knew of only one Mr. Winston. Stanley, Milton's good friend. As soon as the girl said his name, the feeling of unease came rushing back to me. I thanked her and turned to my mother like a zombie.

"Milton's dead," I said, my voice totally flat.

My mother was as stunned as I was. She watched with her hand over her mouth as I picked up the phone to call Stanley. He answered on the second ring.

"Toni, I have something terrible to tell you."

"Yes, I know. Milton's dead."

Stanley freaked. "How do you know? How did you find out?"

"I don't know how, but I know. Tell me what happened."

Stanley told me that Milton, who was on crutches from an automobile accident, had been found dead on his bedroom floor. Stanley didn't provide any further details. I knew Milton had emphysema, which could have contributed somehow to his death. Talking to Stanley in that moment and hearing him say Milton had died created an oddly serene feeling in me. It was the resolution of my premonition. The gentle feeling of accepting a shock I somehow had known was coming.

Did he ever call the insurance company for the kids? No. He never had time.

That should have been the final act for Milton. But in typical Milton fashion, he stuck around a bit longer than he was meant to. A few weeks after his death, Mother told me she could sense Milton's presence in our home. She said she could hear him knocking on the door, she could "feel" him there. Well, the last thing I needed was spirit Milton causing me problems the way actual Milton had throughout my life. I decided to nip the problem in the bud.

I called a psychic named Caroline Lacy. Caroline not only did private readings and taught psychic phenomena at a local university, but she worked for the police department to help locate missing people, so I knew she dealt with the supernatural in a responsible way.

I told her how Mother could sense Milton's presence. "I don't feel it, but Mother does."

Caroline was certain that Milton had something he wanted to say. She asked to come over to hold a séance. While I believed in psychic readings, I was not a believer in contacting the dead and had never participated in a séance before. I could only picture the three of us holding hands and chanting gibberish. Nevertheless, I agreed to the séance only because it would be in my own house where I knew nothing phony could be rigged. I'm not saying Caroline would have rigged anything, but like everyone else, I'd heard stories of trickery and deception in connection with contacting the dead. At least in *my* house, I knew there would be no wires hanging down from the ceiling, no lightbulbs turning colors, and no hidden machines going "woooooo-wooooo" in the background.

Caroline arrived the next afternoon and we sat down at the dining room table. At Caroline's request, there was no cloth on the table, a large oval made of solid oak with a thick top and heavy, turned legs. If I had legs like that table, I would never go out of the house. Caroline placed a pad of paper and a pen on the table beside her, and told us to hold hands. We did as instructed, and Caroline called to Milton.

"If you have something to tell us, please do so now," she said firmly. She repeated this several times.

Suddenly Caroline started talking in tongues. She spoke in a language I had never heard before. Her hand moved the pen on the paper at a frantic pace in all sorts of weird directions. Being a skeptic, I thought, *This is some good theatre,* but I'll admit, a part of me was a little scared. I couldn't tell what she was writing and I couldn't ask her because she seemed to be in a trance-like state. Finally, the strange talk ended and she looked up toward the ceiling as if Milton were actually floating around up there.

"Milton, if you're here...give us a sign," she commanded, this time in English. "Raise this table. Raise...this...table."

I was about to laugh out loud at the absurdity of it when the table suddenly shook and came up off the floor. Without letting go of anyone's hand, I ducked my head under the table to see if maybe Caroline was lifting it with her knees, but she wasn't. Not only that, the table was much too heavy to even think she could. There was nobody and nothing under the table, except maybe Milton—but I certainly didn't see him. Caroline just sat there holding our hands as the table lifted at least eight inches off the floor before it settled back down. Milton—or his spirit—was definitely in that room. And Caroline had known exactly how to contact him.

As the table came back to rest, Caroline told us that Milton wanted to say he was sorry. He wished he had left money for the kids and he felt terrible he didn't. I hadn't told Caroline about the money situation, so there was no way for her to know about it, and I know Mother hadn't mentioned it either. So how did Caroline know? And how did the table lift off the ground?

There was only one answer: Milton.

CHAPTER TWENTY-FIVE

Richard Burton

One day I received a call from a woman who identified herself as the public relations person for Richard Burton. My first thought was *Oh, God, I'm in trouble.* After all, I was the one who told the world I thought Mr. Burton would make a marvelous centerfold for *Playgirl* magazine.

"Mr. Burton heard all the wonderful things you said about him. He's very flattered...and he's very anxious to meet you," said the woman.

"Really?" I responded. By this point in my career, the word "really" could mean just about anything I wanted it to. In truth, I was the one who was flattered.

"Yes, really. He's currently in St. John's Hospital in Santa Monica, but he can come out for a few hours. And he'd like to invite you for dinner."

I knew Burton was in St. Johns "drying out." While I had a rule for myself not to date actors, there's an exception to every rule. After all, this was Richard Burton. I had no reason to believe this would be anything more than a meet and greet, not a date.

"I'd be delighted," I told his PR woman.

I figured Richard Burton must love lavender since Elizabeth Taylor's love affair with lavender was well known. So instead of creating my own look, I stupidly ran out and bought a lavender skirt and matching top. Probably my least sophisticated move to date.

I got a call later in the day that a limousine would pick me up. Scott would be the driver. At precisely six forty-five, Scott arrived. I said good-bye to Mother and off I went.

"Where are we going?" I asked the driver. He wasn't very talkative but did manage to tell me he was taking me to Mr. Burton's favorite restaurant. Ever the drama queen, I remember on the way there I couldn't help thinking, *I hope he's not kidnapping me.*

At seven o'clock sharp the limo pulled up in front of a little French bistro near Pico and Robertson, just south of Beverly Hills. A small man in a light gray suit opened the limo door. "Ah, Miss Holt," he said, taking my hand. "Mr. Burton is waiting for you. Please come inside. We're so happy you're here."

He ushered me inside and led me through the dark restaurant to the far end…and there was Richard Burton, sitting by himself at a booth in the corner.

I immediately noticed how handsome he was. He was wearing a gray jogging suit, with a thin red stripe going down one sleeve. The other arm was in a sling.

The introductions were a little awkward. He offered me a drink and I ordered my usual, ginger ale. Burton explained he wasn't allowed to have any alcohol, and simply asked for a glass of water. Like most people, my perception of Richard Burton was that he was a wild man, an acting genius, a manic-depressive of the first order who seemed to revel in booze-filled orgies and sexual encounters with beautiful women all over the globe, not to mention his on-again-off-again-on-again-off-again marriage to Elizabeth Taylor. I was amazed at the reality of him—he seemed like a quiet and soft-spoken man with his own share of reservations. Either that or not drinking had curtailed his personality.

As the conversation began, he said, "I must tell you about myself."

"I'd love to hear," I replied truthfully, and that was all it took.

In the next two and half hours, I don't think I said more than thirty words. The only time I spoke was when the waiter brought the menu and asked what I wanted for dinner. The extent of my conversation went something like this: "Oh, really?" "My goodness." "That's incredible." "You're kidding." "That's fabulous."

Burton carried on and on about his life…how he was born in Wales…how he loved acting…how he loved the theatre...more about his life…but nothing about Elizabeth Taylor. Then he asked if I knew he was in St. Johns to dry out, self-admitted, of course. He told me he was doing fine…that they'd given him a complete physical and he was in good form. Well, being only a foot away from him that night, I can honestly say his form did look pretty good.

He told me he owned a home in Puerto Vallarta and he was going there just as soon as he got out of the hospital. He talked about how his house was very near the Hotel Garza Blanca, and how he loved to spend time walking along the white beaches and eating in the beautiful restaurants that overlooked the ocean. With that deep, resonant voice of his, he painted a romantic picture of a lush, tranquil spot just this side of paradise. I couldn't help but feel captivated by his speech. He could have read the phone book to me and I would have felt the same way. I've never heard another voice like that.

The time flew by. It was well past nine thirty. Burton had mentioned earlier that he needed to be back to the hospital by ten. When I pointed out the time, all he said was "Don't worry, don't worry."

"No, you must get back on time," I said, nervous for him. I knew how serious hospitals were in their rules, and the last thing I wanted was for Richard Burton to get in trouble because of me. "They let you out on the honor system," I reminded him. "You want them to know you care, that you appreciate what they're doing for you."

After a little more pestering, Burton agreed and we left the restaurant. On the way to the limo, he told me about the red stripe on his jogging suit. He said he always wore a touch of red when he felt something important was going to occur in his life. That should have been a tip-off for what was about to happen, but—naïve as I was—I never saw it coming.

"Let me take you home," he said as we stepped into the limo.

"No, no, no…let's get you back to the hospital first. Then Scott can take *me* home."

But Burton resisted. It had to be his way. "No, please…I want to take you home."

There wasn't much I could do to change his mind. When we got back to my house, Burton got out of the limo with me. Like two kids on their first date, we walked up the path to the house. As we neared the front door, I told him my mother was inside—I wanted him to know that. I unlocked the door and called upstairs just to prove it.

"Mother! I'm home," I yelled, and gave Burton a smile. He smiled back, but our gaze was interrupted by Mother's less than subtle response.

"Well, did you have a good time with that jerk? I don't know what the hell you see in him!" her voice boomed from upstairs.

I could have melted into a puddle right then and there. I was absolutely mortified, horrified, and wanted to be liquefied. For some reason Mother didn't like Richard Burton. She didn't think he was an attractive man and didn't much approve of his lifestyle. She saw no reason for me to have gone out with him. I had to hand it to Burton, though. He didn't even blink. He remained a total gentleman.

I called up again, my voice at least twenty octaves higher this time. "Mr. Burton is downstairs with me, Mother. He'd like to meet you."

I heard a faint "ohhh" from the top of the landing, but she never came down.

Looking to find some way to make amends, I remembered what Burton said about wearing red whenever something important in his life was about to happen.

"Please, stay here for a minute. I want to give you something."

I bounded up the stairs to my bedroom, where I rummaged through my dresser drawer until I found a red scarf. I ran back down the stairs. When I reached Burton I said, "Do you mind if I change your sling?" (My God, did I really say that? Yes, I did.)

Thinking back, I'm sure that line never would have made it into the final script. But Burton was thrilled. "I'd love it."

A few minutes and much amateur knotting later, he was fully set up with a new red sling. I felt as though I'd done something really important. As he started to leave, he turned and said, "Toni, I'll be leaving the hospital in a couple of weeks. I'm going to my house in Puerto Vallarta. I want you to come with me."

I was certainly flattered, but after my encounter with Aristotle Onassis, I was starting to get the hang of this sort of thing. I told him I appreciated the invitation, but I had a commitment to my job and my children.

I couldn't justify running off with Richard Burton to a tropical getaway. Plus, I remembered reading that the house in Puerta Vallarta belonged to Elizabeth Taylor as well. It was all quite whimsically scandalous. I could have made a movie out of that mental picture.

Burton waved away my excuse. "You don't have to work anymore," he said. "Come with me. Just come with me. Tell them you'll be back some other time."

Once again, I turned down his offer. I'd be lying if I said it wasn't thrilling to be invited to be his traveling companion—his girlfriend—or whatever you want to call it. He wasn't married then, so he was properly up for grabs. But I couldn't do it. I wasn't grabbing.

He kissed me good night—not a passionate movie kiss where bells sounded and lights went off, but a kiss just the same. Like Onassis, Burton gave me his number and told me if ever I changed my mind to call him. What is it about these guys? Do they think all they have to do is ask, and we'll fall at their knees?

As it turned out, that was the last I saw of Burton for a few years. Sometime later while on a vacation at the Hotel Garza Blanca, I saw him on the beach. We exchanged greetings and he invited me to have dinner at his house, but I was with friends. It just wasn't the same feeling. And quite honestly, he didn't look as good in his bathing suit as he did in his jogging suit. The electricity and the excitement generated that night at my house were gone. The moment had passed and it couldn't be recaptured. I never regretted my decision. I was growing up fast.

I also pushed my lavender outfit to the back of my closet, where it stayed for a number of years till I gave it away.

CHAPTER TWENTY-SIX

My Frenchman

I don't know how Mother and I managed financially, but we needed a break—a real vacation—and Paris was beckoning. We stayed at the quaint Place Vendome Hotel, a few doors down from the elegant Ritz. The hotel was recommended by a friend, Shirl Goedike, an American artist who lived in Paris. The hotel didn't have room service. The elevator was reminiscent of the kind you see in old movies, tiny and shaky. Nobody spoke more than a few words of English...but so what? We were in Paris! What could be better?

Painting by Shirl Goedike, his France period.

The room itself was huge, with red carpeting, my favorite red-flocked wallpaper, and a huge crystal chandelier that provided a regal atmosphere. It was so French that I half expected Leslie Caron and Louis Jourdan to show up for breakfast. The end tables didn't match and they each had a different lamp. I thought it was fabulously chic and original.

Mother and I shared the king-sized bed, but neither of us cared. In the middle of the night I had to go to the bathroom. I didn't realize there was another door on the other side of the bathroom. I was about to lift my negligee when suddenly the connecting door burst open and a man in his pajamas came barging in. I let out a scream that could have collapsed the Eiffel Tower, and he let out a scream to match. Mother came running in as the man bolted back to his room and slammed the door shut. It was hysterical. Like something out of a Feydeau farce.

So yes, our accommodations were "offbeat," but we couldn't have been more thrilled to be there. The last time I was in Paris, I was working for *Playgirl*. Then, other than an excursion to a transvestite nightclub, Elle et Lui (He and She), where they brought me onto the stage with the performers and snapped my picture, I never got to see the beautiful city.

Our first day we walked down a street lined with haute couture shops. I've said before how fashionable I think the French are, and looking in the windows of those shops that day, I was never more certain. Clothes have always been extremely important to me. They aren't simply items to cover my body, but rather pieces that reflect my mood and who I am.

As we walked along the shop-lined street, I breathed in the splendor of Paris. With each step I felt a growing sense of familiarity about the place. I'd never been to the area where we were walking, but somehow I felt like I had.

It became such an overwhelming feeling of déjà vu that I thought I might burst. "Mother, I feel at home here. I feel like I've lived here before."

"What do you mean?" she asked, taking my arm in hers.

"I can't explain it, I just...I just know it."

We walked a little further when I suddenly felt the urge to deviate from our path. "Turn left here," I said, pulling her across the street.

Toni and her mother in Paris.

When we reached the other side, I told my mother about another street—a street I'd likewise never been to but could somehow describe in perfect detail. I told her about the buildings and shops on the road and about a small church on the corner. It was like a fever was rushing me on as I described it.

"Toni, you've never been here. How can you possibly know all this?"

"That's the point, I don't know! But I can see what I'm describing so vividly. Please, come with me."

We turned a corner, and there—just beyond another shopping area—was the exact road I had described. There were the exact shops and buildings, and that church on the corner. Everything situated precisely as I'd seen it in my head.

My mother was awestruck, as was I. We came to dead stop, each absorbing what had just happened.

"I need to marry a Frenchman," I said, a twinkle in my eye.

There was a message in all this and I needed to find out what it was.

* * * * *

My dear friend Leonard Ross invited me to Acapulco just before Christmas. Leonard was a handsome, immensely wealthy young man who was completely devoted to his family. No one ever knew exactly what he did or how he made his fortune, but it didn't matter.

Among his investments, he owned the incredible Marian Davies estate in Beverly Hills. Davies had been the mistress of the legendary publisher William Randolph Hearst, who established a publishing empire in the early 1900s. He was dedicated to making Davies a movie star. Hearst himself was the inspiration for Orson Welles' amazing 1941 movie, *Citizen Kane*. They say Davies was an avid reader and drinker, and that she kept bottles of booze hidden in the tank of her toilet. Who knows if that's true, but it sure made for some good gossip in the 1930s.

In my days of antiquing, I came across a crystal chandelier from Marian Davies' Santa Monica beach estate. Yes, she had that too. I bought it on the spot and it's hanging today in my home in Bel Air. When I find something beautiful that has a history to it, I regard it as a treasure. Davies' chandelier is exactly that: a treasure I will never sell.

I was as single as a gal can be, so I flew to Acapulco. The "house" Leonard had rented was more of an estate than a simple home. Overlooking a shimmering bay, the place was once the residence of the stunning actress Merle Oberon, best known for playing Cathy opposite Laurence Olivier's Heathcliff in the classic movie *Wuthering Heights*. Years later I bought a turquoise and diamond brooch that came out of Merle Oberon's estate. Another treasure.

Our fourth day into the vacation was the New Year celebration, and we were all set to attend a big New Year's Eve party. My mother instilled in me a superstition that how you spend New Year's Eve is an indication of how the coming twelve months will turn out.

With that in mind, I was determined to dress and feel my best. I laid out my outfit: a pair of turquoise gabardine pants coupled with a beautifully crocheted turquoise sweater I had bought on the Champs-Elysees in Paris. Accenting the outfit was a spectacular turquoise Indian necklace I had purchased in Palm Springs a year or so earlier. When I was all set and put together, I sparkled like the Mediterranean.

Leonard, his girlfriend Barbara, my gal pal Lee, and I arrived at the New Year's party together. I was immediately awestruck. The "party" house was glamorous, hidden behind gates, and set right on the water. The view was magnificent. As we made our way inside, my eyes lit up at the luxury of the scene. Dimly sparkling lights illuminated the crowds of elegantly dressed people who chatted away while sipping their cocktails. Everyone was tan from the Acapulco sun, and the energy in the room was absolutely vibrant. I stood in the entryway for a moment, soaking it all in.

When I finally tore my eyes away from the splendor, I noticed that I had somehow lost Leonard, Barbara, and Lee. I walked through the crush of partygoers, looking for my friends, but they were nowhere to be found.

I decided to wing it and made my way through the spacious patio. The crowd seemed to part before me. There in the clearing, slouched on a sofa, was a handsome man with dark hair. He had apparently nodded off, his head slightly tilted to the side. I recognized Liza Minnelli seated on his right and Alana Hamilton, George Hamilton's wife, on his left. The women were chatting away, seemingly unaware that the man between them was in dreamland. I just stood there, enthralled with the picture of this man peacefully dozing between those two high-energy women.

I guess he could feel my stare drilling a hole into his subconscious because he suddenly opened his large, dark eyes. For that instant we were transfixed on each other. Embarrassed, I quickly melted back into the crowd.

After a few more laps around the party, I finally found my friends. I pressed Leonard for information about the man on the sofa, and Leonard didn't disappoint. The man's name was Tony Murray (pronounced Murr-aee), and the house we were in belonged to him.

A few minutes later, the host found me. He spoke with a heavy French accent when he introduced himself.

"My name is Tony Murray. We have not met before."

"I live in LA," I responded, staring once more into his dark eyes. My heart fluttered, but for some reason I felt oddly cool—not nervous or anxious in the slightest. "My name is Toni Holt," I said, smiling at him.

He smiled right back. With incredible charm, he said, "Ah, in that case, we will have to call you Little Ton-ee…and I will be Big Tony."

Like Onassis, he pronounced my name as if it had an "e" at the end. And, he, too, had a head like a kingdom.

Sometime later I learned that Murray was not Tony's real last name, and that Tony was just a nickname for his first name, which was Jacques Gaston. Tony's confident attitude and commanding presence reminded me a lot of Aristotle Onassis, and it didn't bother me at all that his thick, dark hair wasn't his own. For some reason I can't explain, many of the men I've been attracted to wore toupees: "top of the morning hair," I call it.

Right then and there I knew I had found my Frenchman.

With Leonard's help, I learned that Tony owned a lot of businesses, including gas stations in France, an elevator company, a security company, and many others. Besides the home in Acapulco, he owned a home in St. Tropez, an apartment on Avenue Foch in Paris, and a huge yacht that was once a battleship, which he kept in the South of France. He always stayed at the Pierre Hotel when he was in New York.

To say that Tony was immensely wealthy would be an understatement. He was at least twenty-plus years older than I, which fit the bill, as we all know I'm very comfortable with older men. My interest in Tony was absolutely piqued and I couldn't wait to talk to him again…that was, until Leonard told me there was a woman in Tony's life by the name of Dominique. Leonard said that if Tony had been married, Dominique would have been his mistress.

After hearing about Dominque, my spirits fell. I doubted I would ever see Tony Murray again.

Toni and Tony Murray in Acapulco.

CHAPTER TWENTY-SEVEN

Tony Murray

Following an appearance on *The Mike Douglas Show* in Philadelphia, I went to New York on business. I was at the Sherry-Netherland when I received a frantic phone call from my mother.

"Toni, a Mr. Murray is anxiously looking for you. I told him you were in New York and gave him your number. I hope that's okay."

I hadn't told her about Tony, so I understood her concern. I assured her everything was fine. Within an hour, Big Tony called.

"Ton-e, I'm coming tomorrow to New York to see you," he said in his strong French accent.

I remembered what Leonard had told me about Dominique, and I couldn't help feeling a bit annoyed by Tony's assumption that I would want to see him.

"Well, I'm busy," I replied. "I'm working."

Tony wasn't swayed. "Where are you staying?" he asked, blatantly ignoring my reluctance to see him.

The more I tried to put him off, the more determined he became. It was clear he wasn't going to give up. I was being chased, and I liked it.

I let out a hefty sigh. "I'm staying at the Sherry."

"Ah, a very nice hotel...but I want you to stay at the Pierre," he responded smoothly.

Who did this Frenchman think he was? And more importantly, who did he think I was?

"No, no, no," he insisted, "I am not looking to go to bed with you."

Oh. I was a tad crestfallen. I didn't know whether to be happy or disappointed.

"What I am looking for is for you to be comfortable," he continued. "I want you to be at the same hotel I am. You will have your own suite. And I will have mine."

I weighed the options for a moment, letting the silence hang heavy between us.

"Well?"

I caved. "Call me when you get to New York."

"Excellent. We'll go to dinner. I want to talk to you...get to know you."

He seemed genuine. The hesitation I initially felt all but faded away now that I knew his intentions.

Tony called the very next day. He was at the Pierre.

"I have booked a beautiful suite for you. Shall I send a driver?"

For the record, the Pierre is on Fifth Avenue, only one short block from the Sherry. A car was beyond unnecessary, but I liked the idea of it. It sounded so important. "Yes, you may send a driver."

If someone wants to spoil you, why dissuade them?

While I waited for the car, I phoned my mother and told her I was switching hotels. The car arrived at the front of the Sherry, and the doorman loaded my luggage. "Where to?" asked the driver.

"The Pierre, please."

He turned to me as if I were crazy. "You're kidding, right?"

"No, I'm not kidding. Do you expect me to carry my own luggage?"

The driver slammed down the trunk and grudgingly drove me around the corner to the Pierre. I went to the front desk and found everything was already in order. Before I could sign my name, Tony joined me in the lobby and we went up to my suite. He opened the door and gestured inside like he owned the hotel.

"This is yours," he said.

The suite was old but charming. It was done in shades of blue, with an elegant bedroom and living room. Tony definitely had style and knew how to make a woman feel important.

We talked for a while and he told me he had just bought Harold Robbins' house in Beverly Hills. Harold was a best-selling novelist who wrote about sex and power, sex and money, sex and drugs, sex and history, and just plain sex, all with a lot of four-letter words. His books were roundly panned by critics and devoured by his fans. Years later, he and I developed a strong friendship. When he became wheelchair bound from an accident, I built a ramp at my home in Palm Springs so he could easily get in and out when he and his wife came for dinner.

Tony announced that he was taking me out to the Pierre Grill, which was downstairs in the hotel. I told him I had some business to attend to first. Just then the phone rang. It was my mother.

"Toni, I need to talk to you." The tone of her voice immediately worried me.

I turned to Big Tony, who looked at me expectantly. "It's my mother. Would you be kind enough to hang up this phone when I pick it up in the bedroom?"

The urgency in my mother's voice was unmistakable. "I hate to be the one to tell you this, darling, but *The National Tattler* just called. They're going out of business. Your column is finished."

The National Tattler was a minor competitor to *The National Enquirer*. A few months earlier I had accepted a position with them to write a double-paged spread, "At Home with the Stars."

I collapsed on the bed. "What did you just say?"

Mother repeated the devastating news. "They're bankrupt. They're closing the doors tonight. You're out of a job."

"Mother, I have to hang up. I'll call you later." I didn't wait for her response.

My insides were curled in a knot as I returned to the living room. I've always known I don't handle adversity very well, especially when it comes as a total shock. My feelings must have been written on my face because Tony knew instantly something was wrong.

"What is it?" he asked, concerned.

I was embarrassed. I didn't want him to know I had just lost my job. "Nothing…nothing," I told him, rather unconvincingly.

"Toni, I don't want to upset you, but you look like you've seen a ghost."

I sat on the chair by the desk and Tony rushed to my side. "What happened? What's wrong?"

"I don't want to discuss it."

"I want you to tell me," he insisted.

If ever there was an angel on my shoulder, it was Tony Murray. He pulled a chair beside me and sat down. He took my hand and said, "Please, tell me what happened."

I took deep breath, and broke down. I did my best to keep my tears in check, but it all poured out.

"The company I work for, *The National Tattler*, just called my mother and told her they are going out of business tonight. They've gone bankrupt…and I'm out of a job."

"Oh, I am so sorry," he said, stroking my hand with his thumb. Seeing how overwhelmed I was, he raised my chin up so our eyes met. "I feel you are a very strong and talented woman, and I believe in you. I'm going to give you an offer you cannot refuse."

"What is that?" I sniffled. Without answering my question, he went to the desk, a very old and beautiful French desk. He pulled a checkbook from his pocket. I raised my hands in protest. "No, no, I can't take your money."

"How much were you earning with this *National Tattler*?" he asked, ignoring my reluctance.

"Twenty-five hundred dollars a month," I answered, stifling tears.

"Very well," he said in a businesslike tone. "At the first of every month for one year, you will have twenty-five hundred dollars."

I was speechless. "But...why?"

"Because you need help and I can afford to help you. I am very, very rich...and it would be my pleasure to do this for you. I understand you have children...and your mother... I don't want you to feel stressed or upset. Please, I want you to have it."

"I don't have to go to bed with you?" I asked, half joking, half concerned.

"You don't ever have to see me again," he said with a smile.

That did it! I don't think I ever felt more emotionally fragile than I did at that moment, but I quickly recovered and found myself negotiating. "What happens after the first year if I don't have a job? Then where am I?"

His answer was immediate. "We'll make a new negotiation."

Nobody had ever treated me like that. Nobody! Incredibly grateful, I agreed to Tony's generous offer after repeated assurances that no strings were attached.

Tony took me to the Pierre Grill for dinner. A dance floor separated the beautiful bar area from the front of the room. A trio played music, and Tony asked me to dance.

Within minutes, all the panic I had experienced hours earlier was gone. I felt a much-needed sense of peace and a tremendous appreciation for Tony Murray. Fate had somehow brought him to my rescue. I think I was falling in love.

By the way, they say it's a sign of genius when you can see a little bit of white under the color of a person's eyes. I saw that in Tony's.

It was a very romantic evening.

CHAPTER TWENTY-EIGHT

Cary Grant

At the end of that year Tony invited me back to his home in Acapulco for the holidays. I didn't realize it when I first met him, but his house was practically next door to a former president of Mexico. Consequently, there were soldiers with automatic weapons stationed at the entrance to the gate, guarding the private road that led to these palatial estates. I remember getting a sinking feeling in my tummy at seeing all those machine guns. I found it all very unnerving. The former president invited us for dinner one evening, and Tony returned the favor another night.

Believe it or not, ever since I was five or six I could literally smell poverty. It stemmed from a car ride through lower Manhattan with my parents when I began to cry for no apparent reason. My father stopped the car and asked what was wrong. I pointed to the rundown tenements that surrounded us. "It smells…it smells poor," I whimpered.

I don't know where that came from because I was certainly too young to have any realistic concept of what "poor" really was. But I never forgot it.

Without realizing it, that childhood recollection came back to me in Mexico. Maybe it was the sight of the dilapidated houses a block from the gate, or the dozens of hungry, scraggly dogs that ran after our car. No matter how often I drove down that road, I could always detect that same smell of poverty. It permeated the luxury behind the gates like a stain that was impossible to remove.

Tony, a legendary party-giver, had planned a huge affair for Christmas Eve. He loved to give parties, and anybody who was anybody in Mexico was going to be there. I phoned my mother and insisted she fly in for it.

The night of the party I walked around greeting guests, making sure everyone was happy. Musicians played and the staff kept the elegant buffet piled high with the most delicious food. Everyone talked about

Toni's sons, Adam (left) and David, in Acapulco.

where they were going or what they were going to do, and most of them had a second or third home somewhere in the South of France or Italy or Austria or New York.

I did my best to mingle and take part in conversations whenever I could. All that became inconsequential when suddenly I saw this well-tanned gentleman across the room. I looked twice to be sure, but I knew it was Cary Grant. I walked over and introduced myself. "Hello, I'm Toni Holt. Tony Murray's fiancée."

He offered his hand. "My goodness…so pleased to meet you," he said. There it was, that unique Cary Grant phrasing and that captivating smile.

I was so excited to meet him I could barely stand still. Listening to that voice brought me back to the Midwood movie theatre in Brooklyn.

Just then my mother walked by and I grabbed her arm. "Mother, I want you to meet someone."

Not waiting for a formal introduction, Mr. Grant said, "Hello, I'm Cary Grant."

She looked up at him, her head tilted slightly to the side. "Well, you do look a lot like him."

He broke into laughter and I was totally mortified. "Mother, this really *is* Cary Grant."

She was sure I was pulling a joke. I could see there was a moment where she might say something more edgy, but instead she was enthusiastic. "So nice to meet you." She paused, still not a hundred percent sure. "Are you really Cary Grant?"

"Yes, I am." He kissed her on the cheek to seal the deal. For Mother—and me—there didn't have to be anyone else at the party. We had met Cary Grant, and he was beyond charming.

Cary Grant and Tony Murray in Acapulco.

A few nights later we were invited to a dinner party at the nearby home of Serge Semenenko, who had been a guest at our party earlier in the week. In 1956, Semenenko, the former senior VP at First National Bank of Boston, purchased a majority stake in Warner Bros. Pictures along with a handful of silent partners—a deal that came under scrutiny several years later. Russian-born and Harvard-educated, Semenenko led a life of luxury that included a magnificent terraced suite at the Pierre Hotel in New York in addition to his home in Acapulco.

We arrived at Semenenko's after ten. It was eleven o'clock when we sat down to dinner. There were twenty of us seated at a long table in the elegant dining room. The silver was the best money could buy, and the crystal sparkled beneath the glittering chandelier.

Semenenko, a short man and not particularly good-looking, oozed power. He was seated at one end of the table, and I was four seats away. On my left was my new pal, Cary Grant. My first thought was *Omigod, what am I going to talk about?*

Cary Grant was Hollywood royalty. Meeting him a few nights before was easy—but now I had to be entertaining and interesting. I was sure he would be bored to death with me after five minutes. Surprisingly, he turned out to be the most down-to-earth person I could ever have imagined. His date was Maureen Donaldson, a young woman who wrote a Hollywood column. She was seated at the other end of the table, nowhere near us.

Cary—he insisted I call him Cary—remembered me from our party. "Oh, I got such a kick out of your mother. She was very funny. Do you think she believed I was really Cary Grant?" We had a good giggle over that.

Semenenko made a toast. A few others made toasts. And dinner was served. Everyone was happy to be there and the conversation was lively, often drowned out by laughter.

I've always considered myself an inquisitive person, but I guess you've figured that out by now. I like to learn about people. How they came to be who they are and what interests them. It makes me understand them better. In my quest to learn more about Cary Grant the man, I asked him, "If you hadn't been an actor, what would you have been?"

Without hesitation he gave me his answer, a wistful look in his eyes. He spoke as if I had disappeared, reaffirming his innermost feelings. "I know exactly what I would have been. If I could have been anything in the world, I would have been like Father Flannigan at Boys Town. I wish I could have devoted my life to helping orphaned boys. I admired Father Flannigan so much, and I could have done what he did."

Impressed how he always looked so fit, I asked if he had any health secrets to share. "Yes." He laughed. "At one time I went on a strict carrot diet. I bought a blender and ate chopped or pureed carrots four or five times a day. It made me feel fantastic until one day my skin turned a bright orange."

"End of the carrot diet?"

"Oh, yes," he replied.

I felt I was on a roll, and the reporter in me kicked in. The next question was a bit more brazen. "I know I shouldn't ask you this, but you've been involved with some really wonderful women in your life. Which one was your favorite?"

He didn't seem angered at the question, but it took him a little longer to answer it. "Hmm…I'd have to say my favorite wife was Betsy Drake. I was crazy about her."

The more I thought about his answer, the more I understood why. While Betsy might have been considered the least beautiful of all his wives, she was an extremely caring person who wanted to give to others much like Cary. This common ground must have created an amazing bond between them.

Betsy Drake was Cary's third wife. They divorced in 1962 but remained good friends. Betsy was born in Paris and worked in the theatre in London when Cary first met her. He was instrumental in getting her to Hollywood, where she signed a movie contract with RKO. Not really enamored with the movie business, she gave up acting shortly after her divorce from Cary, and concentrated on writing. She subsequently became a practicing psychotherapist in various hospitals in Los Angeles, then had her own office in Beverly Hills. Her grandfather had built the famed Drake Hotel in Chicago.

Cary's second wife was Barbara Hutton, the heiress to the Woolworth fortune, and whose father was the co-founder of the E. F. Hutton stock brokerage. He was also married to actress Dyan Cannon, with whom he fathered his only child, Jennifer. In her book *Dear Cary, My Life with Cary Grant,* Dyan denies the rumors that Cary was gay. There was also talk that Cary was very thrifty and that he could make a box of Kleenex last longer than anybody.

Cary's fifth wife, Barbara Harris, always made sure there was a red rose waiting in the hotel room for Cary when he was traveling.

After the party I wondered if Cary had any idea who I was or that I did interviews and wrote columns about Hollywood celebrities. If he did, he never let on. I only know we enjoyed talking to each other. So much in fact, after everyone had finished dining and left the table, the two of us remained deep in conversation for at least another hour.

CHAPTER TWENTY-NINE

Daddy Wants to Marry You…

Over the next several months, Tony Murray was back and forth between New York, Paris, and LA. During that time we saw each other frequently, and I learned a lot about my Frenchman. He was peripatetic, unable to stay in any one place for too long. Maybe a week or ten days was his limit, except for the summers he spent at his home in St. Tropez when he would take his friends on his yacht to Monte Carlo and Cannes.

I quickly discovered that there were certain things about Tony's past that he didn't want to discuss. If he didn't want to talk about it, I only incurred his wrath if I pried. But thanks to Leonard Ross, who filled in some of the blanks, I was able to piece together a bit of Tony's history.

When he and his sister were young, Tony's father owned a giant cement company in Paris during the time that Hitler was coming to power in Europe. Tony's father, it turned out, had a mistress who he was crazy about. Fearful that the Germans were going to invade Paris, Tony's father sent his wife and daughter off to Nice—a "safe" area for Jews—while he stayed in Paris to run his company. As best as I could put the story together, when the Germans *did* reach Paris, Tony's father learned to his shock and dismay that the brother of his mistress was one of Hitler's top Nazi officers. The mistress was forced by her brother to reveal the identity of Tony's father, and his father was reportedly taken away to the concentration camp in Auschwitz.

Tony never would directly answer these questions nor even confirm if he was Jewish. Warren Avis (Avis Rent-A-Car) once told me that Tony was really born in Tunisia.

The story goes that Tony fled to England and joined the Royal Air Force, where he was among many young men from occupied countries who had escaped the Germans and joined the RAF to fight against the Third Reich. Tony told me that he went into a phone booth in London, opened the phone book to a random page, closed his eyes, and stuck his finger on a name. That's how he became Murray, which he still pronounced with his

French accent: Murr-aee. I never knew his real name because he never told me or anyone I know what it was. To this day Tony proudly wears the Red Rose Legion of Honor in his lapel.

I was still living in the Doheny house when Tony said to me, "I don't see any reason for you to live here. You pay rent and you have nothing to show for it. For the same money you pay rent, you can own your own home. I'll make the down payment, and out of the money I give you every month, you can pay for the house and it will be yours."

The idea sounded wonderful. I took his advice, and with the help of Elaine Young, I found a house on Coldwater Canyon, only a few minutes from Tony's home. To my complete surprise, Tony paid for it in full. The house belonged to me, free and clear.

"Toni, it's time for you to have a new car," he said, sometime later. He took me to the Rolls-Royce dealership in Beverly Hills where we saw the owner, Charles Schmidt.

Seeing Charlie again was particularly sweet for me. Needless to say, Charlie was thrilled to see me walk in with Tony Murray. "I want to put her in a new car," Tony said.

This time I drove out in a shiny new navy-blue Rolls. For the first time in a long time—if ever—I felt secure. Money was no longer an issue. I had my own house for Mother and my boys, and I had my very own Rolls-Royce.

Was I a kept woman? In a sense I suppose I was. In reality I never felt that way. After all, I still had my television show, my column, and was still actively engaged in furthering my career.

At the same time, Tony had great respect for me. Never, in any way, did he make me feel threatened. He was—and is—a very principled man, and was always very kind to me and my family.

One day I was in my dressing room at KHJ-TV when the phone rang. It was Jean Jacques, Tony Murray's eldest son, calling from Paris. He was ten or eleven at the time, with dark eyes and dark hair, and my favorite. I felt a connection to him. Tony doted over Jean Jacques and his younger brother, Jean Pierre. I was surprised to hear Jean Jacques' voice and even more surprised when he said, "Toni, my daddy said I should tell you he wants to marry you."

"Really?" I answered. "But Jean Jacques, why doesn't your daddy tell me that himself?"

CHAPTER THIRTY

I'm That Crazy American

Tony and I were married in the Presidential Suite at Caesars World in Las Vegas. We flew our closest friends in for the weekend, and it turned out to be a fun and glorious time.

Toni and Tony Murray get married at Caesars Palace in Las Vegas.

Toni with her Best Man and Best Friend, Duny Cashion.

Toni and Tony have dinner at Caesars Palace.

After a quick honeymoon, we returned to Beverly Hills. Mother stayed in the Coldwater Canyon house and I settled into Tony's Beverly Drive home. It wasn't long before I had a reality check.

"Now that we're married you can't work every day on television," Tony announced.

"Well, I don't want to quit," I replied, laughing at the absurdity of his suggestion. "I've worked too hard to get where I am. I'm building a good career."

"I need you with me," he said.

I realized then and there how serious he was.

"But what if something happens with us? What then?"

"As long as you stay married to me, you'll never have to worry."

Here we were, newly wed, and already the marriage had a provision. It felt like he was reminding me of the pre-nup I signed before the wedding. It stipulated that if we stayed married for ten years, everything would be half mine. It was an extraordinarily generous arrangement. After all, my Frenchman was worth many, many hundreds of millions of dollars. But it soon became apparent he wanted total control over our relationship.

Almost immediately my need to keep my own identity clashed with Tony's desire to have me with him at all times. I think it stemmed from the fact that I hadn't really wanted to get married in the first place. I felt sort of nudged into it. At the same time, I knew I was probably the luckiest girl in the world. But the issue was out in the open, and the struggle quickly became a bone of contention.

That wasn't the only rough spot. To be sure, I was Madame Murray—Tony's Madonna. He would say to me, "Ton-e, you are a European-thinking woman, not a bourgeois American. If you ever hear that I am in the company of another woman, you should never let it bother you. It is you I am in love with."

I took Tony at his word and never questioned him. My mindset became one of "what I don't know won't hurt me."

As a result, Tony and I made a compromise. He would be supportive of my career for a year, but if I didn't make it big within that time, I would quit. After only a few months Tony became impatient. "Okay, Ton-e. Nothing has happened. I need you to be with me."

In a way, he was right. Yet I cherished my work, I liked who I was and what I did. I didn't want to be just the wife of a billionaire husband. So, I didn't quit. I simply wasn't ready to give it all up.

But there were other issues. While I was busy interviewing stars like Steve McQueen, Jerry Lewis, and Sammy Davis, Jr., I was having problems at home with Adam and David. My youngest son, Adam, had always had a food addiction, and the problem was getting worse. He was getting heavier by the day. I would find candy wrappers galore under his bed, along with ice cream sticks and dirty dishes covered with stale chocolate sauce.

Meanwhile, David, only eight, and a year older than Adam, had begun smoking marijuana. I'm certain he got hooked when I sent him to an exclusive day camp in Malibu over the summer. He was exposed to someone who worked there. Every time I opened my purse, it seemed like a few dollars were missing from my wallet.

Toni with Sammy Davis Jr.

We sent David off to boarding school as a reprimand, and his marks were excellent. He was an exceptional student who could do anything. Tony told me he wanted to train David to be part of his empire. When he learned that David had a drug problem, he was devastated and furious. He had such high hopes for him, and took the disappointment personally.

Toni's son David.

Tony was a kind man, but also a stern disciplinarian. Drugs in his home were not something he would tolerate. It was Christmas vacation when we discovered David was still smoking pot. How he got it was a mystery. Tony wanted to send him away immediately, back to the boarding school he was attending at the time.

"You can't have David here doing drugs," he insisted.

"Tony, I'm not sending him away. It's Christmas! Besides, the school isn't even open right now. He has nowhere to go!"

Tony wouldn't listen to reason. "He has to go," he argued.

"Well, he's not," I said. My word on my son was final. I still had hope that it was just a phase, something David would get over quickly. I believed if he was home, I could keep a close watch on him, at least for the holidays.

Tony, however, stood firm on the subject. We argued constantly over the next few days, and finally he said, "If you're not going to send him away, I'm going to New York."

"Fine," I said, standing my ground.

Twenty-four hours later, Tony flew off to New York. I was left at home with David, and I knew that I needed to get him straight. I became obsessed with the thought. This was far more important than anything I ever had to deal with in my life. This was my son. It killed me to know he was throwing away his natural intelligence on drugs. I swore to myself I would get him back on track.

While I was at home with David, Tony was romping around New York. He called me a few days after he left and told me he was at Regine's nightclub on Park Avenue.

"I'm sitting between two beautiful girls…and I'm having a wonderful evening." He laughed.

"Good. Have a wonderful time," I said, slamming the phone down.

I was stung by the phone call. I don't think I understood that Tony was trying to make me jealous so I would take a more aggressive path with David and his addiction. In hindsight, Tony was a hundred percent correct.

Years later I knew someone who was having a similar problem with his son. He sent the boy to a mountain cabin away from the rest of the world, hired a bodyguard to keep him safe, kept him up there for a long while...and the boy never did drugs again. I know now that the worst thing a parent can do when a child has a drug problem is to be an enabler and a forgiver. If I had come down harder on David when he was younger, it might have saved him—and me—a lifetime of heartache that I will pay for till my grave.

* * * * *

As time went on, Tony and I grew further and further apart. He continued to pressure me to quit my TV job.

I don't know whether it was Tony's constant harping or a deep-seated sense that he was right, but I was gradually becoming disillusioned. The problem was I still loved doing the interviews. I loved talking to celebrities and getting to know them. But it just didn't feel right anymore.

My current state of affairs came into sharp focus one morning at KHJ. It was one of those rare, unexpected moments when life and career collide like two meteors hurtling through space.

A famous French actress, Danielle Darrieux, was scheduled to appear "live" on my show. Danielle had an illustrious career in the French cinema, starring in over a hundred films. She had a big personality and reddish-blonde hair that framed her beautiful face. I had never met her before, so I took a few minutes to chat with her before we went on the air. Despite the long flight from France the day before, she was bubbly and effervescent. As we waited to go on, she told me about a man she had met on the plane.

"Ohhh," she lamented. "This man was sitting next to me in first class. He drove me crazy...all the way from Paris...he never stopped talking."

"Really? What happened?" I asked, hoping there was a story there that might work for the show.

"He kept repeating that he was married to a crazy American. He told me he is so rich...worth hundreds of millions of dollars...and he was so upset about this woman."

I listened intently as she continued.

"Can you believe this crazy American? She doesn't want to be married to me anymore. I promised her half of everything if she stays married to me for ten years. And she's telling me 'I don't care about your money, I only care about my life.'"

A building didn't have to fall on me to know where this was going.

Danielle continued. "Every time I dozed off, he would jab me with his elbow and say, 'I have more to tell you.' It was a nightmare!"

I couldn't stand it any longer. I put up my hand, and she fell silent. "Danielle, I don't know how to tell you this, but *I'm* that crazy American."

An awkward moment passed as we let the coincidence sink in; then we both broke out in hysterical laughter.

Tony's response when I repeated the story to him set me to thinking. "You don't ever have to divorce me," he said. "I'll take care of you. That way you don't have to worry that anybody will ever pressure you."

The plan made sense, so I moved out of Tony's house and moved back to the Coldwater house with my mother. The separation meant I didn't have to listen to Tony badger me to give up my career, but I felt something inside of me had changed. I wasn't as driven. I felt unfulfilled and empty.

I can't say exactly what changed, but I think maybe the financial security Tony provided me had stolen away some of my fire. I didn't need to be working myself ragged anymore. I lived in a lovely house and drove a Rolls-Royce. But there was more to it than that.

When you're young, you never think you're going to die. You never think you'll get sick, and you never think the world will move on without you when you're gone. You have a different feeling about things, a feeling of invincibility that underlines everything you do. Well, I was getting a little older, and seeing David plunge into the abyss of drug abuse shocked me into reevaluating life. I had spent so long wrapped up in my career that I had missed things developing right in front of me. I realized my priorities should be with my boys.

I gave up my morning show on KHJ, and called CNN to tell them I wasn't going to tape anymore segments of "Toni Holt in Hollywood," a show they were carrying five days a week.

I totally lost interest in my career. Time and time again Tony asked me to reconcile, but no matter what he said, I knew he wasn't going to change his ways. In truth, Tony knew it too. We were incompatible for a variety of reasons and it simply wasn't going to work.

It's a dreadful experience for a woman to openly confront the good and bad of her relationship with her husband and her children. But not facing the problems can lead to an even bigger disaster. As difficult as this is to say, sometimes the problems are so great there is no way they can be repaired.

Despite living in separate houses, Tony and I stayed married for the next few years. True to his word he continued to support me in style.

This "downtime" was a period of great reflection. I wondered if things might have been different had I had a formal education. As it was, my ingenuity had become the solution that led me to many of the destinations in my life. I knew it was time to move on to the next stop. I'd outgrown what I was doing. I didn't care about it anymore. I was fed up with being called a "gossip columnist" when I considered myself a reporter and a storyteller.

My mother would say I was like a little girl peeking out from behind a wall, always eager to see what was on the other side. I had been through so many crazy situations in my personal life in addition to the ups and downs in my career that I was always in search of the next thing that was going to happen.

At this point, I wasn't sure what it was, but for some inexplicable reason I felt drawn to the political arena. "Toni Holt in Washington"... why not? After all, politicians are nothing more than actors turned inside out—and I certainly knew how to converse with actors.

CHAPTER THIRTY-ONE

Thirty Rehabs and Counting

With my next big move not yet planned, I decided I needed some time to regroup, to get away from everything that was weighing me down. So I took off for my favorite getaway—Palm Springs.

Before meeting Tony I had purchased a condo not far off the main drag. While it was small, it was large enough for Mother and me as well as my boys when they visited from boarding school.

Over the years David has been in more than thirty rehabs. Even during the worst of times, when he was full bore into drugs, I never gave up on him. It became a battle of his will against mine. I would put him in a facility for a few months, and he'd come out clean. I would pray and hope for a miracle only to have him relapse and be right back where he started. The constant back-and-forth struggle for David's well-being would be one of the most heart-wrenching aspects of my life, and continues to this very day.

If you've ever had a relative or friend grappling with addiction, you know how emotionally, physically, and financially taxing the situation can be. Being the mother of an addict is possibly the worst role to assume of them all. Here is the child you love unconditionally and have cared for beyond all measure, and you're forced to watch as they lie to everyone and throw away their potential in return for a bag of drugs. I'd already seen what addiction could do to a family growing up with my father's gambling, and to have to go through the same cycle of emotions again as a parent has been devastating. Above all, it is gut-wrenching pain and anger.

David was a total charmer from day one. I remember holding him in my arms for the first time, and I couldn't stop staring at his green-blue eyes and incredible eyelashes. He was just so handsome, so mind-bogglingly perfect to me that I instantly fell in love and felt fulfilled. He had the sweetest disposition, always smiling, always vying to be held and hugged. It was impossible not to feel drawn to his fiery little spirit.

When he was about a year old, I had a fright and a premonition I will never forget. I was standing at the window of his bedroom on the second floor of our house on Next Day Hill Drive in New Jersey, looking down into the rose garden at his little figure laughing and crawling about when I suddenly felt my blood run ice cold. It seemed that time itself had frozen, and a feeling of terror overcame my whole being. I didn't know why or how, I just knew in my soul there was something terrible at work inside my son. I felt I could see deep inside him for that single moment, and what I saw was the Devil. It was only a flash, a few seconds of fear. Then it disappeared. It was a warning, and sadly it was right. Every time something awful has happened with David, that horrible moment comes rushing back like it was yesterday.

Once David started abusing drugs, I tried everything under the sun to help him, but nothing seemed to work. When he was fifteen he was in a rehab in Idyllwild, a mountain retreat just outside of Palm Springs. He became so violent he was committed to Brea Psychiatric Hospital in Brea, California. It was an incredibly dark period in our lives. Not only was I terribly frightened *for* him—I became frightened *of* him. His temper tantrums were out of control, and he would pick up anything that wasn't nailed down and throw it. Only a handful of years had gone by since he was a child, but my perfect son was gone forever.

We all had a hard time saying no to David, and my mother bore the brunt of it. As soon as David would get out of a rehab, he'd ask my mother for favors. She would indulge him with whatever he wanted because she felt sorry for him.

"Mother, if his mouth is moving, he's lying," I would plead. She would nod with understanding, and give him money anyway. It got so bad that David began to depend on my mother for funds.

At one point he got involved with a gang who lived out in the desert near Indio. David was working at Radio Shack at the time and somehow got my mother to give him her credit card. Then he allowed one of the gang members to charge two thousand dollars' worth of electronics on the card. In return, David got drugs. And guess who got stuck with the bill?

One evening I came home to my condo and found the French door leading inside wide open. The glass above the lock was broken and lying in shards outside. My mouth dropped open in shock when I saw that the place had been all but emptied out. I didn't suspect David because he had a key to my condo, which meant he could come and go whenever he wanted—no need for him to break in. Besides, I thought there was no way he would ever rob his own mother.

My first call wasn't to the police—it was to a retired gangster I knew in Palm Springs, an older man who got around with the aid of a cane and a bodyguard. I trusted him and I trusted his word. I told him what happened and said I was mostly interested in getting my property back. He said he would have his driver bring him to my condo right away. He told me not to call the cops and make a police report until he got there.

When my friend arrived he checked my place over from top to bottom, including the broken glass on the patio by the French door.

"This is an inside job," he said. He pointed to the glass on the ground. "See? The glass is broken the wrong way. It was broken from inside the house, not outside."

He explained how the robber or robbers tried to make it look like they jimmied the lock and broke in. When the police got there, they confirmed his theory. I knew then that David was responsible for the robbery, but I didn't say anything to the police.

My next call was to David. "How could you do this?" I screamed at him, the rage causing my voice to tremble. "After all I've been through with you…after all the years I stuck by you…how could you do this to me? I don't ever want you around again."

When he finally spoke he denied his involvement. "Liar! Liar!" I kept repeating. He cried when I said I didn't want him in my life anymore.

After a few days David admitted his guilt. He said the robber was a guy he knew who worked in a gas station, and that he had given him his key and my address. Within days, David was back in rehab.

Years later, another gang David was involved with tried to extort money from me. They threatened to burn down my new house in Palm Springs and kidnap me or my mother if I didn't come through with the cash to pay what they claimed David owed them for drugs. They had beaten David to a pulp, and he needed all sorts of x-rays, including a brain scan. The Palm Springs police said there was nothing they could do.

I was frustrated and terrified, not only for myself but for David. By that time, I had been reduced to an emotional mess and realized I had no choice but to take a stand. I don't know where I got the courage, but I told the gang, "Come on and get me! If you think you can do it…come get me."

Yes, I was quivering in my boots when I called their bluff, but I knew if I started paying them off, they would have me. My stance caused a lot of friction with my mother because she was deathly afraid that something terrible would happen to me, but I knew in my heart I did the right thing.

After that, I took extra precautions, like only getting into my car in the garage and locking the doors before driving away. I was always watching in my rearview mirror and I never went anywhere alone. I was in a state of constant fear, and it was all because of David.

Over the years, my son has overdosed too many times to count. He was arrested…spent time in a Mexican jail…spent more time in jail in LA…and I can't even remember all the times he was in trouble.

In truth, he should have been dead many times over.

CHAPTER THIRTY-TWO

My Brother

Someone told me about a psychic who lived in Indio, a small town about twenty-five miles east of Palm Springs in the Coachella Valley. The woman had a great reputation of seeing things nobody else could. Being a strong believer in psychics (If you are lucky enough to find the right one), I wanted to know what she saw for me in the future.

Despite being in a desolate area, her house was extraordinarily clean and neat. I could tell she took great pride in her home and thought of it as a special place. The walls of the dining room, where she conducted her readings, were lavishly painted with biblical murals. The centerpiece was a huge portrait of Jesus. The ceiling was covered with images of God and scenes from the Bible. I wasn't just sitting in a room with a painting; I felt like I was sitting inside the Sistine Chapel.

The psychic, probably in her fifties, was a smallish woman, maybe an inch or two over five feet tall. She wore a navy-blue suit, cream-colored blouse, and stacked heels—a most unusual outfit for someone who lived in that area of the desert. Her hair was brown, short, and curly, and she had obviously gone to the beauty shop because her "do" had enough spray on it that not a strand would move for the next two weeks. She wore lipstick and mascara but otherwise very little makeup. While she wasn't glamorous, there was a certain class about her—I thought she could have passed for a Washington congresswoman or a Boston attorney. All factors combined, a surprise on all fronts.

She worked with Tarot cards. At the start of the reading she laid them out delicately on the dining room table. I didn't tell her anything about myself nor did I tell her what I wanted to know. In fact, I didn't even use my real name when I made the appointment.

She told me I had a lot of decisions to make. After a while I asked, "Is there a new man in my life?" She really didn't give me a definitive answer but told me everything would work out as it was supposed to.

"You have someone on the other side looking after you," she said.

She had my full attention. "I do? What do you mean? Who is it?"

"Your brother," she said emphatically.

I smiled sadly. "Oh, no, you're mistaken. I don't have a brother. I'm an only child."

She shook her head. "No, no, no...you have a brother...or you *had* a brother. In fact, his name begins with the letter 'P'...and he's definitely looking after you from the other side."

My confidence in her ability completely vanished. I knew that my mother didn't marry until she was in her early thirties, which was fairly old for those days, and for her to have more than one child at that age would have been most unusual. Besides, my mother and I were so close, she would have told me if I had a brother. There was no way what the psychic said could be true.

As I drove home I couldn't shake what she said from my mind. I stopped at the first gas station I saw and rushed to the phone booth. I dropped a coin in the slot and called my mother.

"Mother, I just saw a psychic. Did I have an older brother?"

I was sure she would laugh at the question and reprimand me for using an unreliable psychic. It was just too absurd. But no laughter came. Instead, there was a long silence. I didn't even hear her breathing. A moment later, she spoke.

"How do you know?"

I was so stunned by her response, I could hardly speak. "I have an older brother and you never told me?"

"He's not alive," she said, her voice not much more than a whisper. "I lost him."

I was confused, angry, and sad. For a moment the world seemed to fall out of focus. "Did he have a name? Did it start with a 'P'?"

"Yes," she answered.

I pressed her for more information but she cut me short. "Toni, I don't want to discuss it on the phone. We'll talk about it when I see you."

I sped home, my thoughts racing as fast as my car. The minute I walked in, I could feel my mother had already put up a barrier between us and the subject was closed, but I'm certain I had a brother who died shortly after his birth. It must have been a terrible time for my mother. I could understand why she didn't want to revisit it. I felt badly, as though I had trespassed into her personal life. I was overcome with a strange, misplaced sense of shame that I hadn't known about this huge tragedy in her life.

It's amazing what you don't know about the people you love. Learning about this adversity in Mother's life reminded me how truly strong she was. It also made me understand why she loved me so much. Having been robbed of her first child, I was an even greater gift.

CHAPTER THIRTY-THREE

Two Quick Ones

After my marriage to Tony Murray, I had two brief marriages before I met the love of my life.

One to John Yantis, a wealthy and charming southerner who owned a couple of major companies and had real estate holdings in Texas and Arkansas. John showered me with attention at a time in my life when that was exactly what I needed.

"I know you're the woman for me," he told me. "Just give me the chance to prove how much I love you. I want you to have everything beautiful."

He backed up his words by buying me a fabulous house in Palm Springs, and put it entirely in my name. He even convinced me to divorce Tony, thus giving up the financial security Tony had assured me would be mine. Tony couldn't understand why I would do such a thing, but he reluctantly agreed. After John's divorce was final, he and I said our vows.

I questioned if this was a mistake the night before our wedding, but I went through with it anyway. Almost immediately, everything went south. Much of what John had told me turned out not to be true. I learned that he had a drinking problem, and he reneged on many of the financial promises he had made to me. In short, our marriage was a giant mess. And so was I.

When deciding to divorce from John, I met the suave, elegant, famous Beverly Hills attorney Arthur Crowley. It took all of Arthur's skill, plus diligent investigative work on my part, to extricate me from the web of deceit John Yantis had woven to entice me and make me feel secure. As a bonus, I became Arthur's wife. The courtship was brief, and the marriage even shorter. Nevertheless, Arthur was there for me when I needed him the most.

(left to right) Jean Richmond, Auntie Shirl, Toni's mother, Toni, Sammi Vudgrovik at Toni's wedding to John Yantis.

Toni marries Arthur Crowley (right) at Palm Springs home of Carol and Rod Taylor.

CHAPTER THIRTY-FOUR

Marlon Brando and Anna Kashfi

On May 16, 1990, Marlon Brando's son, Christian, shot and killed his half-sister's boyfriend in Marlon's home on Mulholland Drive, high above the city of Los Angeles. By this time, I was no longer working on TV on a regular basis, so I was surprised when I received a phone call from one of those Hollywood celebrity news programs asking if I would interview Anna Kashfi, Christian Brando's mother.

I knew it was a hot story, and I knew everyone in town wanted the interview with Anna. "Why me?" I asked.

"Because she told us you're the only one she'll talk to," replied the caller.

I had met Anna a number of years earlier at a Hollywood party where she complimented me on my Indian-style dress. She loved my dress so much that I felt the need to send it to her. Soon after, circumstances changed and we lost touch. Needless to say, the phone call about the interview was totally out of left field.

Anna was born in India and raised in Calcutta. Her real name is Johanna O'Callaghan. An exotic beauty, Anna moved to London, where she became a model, then an actress, and starred in several movies in the late fifties with Rock Hudson, Spencer Tracy, Robert Wagner, Glenn Ford, and Jack Lemmon. It was during that time that she met and married Marlon Brando. The marriage lasted less than two years, but long enough for them to produce a son together, Christian. Christian was about thirty-two at the time of the shooting.

Accompanied by a cameraman, I drove to San Diego for the interview. To my utter shock, we were directed to a trailer park, and not a very nice one at that. It was incomprehensible to me that a gorgeous woman like Anna Kashfi, a former movie star and the former wife of Marlon Brando—arguably one of the most important and successful actors of our time—could be living in a small trailer. But yet, there she was.

Anna was in her late fifties by then, and heavier than I remembered her. I'll never forget she was wearing navy-blue polyester pants and black lace-up shoes that looked like orthopedic clodhoppers, the kind elderly people wear. This was not the movie star I remembered, and it tugged at my heart big time to see her this way. Still, Anna couldn't have been more gracious and happy to see me. Her clipped English accent was a pleasure to hear once again.

She told me she did charity work at a senior citizen-type village, and didn't even have a car to get there. "Christian was going to buy me one, but that isn't going to happen now," she said wistfully. Anna talked about her son and the shooting, obviously distraught by what had happened.

As I did the interview, I thought, *Oh my god! Look what happened to this poor woman's life*. To paraphrase Marlon Brando's famous line from *On the Waterfront*: After all, Anna Kashfi *was* "somebody."

At the same time, I was impressed about the way she handled her diminished circumstances. She came across so regally, not the least bit sorry for herself. We finished the interview and she told me how much she enjoyed helping the older people at the village where she spent her days.

She took me into her little bedroom and showed me a framed picture on her dresser, the only picture in the room. I was shocked to see she was wearing the very same dress I had given her a number of years earlier.

That moment touched my heart, and has been embossed in my memory ever since. For me, the personal twist of that photo and the dress transcended the story I was sent there to cover.

If not for that dress and what it meant to her, I'm sure Anna wouldn't have trusted me to do her interview.

Toni wearing the dress she gave Anna Kasfi, with John Wayne.

CHAPTER THIRTY-FIVE

Robert Kramer

I was meeting Zvia Holmes for the first time. A friend of mine in Palm Springs said she was the best psychic he had ever been to. Always on the lookout for a good psychic, I couldn't pass up the opportunity.

Toni meets Zvia Holmes in Palm Springs.

It was early evening when I arrived at her house. Before getting there I had slipped my diamond ring off my finger and placed it in a zippered compartment inside the tapestry handbag Mother had given me for Christmas. I didn't want to give Zvia any clues about who I was.

Zvia, a former gun-toting Israeli soldier, didn't use Tarot cards to do her readings. Instead, she gave me a cup of espresso. When I finished, she turned the cup upside down in the saucer and read the murky grounds of the coffee. Certainly a different approach than I was used to.

Among her predictions Zvia said I would meet a couple. At first I would like the wife but not the husband. She said the couple and I would start a new TV series together, and I would team up with another woman to do the show.

As we sat in her "reading" room, Zvia predicted I would meet someone else. "He was married...you were married. Now you're single...and he will be single. You will run into him randomly—this is the man you are going to marry...and this is the one you will stay married to. You will never, ever divorce each other."

Great, I thought, *what a novelty.* But I had no idea who she was talking about.

I was about to leave when she said pointedly in her strong Israeli accent, "When you come again, you don't need to hide your diamond in your purse."

I was flabbergasted. How could she know? I never once opened my purse in her presence, and even if I had, the ring was well hidden in the zippered compartment. That single moment served to confirm Zvia's credibility as a psychic. I told her I would be back and I did go back. I'm still going back. As the years went on, many of her predictions turned out to be incredibly accurate, and we became good friends.

Not too long after that reading I was at Trader Vic's restaurant in Beverly Hills having dinner with Ruta Lee when I ran into Robert Kramer—Bobby, as everyone called him. We had met a few times in the past, and every encounter—though brief—was always fun. Bobby, the owner of major car dealerships and auto-related businesses in and around Los Angeles, was a soft-spoken gentleman, a quality I was definitely ready to enjoy.

After dinner, Ruta and I went back to my house to discuss the projects we were working on when the phone rang. It was Bobby.

"Hi Toni. Listen, it was so great running into you at dinner tonight. I was just wondering—if it's not too late, maybe I could stop by?"

"That would be wonderful, but Ruta and I are working right now."

"Oh," he said. The sound of disappointment in his voice was evident. "I just thought it would be nice."

Truth be told, I was thrilled Bobby called, and I really did want him to come over. I covered the phone with my hand and asked Ruta if she would mind if Bobby Kramer came over for a little while, promising his visit would be brief.

"No, not all," said Ruta, giving me a mischievous smile. "Tell him to come. He's a nice guy…and I think he likes you."

A short time later Bobby arrived. His visit definitely wasn't brief, but neither Ruta nor I minded in the slightest. After a while Ruta excused herself and went home. Bobby stayed well into the early morning hours. We continued to talk and talk and talk…and Bobby never left. We've been together ever since that night.

That was June 4th turning into June 5th of 1991. We celebrate both days as an anniversary.

Toni and Bobby have dinner at the Bistro Garden.

CHAPTER THIRTY-SIX

The Elopement

Bobby and I made arrangements to have a big wedding at my home in Beverly Hills. A woman named Alice Rand had built the house some thirty years earlier. The unique compound included a tennis court shared by four other houses that were at one time the homes of Alice's large family. I owned the one Alice built for herself, perched high on a hill with a view overlooking the entire city.

The plan was to have our wedding ceremony on the tennis court at three o'clock on the afternoon of August 2, 1992, followed by a reception. We invited about two hundred friends and family, and I asked everyone to wear white. Yes, I said everyone.

It was the end of July. As the date approached, LA was sweltering in the midst of a terrible heat wave. Bobby had visions of our guests frying in their white gowns and jackets.

Two weeks before the wedding, with no relief in sight from the heat, we agreed to change course. Rather than getting married in the middle of a hot, steamy afternoon, we decided to elope to Santa Barbara. We'd still have the reception at the house—only we'd schedule it for five o'clock instead of three, when the air would be much cooler.

I was okay with the last-minute change except for one point: I didn't have a thing to wear. I had an amazing Oscar de la Renta gown and a dramatic hair ornament that I was going to wear, but that was for a formal wedding. I couldn't wear a triple-tiered white organza Oscar wedding gown to an elopement. It just didn't match the "spur of the moment" nature of the event. Not only did I not have a thing to wear, I didn't even have time to go shopping.

Then I remembered Gary.

Gary Rome was the best salesperson at I. Magnin in Beverly Hills. He was one of their top sellers, and all of the women loved him—especially me.

"Gary, it's Toni. I'm getting married the day after tomorrow and I'm running to buy a hat. I'll call you from there…tell you what color I bought. Can you put an outfit together that will match?"

"Toni, of course," he assured me with his usual calm.

Mother and I immediately left for a little hat store on Santa Monica Boulevard. I stormed through the shop like a tornado, and after a few moments, my eyes fell on a light pink, organza movie star hat with a big pink rose in the center of it. "Ah, this is gorgeous." I held it up for Mother's approval. Being the Pink Queen, she was thrilled at my selection.

I bought the hat and immediately called Gary. "It's pink. I'll be there in a few minutes, but I need a drive-by. I don't have time to come up. I'll take everything home and deal with it there."

Gary knew exactly what I meant. Mother and I hopped into my Rolls and high-tailed it to the alley that ran behind Magnin. Gary was there waiting, arms spilling over with outfits.

"Oh, darling, I know one of them will be perfect," he said, kissing me lightly on either cheek.

I laid all the outfits out on my bed and began trying them on. Gary had phenomenal taste, but as each outfit failed to captivate me, I began to feel nervous again. The pile of clothes got smaller and smaller, and I furiously sorted through the remaining outfits, praying I would find the perfect look I needed for my special wedding day. Finally, I hit the jackpot—a pink suit, a perfect match to my new hat. The stress of the elopement lessened instantly.

After dinner, Bobby and I drove to Santa Barbara and checked into the Biltmore Hotel for the night. Despite both of us having been married before, there was no anxiety about getting married again. We both knew in our hearts that this time it was going to work.

The next morning we went to City Hall to pick up the marriage license and certificate. Everything was going according to plan, but as I went to slip my ID back in my purse, I realized I didn't have the right lipstick. It was a small detail, but I wanted the entire day to be perfect. I couldn't brush it off, typical behavior for an A-type personality. Detail… detail…detail.

"Oh dear, Bobby, we can't get married yet!" I said, rifling through my bag.

"Why not?"

"I don't have a pink lipstick to match the pink outfit!"

"You're kidding, right?" He smiled.

I often think about that moment before our marriage and cite it as evidence that Bobby is my perfect match. He could tell I was serious and, without any protest at all, said to me, "Well, c'mon, let's get you some pink lipstick."

One hour and three stores later, we found it. I figured if Bobby didn't leave me after that fiasco, he never would. But as silly as the whole thing was, Bobby understood that my compulsion was fueled by an insatiable drive for perfection, attainable or not. We were getting married—and I wanted to look perfect for my husband.

Toni and Bobby get married in Santa Barbara.

Before we left LA for Santa Barbara, we had made arrangements for a local rabbi to marry us. We met him and completed our vows in the presence of a small group of family and friends. When I said "I do," I was sure it was for all the right reasons.

The ceremony was brief. Afterward we had a wonderful dinner party at the iconic San Ysidro Inn before going back to the hotel. In the morning, we drove home to Los Angeles.

That night we decided to have dinner at Jimmy's in Beverly Hills, the "in" restaurant at the time. Nobody knew we had gotten married, and I wanted to make a grand entrance and make the official announcement to our friends. I remember what I was wearing like it was yesterday: a full-skirted, white-and-black Yves St. Laurent dress with leopards dancing on it.

We swept into the restaurant, and Bobby stopped off at the first table, where a woman and a younger man were having dinner. We knew her but not him, though we'd heard that her husband had recently been killed in a drive-by shooting on one of the LA freeways. Bobby took the woman's hand, offered his condolences, and said, "Toni and I just got married."

The woman smiled and congratulated us.

"It's so nice to see you out with your son," Bobby said, in a voice meant to make her feel better.

The woman glared at Bobby as if he had poked her in the eye with a stick. "He is *not* my son." The force of her voice could have broken glass.

Bobby was so embarrassed, he wanted to crawl under the table. To make amends, he reached out to shake the young man's hand and proceeded to knock a glass of red wine all over the new widow and her escort. "I think we should go," I said, pulling Bobby away from the table by his jacket, apologizing profusely as we backed up.

It was a total Lucy and Desi moment. A grand entrance indeed.

* * * * *

On August 2, 1992, we held our wedding reception at the house. The heat wave was still in full swing, so I was really glad we cancelled the official ceremony, as were our guests, family and friends. We dotted the tennis court with big green trees and thanks to talented designer Dan

Klemuk, we had white latticework strategically placed to set the scene. The overall effect transformed the tennis court into something out of a picture book. It looked like the garden at Versailles.

I wore my white lace Oscar hi-lo dress, short in the front, long in the back. The style is back as I write this. As requested, everyone wore white. Everyone, that is, except for my psychic Zvia. She came in a black dress, but since she was the one who predicted I would meet and marry Bobby, I forgave her.

The party was spectacular, a star-filled reception with entertainment worthy of a Las Vegas show. Gene Barry, who had been starring on Broadway in *La Cage aux Folles* at the time, sang "The Best of Times." Debbie Reynolds and Helen Greco both sang, and Ruta Lee cracked jokes. Comedian Jack Carter also performed, telling some really funny stories. All of the humor was aimed at Bobby and me, of course, and we greatly enjoyed it.

Amongst our swarm of guests was also the great actor Cesar Romero. An incredibly dapper man and dear friend, Cesar had a shock of gray hair that never seemed to move. He never married, and was a popular escort for many of Hollywood's most beautiful movie stars. He was always very attentive to me, and we would laugh and giggle, as good friends tend to do. About a year earlier, Cesar and I shot an episode of *48 Hours* together. It was his birthday when we did the show. The cameras followed us around all day as we toured Beverly Hills, then into the night for the birthday party I threw for him. I had a giant black-and-white photo of Cesar blown up, and all the guests, including Danny Thomas, signed it with birthday wishes. He loved it.

Years before I had interviewed Cesar at his Brentwood home for one of my columns, and he showed me a black-and-white photo over his bed of twice-married Tyrone Power, the swashbuckling movie hero of the forties and fifties. Around that time a story circulated that Cesar and Ty had been lost at sea together on a yacht, but Cesar told me it wasn't true, at least not the "lost" part. Power was only forty-four years old when he died from a heart attack. When I first saw the photo of Ty Power, I was reminded of the photo over Rock Hudson's bed, but the identity of the man in Rock's picture will remain my secret forever. Or… at least until that star is gone.

The happy couple celebrates their marriage at home with friends.

Holt-Kramer Wedding

"A Vision in White"

Toni Holt-Kramer, asked everybody to wear white because it was supposed to be the wedding, but Tony and Bobby ran off to Santa Barbara to get married and surprised everyone! The celebration at their beautiful Beverly Hills home became a wedding reception, and what a reception it was. Everyone honored Toni's request and wore something white. The reception was held on the tennis court that was decorated by Dan Klemeck in green Ivy woven through white lattic and spectacular white centerpieces of roses on a lighted stand. Then came the show, with this line up: Ruta Lee, Debbie Reynolds, Gene Barry and Jack Carter. You would have thought you were on Broadway in New York, they all performed. Robert never seemed happier. We wish Toni and Bobby a wonderful life together!

Photos by Todd Vitti

Bride and groom Mr. and Mrs Robert Kramer

Photos by Todd Vitti

Roxanne and Jack Carter. He said, "he never saw so many Jews in one week shopping for white suits."

March Schwartz and his gift, true to March, a 1940's toaster, and Suzanne Allen

Ceasar Romeo and Bride

Spencer and Mr. Blackwell

Everyone wore white.

Freddy Otash, the famous private detective who often plied his trade for the Kennedy family, also came to the wedding. The man I called Uncle Freddy—and had known for years—had flown in from his apartment in the South of France just to be with us.

Cesar Romero with signed photograph.

Toni with Danny Thomas.

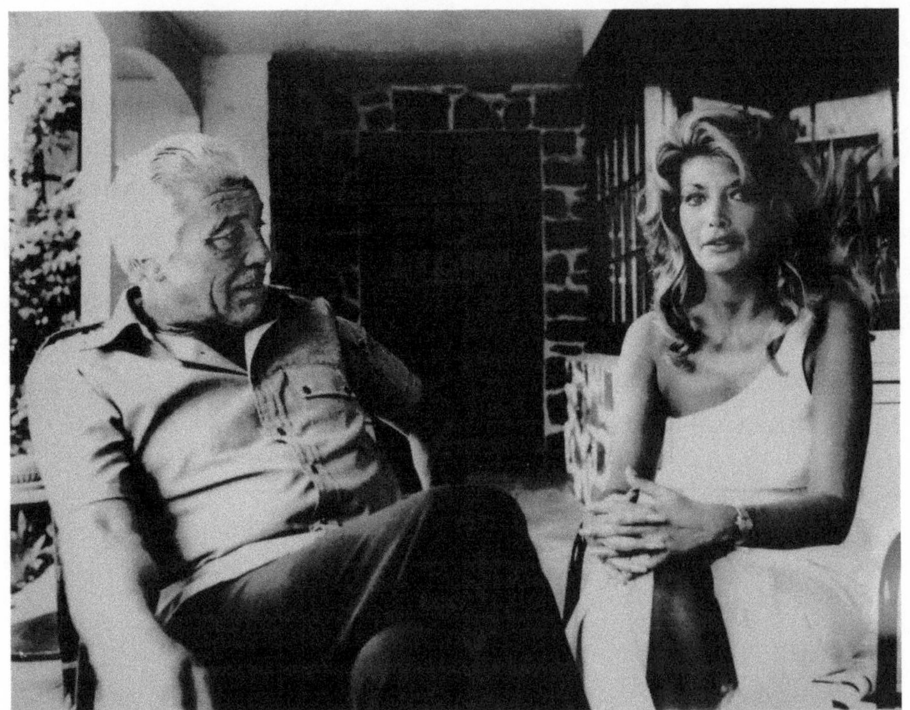

Toni with Cesar Romero.

It was more than just a wedding reception. It was a picture-perfect, very loving, fun-filled extravaganza that became the talk of the town. Hmm, what a good title for a TV show.

* * * * *

Bobby and I were watching President Clinton's inauguration on television as the cameras captured a number of parties the Clintons attended. One moment in particular struck a nerve somewhere deep in my soul.

I saw Pamela Harriman, soon to be appointed the United States ambassador to France, looking elegant and radiant—"helmet hair" and all—greeting Hillary and Bill with incredible grace at her home in a posh section of Georgetown. Pamela was dressed elegantly. Hillary was wearing an indigo-colored gown that made her eyes even bluer than they are.

All of a sudden what they were wearing was no longer important—it was all about what was happening. The pomp, the circumstance…to me, those people were true royalty. Hollywood stars seemed like pretenders by comparison.

At that very moment, I realized I wanted to be in Pamela Harriman's shoes. I wanted to do what she was doing. I turned to Bobby. "I could do that. We should be involved in Washington."

Bobby laughed, but sensed my earnestness. "Well, that sounds like fun. Someday we'll try it, if that's what you really want."

CHAPTER THIRTY-SEVEN

Talk of the Town

The Bistro Garden Restaurant in Beverly Hills was *the* celebrity hangout from the 1960s well into the 1990s. It was a second home to me. I absolutely loved going there. The garden-like setting provided the perfect atmosphere for those who wanted to be seen as well as those who simply wanted to see who they could see. Star-gazing is still the number one occupation in LA.

Having the right table in the right section of the Bistro was a must, and there were only a few "right" tables. The number one table was just past the piano on the right as you entered, and that's where Linda Tallen sat every day for lunch at noon. If you walked in or out of the main entrance, you couldn't miss her and she never missed you. For years she was known as the Queen of the Bistro Garden.

Linda was the host of a syndicated television show called *The American Jewish Hour.* Oddly enough, I'm sure she was very Catholic. Linda had platinum-blonde hair, beautiful dark eyes that she accentuated with heavy black eyeliner, and lips that were painted bright pink. You couldn't miss her if you tried. There were always two or three of the most important people in town lunching with her, including movie stars, producers, directors, studio execs, and even judges.

Linda was convinced that eating broccoli would prevent cancer, so she ate it every single day for lunch. Even though Linda was a little quirky, everyone liked her for one reason or another.

Linda's on-camera partner and the backer of *The American Jewish Hour* was David Paul Kane, founder and owner of a major financial company on Wilshire Boulevard called Kennedy Cabot. As I understand it, David, a successful stockbroker, took the name Kennedy, added another famous Bostonian name, Cabot, and put them together to give his company a powerful, rich-sounding name. And it worked.

David and Linda were together as a couple, but didn't live together. And I don't believe they had much of a sexual relationship, if any at all.

Ironically, *The American Jewish Hour* had very little to do with religion. Sometimes a rabbi appeared on the show and there would be a discussion about Israel, but primarily Linda would go to glitzy charity events, award shows, and parties in and around LA and Beverly Hills. The format of the show was to tape interviews with as many celebrities as she could get her hands on. It was a successful format to be sure, one that was mirrored years later by many broadcasters, including the E channel and the late Joan Rivers and her daughter Melissa.

Linda interviewed me when I was working on television, and whenever I saw her, she would say, "Oh, Toni, you're so happy when you're on television. The minute a camera points to you, you light up like the Fourth of July. You really do have to go back to work."

Going back to work was just about the last thing I wanted to do at the time. After a string of short-lived marriages and all the problems with my son David, my new marriage to Bobby was the most important thing in my life.

A few months later Linda called and sounded desperate. "Toni, I'm doing this event and I need your help. I can't do one interview after another; it's just too hard for me. Could you please come help me? I'd be so grateful."

Well, if the universe was so set on me stepping back into the game that it was going to throw opportunities like this at me, who was I to turn them down?

The event was the annual Thalians Ball, a charity Bobby and I had already become involved in. The Thalians, named after Thalia, the Muse of Comedy and the shepherdess of stray lambs, was started in 1955 by a handful of young actors and actresses. The very first meeting was held at the Pink Palace, the Sunset Boulevard home of Jayne Mansfield, at which time the group decided to devote their time and money to children with mental health problems. In 2002, and again in 2003, Bobby and I chaired the annual Ball.

Debbie Reynolds, Ruta Lee, and Hugh O'Brian were at the helm of the Thalians almost since its inception. Debbie's recent death was a shock to all who knew her. To most she had what appeared to be a

(Top right) Ruta Lee, Toni and Debbie Reynolds at the Thalians Ball.

Toni and Bobby with Linda and Fred Wiliamson at the Thalians Ball.

perfect life, but it was filled with lots of ups and downs. Ever caring and generous, Debbie gave everyone she knew a helping hand, both emotionally and financially, if needed.

Of all her husbands, Debbie said Eddie Fisher was the best of the lot. She wanted very little for herself and didn't need to be showered in luxury. The image that remains etched in my mind is when Ruta and I arrived in Las Vegas to see the hotel she had just purchased. We found her in one of the suites, her hair wrapped in a head scarf, standing on a ladder, washing the windows. That was the real Debbie.

By her later years, Debbie had lost most of her close friends. I recall in 2003 being at her house and seeing the walls literally blanketed with inscribed photographs of her celebrity pals. "Almost all of them are dead now," she said. It was a heart-stopping moment for me.

Debbie lived for her two children, Carrie and Todd. Knowing how close she was to them, when I heard on the news that Carrie had suffered a heart attack on a trans-continental flight from London to LA,

Toni with Debbie Reynolds backstage on Broadway.

I said to Bobby, "If Carrie doesn't make it, Debbie will be right behind her."

Sure enough, just a day apart, both were gone. Mother and daughter were laid to rest together at Forest Lawn Memorial Park in the Hollywood Hills. Three months later, Ruta Lee held a touching memorial for her close friend.

Elizabeth Taylor died in 2011 and left some jewelry to Debbie. I have to believe it was her way of saying she was sorry for stealing Eddie Fisher from her. I suppose we'll never know.

I truly had no expectations the night I worked the Thalians event with Linda, but it felt good to be in front of a camera again. As usual the event was a star-studded affair, and I interviewed a lot of old friends while making some new ones. I had a great time, and when the program aired, there was a very positive response to my appearance on the show. So much so, in fact, that Linda started calling me to co-host with her more and more often. And Bobby was all for it.

A year or so later, Linda became very ill. For months and months she complained about stomach pains and not being able to eat. The doctors kept saying it was due to nerves or stress, until Dr. Donald Morton, a world-renowned cancer specialist at the John Wayne Cancer Institute, became involved. Linda insisted I go with her to see him.

As she signed in, Linda glanced at me with a look of resignation. "You know, Toni, I'm going to die. I have pancreatic cancer."

I didn't know what to say. I did my best to be supportive, and we went in to see her doctor. Linda had x-rays taken, and afterward Dr. Morton put the pictures on a screen. He pointed out exactly where the cancer was and explained that if the cancer had been in a different position in the pancreas, Linda would have a better chance of survival. It was all so personal, but for some reason Linda wanted me to know.

Before she was diagnosed, Linda and David Paul Kane had gotten married, as much for business reasons as anything else. David became ill and sold his company to Gloria and John Gebbia, a stock entrepreneur. As a result, John and Gloria became the producers and funders of *The American Jewish Hour*.

The instant I met the Gebbias, I realized they were the very couple my psychic Zvia predicted I would meet. I recalled Zvia saying that I would like the woman but not the man—not at first, but I would eventually grow to like him. That was exactly what happened. It took a while, but today I regard them as family. Zvia also predicted I would do a new TV series with them. I didn't know it then, but that, too, would unfold in short order.

The next show Linda and I were supposed to do for *The American Jewish Hour* was the Academy Awards. We made plans to tape our show at the annual Oscar party to be held at Chasen's Restaurant, one of several Oscar parties to be held that night in and around Beverly Hills for celebs who didn't go to the formal ceremony.

Chasen's had been a popular haunt for A-listers since it first opened in 1936. It was nothing more than a shack at the time, and the story goes that Frank Capra, the three-time Oscar-winning director, had to loan the restaurant his silverware so they could stay in business. After the death of its founder, Dave Chasen, the restaurant was taken over and run by his wife, Maude.

One famous story had Elizabeth Taylor, a regular at the restaurant, order cartons of Chasen's signature chili shipped to her in Rome, where she was filming *Cleopatra*.

Fred Astaire was a regular at the restaurant, and I'll never forget the night he came over to my table with his best friend and great choreographer, Hermes Pan.

"Excuse me, I'm Fred Astaire," he said politely as if I didn't know who he was. "I just want to tell you I'm one of your biggest fans. This is Hermes Pan. He's a fan too, and he never misses your show." I had to pinch myself when they left to be sure it really happened.

Despite its popularity and after a long run as a star-studded hotspot, the restaurant began to lose its luster with the rise of eateries like Spago, which catered to the younger Hollywood crowd. Chasen's eventually closed.

As much as Linda wanted to be at Chasen's with me on Academy Awards night, she wasn't well enough and wound up in the hospital the day before the taping. John and Gloria knew what was going on with Linda, and they were with her constantly at the hospital.

On her deathbed, Linda asked them to please continue *The American Jewish Hour* in her memory, with me as the host. Linda knew of my friendship with Ruta Lee, and suggested that Ruta could be my partner in taking over the show. Ruta and I had been friends for years and always worked well together, so I knew she would be thrilled with the opportunity. And she was. Score another one for Zvia.

Linda passed away a few hours before we were to do the Awards show. We thought about canceling the whole thing, but Gloria and John insisted we go ahead and do it, saying that Linda would want it that way. As they say in Hollywood, the show must go on, so we went on as planned.

Ruta and I arrived early to set up, the paparazzi clicking away outside as the stars made their way into the restaurant. The actual Awards show was shown on television sets placed around the restaurant, and during the course of the evening, Ruta and I interviewed the various celebrity guests, along with some of the eventual winners and nominees who came by after the Awards show was over.

Ruta and I both love to talk, and we fed off one another with such ease that we never needed a script. All in all, the show went off without a hitch and everyone loved it. It turned out to be the birth of a show that Ruta and I would do together for the next seven years.

Ruta's husband, Webb Lowe, and my husband, Bobby, became like stage-door Johnnies. They were good friends, and wherever we were taping, they would sit at the bar and watch, bringing us a glass of wine whenever we took a break. It became a tradition.

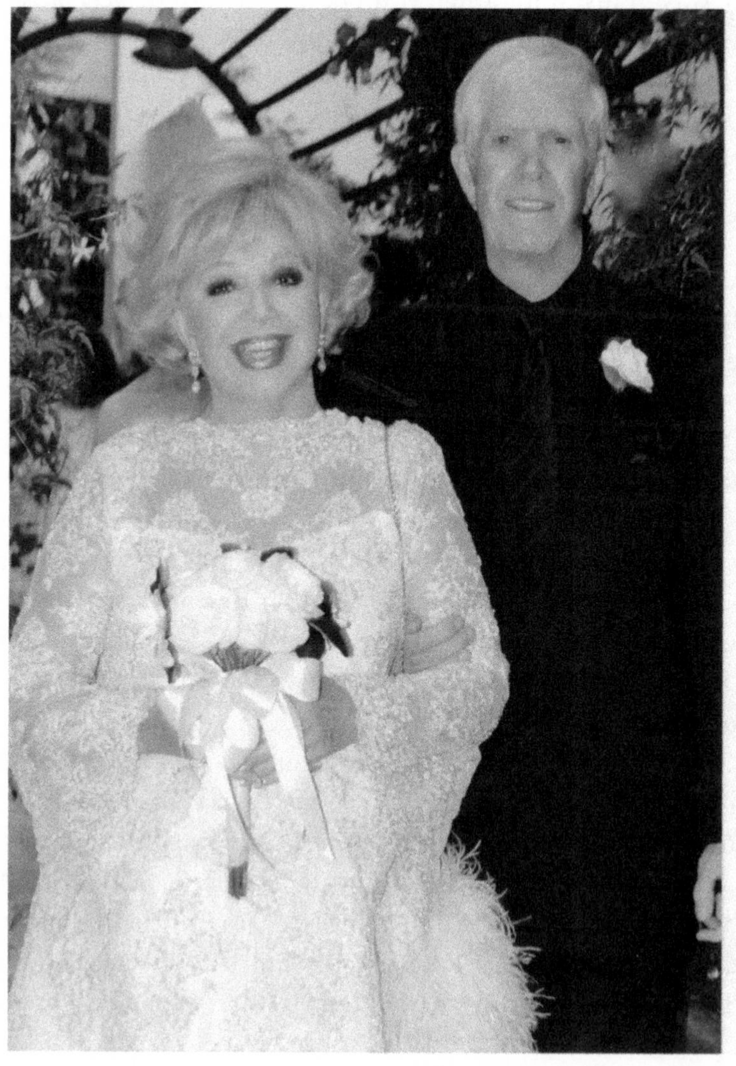

Ruta Lee and her husband Webb Lowe.

Ruta and I co-hosted a few more shows under *The American Jewish Hour* banner; then Gloria changed the title to *Talk of the Town*. The interview format remained the same, and the commercials were still done by Kennedy Cabot, now John and Gloria's company. They featured the familiar phrase "...brought to you by the good people of Kennedy Cabot."

Ruta and I formed a production company called Blondes Have More Fun with John's wife, Gloria. Gloria proved to have terrific talent as a producer, which probably stemmed from the fact that like me, she had a tremendous love of movies and movie stars from the time she was a little girl. The Gebbias had a rock-solid marriage and close-knit family, and lived in a beautiful house on the East Coast on Long Island Sound. John and Gloria eventually moved to the West Coast and continued to back the show financially, while Ruta and I delivered the creative goods that made the show extremely popular.

Toni and Ruta shooting Talk of the Town.

Cover Story... The American Cinematheque The 12th Annual Moving Picture Ball Honoring John Travolta

Top L-R, Celebrity Talk Show Hostesses Ruta Lee and Toni Holt Kramer; John Travolta and Kelly Preston. Bottom L-R, Sally Kellerman; Gene Siskel.
Story and photos on pages 8-9.

Toni at the Moving Picture Ball.

As it turned out, *Talk of the Town* took up much of my time, and I had to put my Washington aspirations on hold. I did, however, use the TV series to interview people in politics as well as people in the entertainment business. As a result, I was able to stick my toe into the political waters just a little bit.

All I had to do when the time was right was learn how to swim.

CHAPTER THIRTY-EIGHT

Villa Paradiso

I still had the house John Yantis had bought for me in Palm Springs. Bobby and I spent weekends and holidays there. One day Bobby said to me, "You know, I think we need a house to make our own history in...a house to make our own memories."

I couldn't have agreed more.

"It just so happens I know a house right down the street that has come up for sale," I said with a smile that went from one ear to the other.

It was a house I passed every morning when I'd take my walk up into the hills. I could barely see the top of the house over the big stone wall that surrounded it, but as I walked by, I would religiously chant, "Someday you'll be mine...someday you'll be mine...someday you'll be mine." I did that for eight years, hoping and wishing it would happen.

When Bobby and I went to go look at the property, the inside really wasn't as beautiful as I had hoped. I was disappointed, yet the house still drew me in like a magnet. Built around 1926, it sat on four acres all enclosed inside the huge stonewall that wrapped around the property. The main house was spacious but only had one master bedroom. Through a breezeway constructed by an artisan who worked on the original Mar-a-Lago in Palm Beach was another wing, consisting of three bedrooms, two on the main floor and one on the second floor. It also featured two huge terraces that overlooked the picturesque grounds and majestic mountains. A short distance from the main house was a much smaller house, one of several on the property. The grounds, which included over two hundred palm trees, a pool house, and a swimming pool, were spectacular, and the history of the place was spellbinding.

A well-known Vegas hotel man, Charlie Rich, had owned the estate for a number of years. Cary Grant often stayed in one of the houses, and nicknamed the property "Villa Paradiso" (House of Paradise).

When Cary was off doing a movie, Charlie had the pool house constructed from the ground up in a Vegas-style architecture that didn't really go with the rest of the property, but somehow it worked. Charlie had everything in the pool house monogramed with the initials "AL," which stood for Archibald Leach, Cary Grant's real name.

Donald Duncan, the man credited with the Duncan yo-yo, owned the property before Charlie, as did Texas oil magnate Arthur Cameron. Cameron was married briefly to Ann Miller, the leggy star of many MGM musicals.

Parties were legendary at the estate. Among the famous guests were Howard Hughes, Frank Sinatra, and Ginger Rogers. Oh, if only those seventeen-inch-thick walls could talk.

Villa Paradiso, Toni's Palm Springs estate.

A few months later we bought my dream home. Villa Paradiso was the perfect place for us to begin our memories.

* * * * *

Talk of the Town was always done on location, whether in Los Angeles, Beverly Hills, Palm Springs, Las Vegas, New York, or even Europe. Ruta and I were like the Paladin of interviews: "Have Camera, Will Travel." Over the next seven years, we taped several thousand interviews with Hollywood celebs and political luminaries, many of whom are now gone, but certainly not forgotten. We have the videos to prove it.

By the mid-90s, Bobby and I were firmly entrenched in Villa Paradiso along with my mother. We fixed up a beautiful suite for her in the wing just off the breezeway. We adored living there, and I loved walking up into the mountains, going up and down the hills, breathing in the fresh air, and watching the mountains change colors as the sun sweeps across them. My standard poodles became great hikers.

While the desert nights were filled with stars, so were the days. Across from my house was the former Dinah Shore residence where Nancy and Ronald Reagan lived for a while. Years later the house was owned by legendary musical genius Jerry Herman. After he moved, it was purchased by David Lee, the Emmy award-winning writer/producer/director who created the TV series *Frasier*. And now Leonardo DiCaprio is the latest in a stream of celebrity owners.

One time MCA/Universal Studios chief Lew Wasserman was also a neighbor. Mike and Bob Pollack, who wrote episodes for the *Dynasty* series, lived a stone's throw away, as did Sidney Sheldon, Harold Robbins, Kirk Douglas, and Liberace.

These legendary estates are rich with stories, many of which Ruta and I captured in a series of videos we called, "The Tour Bus Stops Here." Living in Palm Springs has been a dazzling experience, filled with unforgettable characters and indelible memories.

In April of 1995, I was honored with a sidewalk star in Palm Springs. Along with the people from the Palm Springs Star Association, the hosts for the event were my partner Ruta Lee, actor Gene Barry, and Mr. Blackwell, the fashion commentator.

Toni and Bobby with Palm Springs residents Betty and President Gerald Ford.

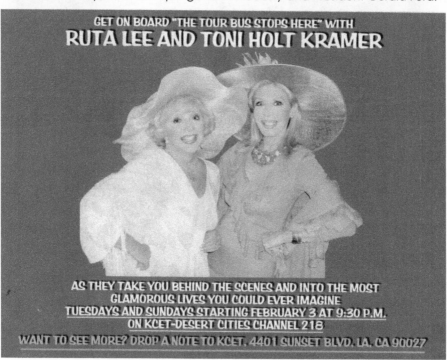

GET ON BOARD "THE TOUR BUS STOPS HERE" WITH
RUTA LEE AND TONI HOLT KRAMER

AS THEY TAKE YOU BEHIND THE SCENES AND INTO THE MOST
GLAMOROUS LIVES YOU COULD EVER IMAGINE
TUESDAYS AND SUNDAYS STARTING FEBRUARY 3 AT 9:30 P.M.
ON KCET-DESERT CITIES CHANNEL 218
WANT TO SEE MORE? DROP A NOTE TO KCET, 4401 SUNSET BLVD. LA, CA 90027

Toni and Ruta, "The Tour Bus Stops Here".

Shortly before the day of the ceremony, I received a phone call from my aunt Miriam in Walnut Creek, California. She told me my cousin Enid had been trying to reach me, and she gave me her phone number in New Jersey. Excited to reconnect with my favorite cuz, I called Enid immediately. We were thrilled to be speaking to each other after so many years of no contact. I invited Enid and her husband, Dr. Louis Rogow, to come to Palm Springs for the unveiling of my star on the Walk of Stars. They were on the next plane to California.

Toni gets her star in Palm Springs.

Toni and cousin Enid.

I don't have a lot of family, so the idea that my cousin was coming to share this honor with me made it even more special. When Enid arrived and I looked at her for the first time in many years, I felt a surreal camaraderie. I realized we look nothing alike, but people always think we're sisters. While we're both tall and slim, I believe it's our mannerisms and matching outgoing personalities that make us appear similar. The instant I saw her I could see our entire family.

For most of my career, I reported on stories and events that involved Hollywood celebrities at different times during their lives, so for me to *be* the story was a totally different experience. Hundreds of people turned out to support me and see my star revealed on the sidewalk. To be recognized for my contribution to the industry I loved was both gratifying and unexpected, an honor I will cherish for the rest of my life.

After the ceremony, our friends came back to our house for the party. The Cary Grant pool house was open for all to enjoy. Everyone loved the work of muralist Sharon Whisnand, whom I had hired to create a trompe l'oeil tribute to the twenties and thirties: lots of greens, a few monkeys, a bumblebee, and strategically placed flamingos set against a blue sky and fluffy white clouds. All in all, it turned out to be a glamorous Palm Springs bash.

During the party I took Enid by the hand and proudly introduced her to my friends. From that day on we agreed to stay in touch. Sometime later, Bobby and I went to New Jersey, and Enid and Louis introduced us to their friends. Subsequently, Enid and Louis moved to Florida.

The more Enid and I spend time together, the more we realize how alike we are—how much our brains are in sync on a myriad of diverse topics, from politics to finance to fashion.

After so much lost time, it feels beyond amazing to be a real family again.

CHAPTER THIRTY-NINE

If You Die, I'll Kill You

In 1998, Bobby and I went to Gothenburg, Sweden, for a Volvo convention. Bobby was one of the first to own a Volvo dealership in the United States. We were staying at the Hilton Hotel and it was sometime in the middle of the night when my mother came to me in my dream. Her image was incredibly vivid. "I've come to say good-bye," she said. "It's time for me to go."

"Mother, what are you talking about? You can't go. You're not going anywhere."

"Yes, Toni," she said firmly. "I have to go. It's time."

I could tell she was serious, and my entire being was filled with dread. I was in a total panic. "No! No! I won't let you go!" I shouted. I could feel myself reaching out to her and grabbing a firm hold. I squeezed onto her with all of my might so she couldn't leave. "Mother, Mother…you can't go! I won't let you go!"

The next thing I knew I awoke, trembling. The image of my mother was still sharp in my mind. I shook Bobby awake. "Bobby, something terrible has happened to Mother!"

"Oh, Toni," Bobby answered, still half asleep. "Nothing terrible has happened. You've just had a bad dream. You probably had too much dessert…or dinner was too heavy."

"No, no, no!" I said, my voice rising. "Bobby, this was not a nightmare! This was real. You have to believe me! I saw her! I know something awful has happened!"

I reached for the phone to call her, but Bobby stopped me and pointed to the clock. "Toni, it's two o'clock in the morning in California. You can't call now. Let's get dressed…we'll get something to eat…take a walk…by then it'll be six or seven in the morning there and you can call her."

We dressed and left the hotel. It was a Saturday, and I remember as we walked along the shop-lined streets we could see TVs airing footage of the O.J. Simpson trial. We stopped somewhere for a bite, but I just didn't feel right. My stomach was in knots and I was haunted by the image of my mother saying it was time for her to go. We stopped at a bookstore and I bought a Sidney Sheldon novel. We stopped at another store and I bought a pair of sneakers. We did anything we could to make the time go by. When we arrived back at the hotel, one of the girls representing Volvo at the hospitality desk came running up to us.

"Mrs. Kramer, Mrs. Kramer!" she yelled. "Did you get your emergency phone call from home?"

I let out a scream that scared the hell out everyone in the lobby, then quickly switched into action mode.

"Bobby, go to the desk and check us out. Get us out of here now… no matter what you have to do." It was exactly 3:25 in the afternoon in Sweden—6:25 in the morning in California. I raced up to our room and called our house in Palm Springs. Emma Santana, my secretary at the time, answered. I knew immediately something was wrong because Emma didn't work on Saturdays. "Emma, what's wrong? Why are you there? What happened?"

Emma responded as if she didn't have a care in the world. "Oh, Toni...it's beautiful here today."

I was gripping the phone so tightly I thought it would crumble in my hand. "Emma! Do you hear me? What's wrong? Tell me!"

"Well, Toni…"

"Emma, get to the point!" I screamed. "I'll climb through this phone and strangle you if you don't tell me!"

Finally, she told me the truth. "Toni, your mother is in the hospital."

"What happened to her? For God's sake, tell me!"

"Well, they don't know. They're doing tests. She's at Desert Regional."

"When did this happen? How many hours ago?"

"Around eight or nine last night."

I knew it! That would have been around four or five in the morning my time, when I was sleeping…when I had the premonition. "Who's with her?" I asked.

"Isobel."

Isobel was Mother's companion. After getting the room number from Emma, I called the hospital. Isobel answered the phone. I'm sure my voice was trembling when I asked, "How's my mother?"

"She's asleep right now. They think she had a stroke."

Isobel's words went through me like a knife. "Is she in a coma?"

"I don't know."

"Isobel, put the phone to her ear. Do it now."

Isobel did as I asked as Bobby entered our hotel room. I spoke to my mother in a strong, clear voice. "Mother, listen to me. Listen to what I tell you. I'm on my way home. You must not die. You are not going to die. If you die, I promise I will kill you!"

I'll never forget saying that. Isobel got back on the phone. "Did my mother show any signs that she heard me?" I asked.

"Her eyes flickered a little when you were talking to her. They didn't open…but they flickered."

I told Isobel we would be in touch, hung up the phone, and brought Bobby up to speed on what happened.

"I have some bad news," he said. "The next flight out of Gothenburg isn't until seven thirty tonight."

That wasn't going to work for me. Bobby's son, Steve, had a great travel agent in California. I dialed Steve's number in LA and asked if he would call in any favor he could to get us out on an earlier plane.

I literally threw our clothes into our suitcases. We raced out of the hotel and into a car that took us to the airport. When we reached the waiting room, we received more bad news. Our plane would be arriving late and there was no other flight out of Gothenburg. That meant we would miss our connection in London. I called Steve again, absolutely frantic, and he solved our problem by getting us booked on Air Canada out of London into Dallas, then a connecting flight into Ontario, California, about an hour out of Palm Springs. Our houseman would pick us up in Ontario and drive us to the hospital. The connections would be tight but at least we were booked.

The plane from Sweden to London landed at Heathrow. It was a major terminal change to make the Air Canada flight to Dallas. We had no choice but to take a shuttle bus or we'd never make the connection, which meant we couldn't wait for our luggage to come off the flight from Sweden. "Forget the luggage," I said to Bobby. "It's only clothes."

We were in such a hurry that we didn't even tell the airline where to forward the luggage. We just left our bags at the terminal and raced to the shuttle. We boarded the bus and told the driver where we needed to go—only the bus didn't move. The driver just sat there like a wooden Indian.

"This is a life-threatening situation," Bobby said, urging the driver to get going.

"I'm very sorry," said the driver, a proper Brit. "I have to wait for the other people." Other than kicking the driver off the bus and driving it myself, which truly went through my mind, there was nothing I could do or say to make him deviate from the rules.

We were hysterical. Should we wait? Should we take a taxi? All I could think of was my mother lying there in the hospital. My heart was racing out of control from fear that she might die and I wouldn't be with her. Five...ten...fifteen minutes went by and finally, he started the bus and drove us to our terminal.

We jumped off the bus before it could even pull to a full stop. We raced through the terminal and finally reached the Air Canada counter. Bobby sped through our flight confirmation code, and we were all set to head on to the plane, but the desk attendant simply shook her head. It was too late, she told us. The door to the plane had already been closed and we couldn't possibly board.

"But you have to let us on, you just have to," I cried. It seemed like the end; all our legwork and rushing had amounted to nothing. I was totally panicked that I would never see my mother before she left this world for good. This was the true nightmare, one where you have someplace to be but can't seem to move fast enough to get there, where the whole world refuses to acknowledge your emergency and your feet seem rooted in cold molasses.

I was in near hysterics. Bobby pulled the desk attendant aside and explained the situation. After much urging and cajoling, the employees finally called the plane to see if we could still get on. The pilot agreed. A sense of relief instantly washed over me. Things would be all right.

We collapsed into our seats in first class, mentally and physically drained from the ordeal. The flight attendant offered us a drink, but I declined, knowing I needed to keep my mind clear. I opened my Sidney Sheldon novel and got lost in his storytelling.

At one point the pilot came back to see us and said he was sorry to hear that we were racing home for a medical emergency. "I certainly hope everything will be okay. I have an idea," he said. "Why don't you and your husband come up and sit with us in the cockpit for a while. It'll give you a whole different look at the world, and maybe it'll distract your mind for a bit."

I thought it was a great idea, so Bobby and I followed the pilot into the cockpit. For sure that would never happen today.

It was nighttime by then, and the view was absolutely breathtaking. We were flying over the ocean, but all you could see was a sea of black enveloping the plane. The stars looked so bright, twinkling all around us, that I felt like I could reach out and touch them. It was an incredibly spiritual experience, floating there in the sky after such a tumultuous and nightmarish day. It was as if God himself were personally guiding me home.

The plane landed in Dallas a little before midnight. Our flight to Ontario was scheduled for 5:30 in the morning. We had no luggage and only the clothes we were wearing. There was a motel at the airport and we took a room with the idea of catching a few hours of sleep before our flight.

I knew I wouldn't be able to sleep, but Bobby insisted I try. "At least lie down and rest."

I obliged, lying down on the bed with my clothes and shoes still on, ready to pop up at a moment's notice.

After about fifteen minutes I grew antsy and phoned the hospital. I spoke to the night nurse who told me my mother was resting comfortably. I asked her for the name and phone number of the doctor who was taking care of her. It was late at night and she wasn't too keen on giving me his number. I insisted, probably threatening a thing or two, and she finally gave it to me. His name was Dr. Nuzimi, a neurologist, and as soon as I hung up with her, I punched in his number. I apologized for calling at such a late hour, but explained it was urgent that I speak to him.

Over the years I've never trusted anyone more than myself when it comes to making decisions for those I love, whether it's my children, my mother, or my husband. I need to be in control, especially when it comes to doctors because I don't trust too many of them. They say they practice medicine...well, I do too—the only difference is that they have a license and I don't. I'm always up to date on what's current in medicine because I read a lot, and every little particle sticks in my head. With a situation as grave as this one, I wasn't going to take any chances.

"You know, my mother has had a problem," I told Dr. Nuzimi. "I'm not saying this is her problem now, but it could have something to do with it. She's always very low in sodium."

I told Dr. Nuzimi that my mother had congestive heart failure although she'd never had a heart attack, and she was on diuretics to keep her lungs and heart from filling with water. I know that when you take diuretics you excrete a lot of things from your body, including salt. As a result, my mother had been taking salt pills for the past couple of years. I also read that if a person is low in sodium—and their levels get low enough—the symptoms could easily mimic a stroke. I mentioned all of this to the doctor, and he said he would check it out in the morning.

"Has she awakened yet?" I asked.

"No," he said. My heart sank half an inch further into the pit of my stomach.

When I finished with the doctor, I called the hospital again and asked the nurse to put the phone by my mother's ear.

"Mother, it's me, Toni. I'm on my way home...I'm almost there. Stay with me... don't leave me. Please do not die...do not die...do not die..." My voice cracked as I spoke. "If you still plan on dying when I get there, we'll talk about it then. I love you."

The nurse got back on the phone. I asked if there was any response.

"Her eyes flickered," she said.

I was encouraged; she may not have awakened yet, but something was definitely registering.

At 5:30 in the morning our flight left Dallas. We landed at Ontario Airport, and our houseman was there waiting for us. We sped off to the hospital, and as we drove, I called again from the car. Mom was still alive.

When I crossed the threshold into my mother's room at the hospital, I felt a giant weight shift off my shoulders. I was so relieved to have made it to her that it took me a second to realize she was awake and sitting up in bed. "Mother!" I squealed, rushing to her bedside.

She looked up at me with puzzled eyes. "Who are you?"

"You...you don't know who I am?" I asked, crestfallen. "I'm your daughter." I looked around at the nurses, completely bewildered. They returned my gaze but offered no answers. Mom stared me down without the slightest hint of recognition.

I'm not sure where it came from—maybe out of relief or gratitude that she was still alive—but suddenly I felt overcome with anger. "It took me twenty-nine hours to get here...and she doesn't know who I am? I can't believe this! Why doesn't she know who I am? After everything, why doesn't she know?!"

My mother looked up as Bobby entered the room. "Bobby!" she exclaimed.

My mouth dropped open. How could she know who Bobby was and not me? How was that possible? She turned to me. "Dear, you're so lucky you met him first...because *I* would have married him."

Bobby with the loves of his life, Toni and her mother.

Well, that was it. Bobby and I and the nurses all broke out into tears and laughter. It had taken her a second, but Mother was back and she definitely knew who I was. The nurses told us she still had one more scan scheduled, and I asked if I could go with her. They gave their approval, and we wheeled Mother off to get her scan.

I shook hands with Dr. Nuzimi, and he gestured to my mother through the plexiglass window of the exam room. "Nothing wrong with that brain," he said with a wry smile, so I guessed my mother had managed to make a lasting impression on the hospital staff since waking up.

"Low in sodium. Very low in sodium," the doctor stated.

Following the test, my mother all but bolted from the room. "I want to leave here right now," she demanded.

"You can't just get up and leave," protested the doctor.

"I'm fine. I'm going home," said Mother. "I can walk."

Her feistiness was back and I knew she'd be fine. We got her into a wheelchair, wheeled her out of the hospital, and took her home.

We hired an RN to take care of her for the next few weeks. My mother loved that. She loved being waited on hand and foot, and we decided it would be a good thing to have someone living there with her permanently.

My God, she deserved it, after all those years of looking after me.

CHAPTER FORTY

A Walk on the Moon

Charles "Pete" Conrad, a former Navy captain and astronaut, was the third man to walk on the moon. He is remembered for his shout of "whoopee" when he first stepped on the lunar surface.

Bobby and I first met the Conrads in 1996 aboard a yacht owned by my good friend Paula Kent Meehan. Paula began as an actress and had a small part as the hat check girl on the hit TV series *77 Sunset Strip*. Her acting career made a left turn when she and her friend Jheri Redding started Redken hair products in a garage and turned it into a multimillion-dollar business. The "red" in Redken came from Jheri's last name, and the "ken" came from Paula's.

Not too long after her business took off, Paula married John Meehan. Eventually Paula bought out her partner Jheri, and much later sold the business to L'Oréal of Paris for hundreds of millions of dollars.

Paula and John kept their yacht in the Mediterranean most of the time, and Bobby and I were lucky enough to be invited on many, many cruises. Nancy and Pete Conrad were on the boat during one of those cruises.

Pete—along with Buzz Aldrin and some of the other early astronauts—was revered around the world for his amazing courage in outer space. Pete was a star wherever he went. He regaled us with stories about his travels and the grandeur of their life.

The last night on the cruise, we all dressed up for an elegant party. Over cocktails I asked Pete why he became an astronaut. Everyone gathered in close, expecting some deep, zen-like response. Instead, Pete paused thoughtfully and said, "Well, I don't know why the fuck I did it." We all laughed at his answer.

Bobby and I saw a lot of the Conrads over the next couple of years, and we made plans to visit them at their holiday house in Santa Fe, New Mexico. At a psychic reading with Zvia, she looked at the coffee grounds in my saucer and said, "No, you're not going. You will never go to Santa Fe. You'll stay friends...but you'll never be there. It will never happen."

Toni with Pete Conrad aboard Paula's yacht. 1996.

Toni and Nancy Conrad, a great friendship.
Bel Air, CA 2002.

Her prediction frightened me. I wondered what she knew that I didn't. Once again, Zvia was right.

On three separate occasions we made arrangements to go to Santa Fe. Each time something unexpected happened and the trip was canceled. The first time Pete, a big overgrown kid who rode a Harley and loved all kinds of sports, broke three ribs in a skateboarding accident. The second time, I came down with bronchitis. A third trip was planned, but shortly before we were set to leave, I received a phone call that Pete had suddenly died.

As the story was relayed to me, Pete had gone on a motorcycle ride with a group of his biker buddies. They left from Pete's home in Huntington Beach, just south of LA, and headed north toward Ojai. Pete wanted Nancy to ride with him, but she declined. At some point, Pete's bike veered off the road on a curve. The motorcycle flipped up in the air and landed on top of him.

They called the Trauma Hawk, but the medics said Pete wasn't injured badly enough to need the helicopter. Instead, he was driven to a hospital in Ojai, and they called Nancy to tell her what happened. When the doctors finally got Pete into surgery, they discovered internal bleeding and immediately operated on him. A short time later they discovered more internal bleeding. By the time Nancy arrived, Pete was gone.

After all Pete had been through in his life, it was an ironic way for him to die. The man who had walked on the moon lost his life in a freak motorcycle accident. It was less than a month after the four of us celebrated Pete's birthday at a Japanese restaurant in West Los Angeles.

It was the middle of July 1999 when Bobby and I flew on a private plane to DC with Nancy, Ruta Lee, and her husband, Webb. There we went to a military chapel for Pete's funeral service. Everyone in Washington was there. Afterward, he was buried in Arlington National Cemetery in an elaborate tribute that included horse-drawn carriages, a big gun salute, and a flyover by a group of F14 Tomcats.

No doubt, Pete was a true American hero. He wasn't big in stature, but he was definitely bigger than life itself. Nancy really rose to the occasion. A smallish woman herself, Nancy looked six-foot-four on that day. She was so incredibly gracious. I don't know how she did it. She was beyond sad and crying, yet managed to hug and kiss every single person who came to pay their respects to the legendary Pete, the love of her life.

As we flew back from Arlington, we heard the news that JFK Jr., his beautiful wife, thirty-three-year-old Carolyn, and her sister, Lauren Bessette, had been killed when their plane crashed into the Atlantic on their way to Martha's Vineyard. Having just gone through such a tragedy with Pete, it was all too spooky for words. "How could this happen?" I asked.

Bobby, a weekend pilot, provided the answer. "If you're not instrument savvy, sometimes you can't tell what's up or down when you fly into a fog. In other words, you can't tell if the water is above or below you."

It was all so dark, my mind became a blur of tragic images from the past. JFK had been assassinated. Bobby Kennedy had been assassinated. Onassis had died. Onassis' twenty-four-year-old son, Alexander, had been killed in a plane crash two weeks before his father died. Jackie Kennedy had died. And now JFK Jr., only thirty-eight, was gone.

The passing of young John seemed to bring all of those tragic deaths into focus. It made me wonder again about the bad luck that seemed to haunt the Kennedy family.

Some might even call it a curse. Is this what Aristotle Onassis knew in his heart that night in Paris when he wanted to leave Jackie and fly off with me?

CHAPTER FORTY-ONE

Hello, Washington!

Working on *Talk of the Town* increased my exposure to politics and politicians, and my appetite for Washington soon became voracious. I found myself pushing for more and more politicians to come on the show. California Governors Pete Wilson and Arnold Schwarzenegger were among them.

When I was working for KHJ, I conducted a half-hour interview with Nancy Reagan just before her husband was elected president. It was early in the morning when she arrived at the station in a blue denim outfit—a dress, not jeans. I wasn't sure what to expect, but Nancy turned out to be very pleasant and personable. As the interview progressed, I realized she had the question-and-answer game down pat. Every time I asked her a question, she would smile and say something innocuous to give herself time to gather her thoughts and formulate an answer. Not once did she give me a spontaneous response. She was well rehearsed and totally in control.

Whenever I deviated from my comfort zone, I did my homework. That was definitely the case when it came to politics. My knowledge of how local and national politics worked was superficial at best in the beginning, but I was an eager learner. By the time *Talk of the Town* came to an end, I felt my comfort zone was expanding to include the political arena, and I was more determined than ever to find a way inside.

Once again I brought up my desire to get into politics to Bobby. Now that I was no longer working, it seemed like perfect timing to get the ball rolling with a new venture.

"We should go to Washington. Somehow, someway, we have to get involved."

Bobby smiled. "Honey, you figure out the way and we'll do it. It'll be fun."

* * * * *

Flash forward to the year 2000. George W. Bush had just been elected president.

I knew that Nancy Conrad had great connections in D.C. I gave her a call and told her I wanted to go to the Inauguration.

"I don't just want to go to a party," I said. "I want to meet everybody...I want to be noticed. I want to make enough connections in Washington to get my foot in the door. I don't know what I want to do... I just want to get there and let it play out."

"Don't worry," Nancy replied. "I know this terrific man who's with the Republican Party and I'll call him. I'll get you tickets."

For one of the few times in my life, I didn't do my homework. I figured Nancy understood what I wanted and knew how to accomplish it. All we had to do was send the Republican Party a big, fat check. At the same time, I didn't want to be someone who just pays to be at a party. If we were going to dive into the political pool, I wanted us to make a big splash.

"What do you think?" I asked Bobby.

Bobby's answer was optimistic and supportive as usual. "Well, there's no sense in starting at the bottom. We might as well send the check. Everyone will know us. We'll get involved...we'll be accepted. They'll think we can be important to them. They'll keep inviting us to Washington...and eventually you'll get to know your way around. You'll see if you like it...I'll see if I like it. Besides, living with you is the adventure of my life."

Bobby always said that he couldn't get old being married to me because there are always so many new and exciting things I dream up. He always has "missions" that I create for him, and he says they keep him "on his toes." My husband, a rare man, has complete confidence in my judgment and business sense, and in my intuition, which he's witnessed as being spot-on several times. On three separate occasions I warned Bobby about people in his business who would cause him trouble. All three eventually double-crossed him. Bobby knows I don't like to waste money. I don't mind spending it—I just don't like wasting it.

So, we sent a check, and received the invite to the Bush Inaugural. It was late in the game and there weren't a lot of first-class hotels available. Luckily we found one and made the reservation. Nancy went to Washington with us, but told us she wouldn't be attending every event. We were on our own—which was just fine.

Toni and Nancy Conrad go to Washington.

It was straight downhill from the minute we arrived. The hotel was horrible. The carpeting was stained and had a funny odor. I called housekeeping and asked for extra bedsheets. When the sheets arrived I spread them out all over the carpet. It was pathetic. "Oh, God, I can't stay here," I moaned.

"I agree," Bobby responded. "But where do you think we're going to go? I don't know if we'll find anything better."

"I don't know, either. I just know we can't stay here."

Bobby went down to the lobby and spoke to the desk clerk. He explained the problem, gave him twenty dollars, and asked him if he knew anyone to call. The clerk said he had a connection at the Watergate Hotel. Five minutes later we were on our way. We left our luggage behind just in case the new hotel was worse. This time we were going to make sure we liked it *before* we checked in.

We were surprised at how lovely the Watergate was. It had recently been refurbished, and the ambiance was wonderful. It was amazingly cheerful with an exceptionally attentive staff. We were shown a suite with windows that overlooked the Potomac River. The room had a little bay with a table and chairs, and a desk I could convert to my makeup table. I was happy as could be.

We told Nancy about the switch, and she liked the accommodations so much she took the connecting room. Bobby and I went back to the first hotel, got our luggage, and checked into the Watergate. The move to the new hotel and the new room made me feel a lot better.

The Candlelight Ball was that night. We found ourselves surrounded by the entire "who's who" of the Republican Party. We knew no one, but being the gregarious person that I am, we met a lot of people. I've always had the knack of finding a reason to say hello to perfect strangers, and this skill came in handy as we made our way around the ballroom.

One woman came up to me and said in a syrupy Southern accent, "Honey, I just love your black pearls."

Everyone was extremely gracious, but perhaps the most gracious of all were Colin Powell and his wife, Alma. She was charming and lovely, and he was unexpectedly friendly. The evening exceeded our expectations.

The next day, Bobby and I went to pick up our tickets for the Inauguration. As we approached the building, we saw a long line of people that stretched from inside to out on the sidewalk. "This can't be right. I mean, after the check we gave them, certainly we don't have to stand in a line like this."

I grabbed Bobby by the hand, and we ducked into an unmarked door at the side of the building. I cornered a woman at the counter. "We're the Kramers," I said politely. "We've been invited to the Inauguration...but I'm afraid something isn't right."

I told the woman we had sent in a substantial check. She looked us up on her computer. "Oh, my," she said. "Here's the problem. You've been signed up for the Inauguration Committee, not Team 100. That's where you should have been."

She went on to explain that our check was definitely large enough to get us into Team 100, which is what we thought we were joining. But because we were signed up to the Inauguration Committee, we were only entitled to go to the Inauguration and one of the balls afterward. Apparently Nancy had just signed us up for the Committee, which was like taking our money and putting a match to it. She never even told us about Team 100. To be totally fair to Nancy, maybe they never told her the difference. Still, I was miffed, to put it mildly.

The woman behind the counter apologized and clarified further that our check should have been specifically marked for Team 100, definitely not Inauguration Committee. "Well, certainly you can straighten out that problem," I said, trying to control my temper. "You wouldn't want to alienate us and not make any further contributions to the Republican Party...would you?"

"No, no, of course not," the woman said quickly. "But...it's not in my hands to make a change. We don't even have the same offices...the same people...the same anything. When you get back home, you'll have to write a letter."

"A letter? What good will a letter do now?"

My foray into politics was going so poorly at this point, I resorted to shameless self-promotion. I wanted to make the most of our time in Washington and was so disappointed in how things had been unfolding for us that I figured I had nothing to lose. "Do you know who I am? I'm

Toni Holt...from Hollywood," I told the woman behind the desk. "Have you seen any of my shows? Have you read any of my columns? I've done over three thousand live interviews!"

I did everything but stand on my head to get her attention. The more infuriated I became, the more apparent it was that nobody was going to help us. They didn't care who I was or what I'd done. They were there for the president. It was evident that dealing with the Inauguration was a much larger issue than my problems.

Bobby calmed me down and I realized we had no choice but to accept the tickets they gave us. I did, however, manage to get us invited to the Library of Congress's *private* reception for George W. Bush... private meaning only 250 invited guests the night before the Inauguration. It was a small bonus but at least it was something.

By the time we got back to the Watergate, I was in a truly foul mood. I was mortified and angry, steaming and sputtering around our suite. Always looking to find a silver lining, Bobby remarked that there was nothing we could do about the situation, so we might as well make the best of it. "There's no sense in ruining what we have while we're here," he said, sensible as ever. Thank goodness I married such a stable, low-key man.

Deep down, I knew he was right, but in the heat of the moment, there was no rationalizing for me. "It's ridiculous!" I wailed. "This is just really, really awful!"

Just then the phone rang. It was Aaron, a young man we had met a few months earlier. Aaron, heavyset and in his mid-thirties, was a likeable, smooth-talking fellow who had found a niche for himself in Hollywood by becoming the go-to guy when it came to putting on fund-raisers for prominent Democrats. Many celebrities embraced him for his clout and connections on both ends of the political spectrum. If you wanted to be invited to a particular event or access a particular politician, Aaron was your man. Little did any of us know at the time, but Aaron would find himself in big trouble a few years later for allegedly diverting and mishandling funds. He eventually spent time in prison.

"Hey, Toni. Are you having fun?" Aaron asked brightly.

"Actually, no," I said. "It stinks! It's horrible and I hate it! I'm having the worst time! I feel like such a fool!"

The poor guy only called to say hello. Instead, he got an earful from me, and it wasn't even his fault. "I have to go," he said. "I'll call you right back." He hung up. I figured he didn't want to tolerate my complaining and I'd never hear from him again.

I crumpled onto the bed, thoroughly disheartened. Things were already bad, and my attitude was making them worse.

Less than five minutes later, the phone rang again. I snatched it off the cradle. "Hello?"

"May I speak to Toni Holt Kramer, please," said the polite woman on the other end.

"This is she," I said cautiously.

"Oh, hi, Mrs. Kramer, this is Kelly Craighead. I'm the personal secretary and assistant to President and Senator Clinton."

"Oh, how nice," I replied suspiciously. I wasn't about to let myself be fooled by some prankster trying to have a laugh—I was already down in the dumps and didn't need another humiliating event for the day.

"We'd like to invite you and your husband—"

I stopped her. "Miss Craighead, I'm so sorry. I'm on another line. May I have your number and I'll call you back in just a few minutes?"

"Oh…of course," she said, a little taken aback. She gave me her number and hung up.

My doe eyes narrowed to slits as I slammed down the phone. "That was not funny what Aaron just did. Can you imagine? He had somebody call and pretend to invite us to a party or something."

It took Bobby a good ten minutes to convince me to call the woman back. Finally I conceded. I dialed the number and the voice on the other end answered robotically: "The White House."

It no longer seemed like some cruel joke. I held my hand over the phone and whispered to Bobby, "Oh my gosh, it's the White House!"

"Yes, hi. Is there a Kelly Craighead there?" I asked.

"One moment please."

After a couple of rings, the phone was answered and I immediately recognized the voice. "Kelly Craighead."

"Kelly, this is Toni Holt Kramer."

Kelly laughed. "If I were you, I would have done the exact same thing."

"I'm sorry. It's just that I thought someone was playing a joke on me."

"No, not at all. Actually, the Clintons would very much like to meet you and your husband. They're giving me and my fiancé an engagement party on their last night at the White House...and we'd like you to come."

"You're kidding," I said.

"I assure you I'm not. We hope you can make it."

I don't know if I was more surprised or confused, but I wasn't about to let the invitation go by the boards. "We'll be there! What time?"

"Four o'clock. At the White House."

I hung up and repeated the conversation to Bobby, who just sat back and laughed hysterically.

Another angel had just stepped forward to push me closer to where I wanted to be.

CHAPTER FORTY-TWO

President Bill Clinton

It was Friday afternoon and it was snowing in the nation's capital, one of those icy-cold days where I could make smoke rings with my breath. I wasn't prepared for such a bone chilling day. To make matters worse, friends had told me not to bring a fur coat, that it was not politically correct. As a fallback, I brought a taupe and gray tweed coat. It barely kept me from severe frostbite. In truth, my teeth were chattering.

Bobby hired a driver and we left the Watergate for the White House to meet the Clintons. The traffic was brutal. I didn't know if it was because of the Inauguration or if it was just normal Friday afternoon rush hour, probably both.

"Honey, did you bring the camera?" I asked.

"Oh, no! I forgot."

"You didn't bring the camera?" I repeated, hoping against hope for a different answer, but my husband's response didn't change.

"We have to have a camera," I insisted.

"Toni, this is crazy. With traffic like this we're going to be late."

At that point I didn't care about traffic, and I knew somehow we wouldn't be that late. I dug in my heels. "I am not going to the White House without a camera. Nobody's ever going to believe that we were there...not even me. Please, let's go back. Please?"

The last *please* got him. Bobby instructed the driver to head back to the hotel. When we arrived, Bobby ran up to the room. He retrieved the camera and we headed back to the White House again.

We were greeted by a staffer who directed us up a flight of stairs that led to a long hallway. Bobby pointed out a sign that read, "NO CAMERAS, PLEASE." I smiled and touched my purse, where my trusty camera was hiding.

A woman appeared in the hallway and introduced herself. "Hello! I'm Kelly Craighead."

"I'm Toni Holt Kramer...and this is my husband, Bobby."

"Glad you could make it."

"We're honored to be here. Thank you very much for inviting us."

There was something extremely reassuring about Kelly, a sense of calm amidst the chaos that is Washington. Despite being both a hostess and the guest of honor for her own party, and despite it being Bill Clinton's last night in office as president, Kelly was truly cordial and relaxed. "You know, the Clintons really do want to meet you."

"We're delighted." I laughed, not quite sure how to respond.

I have to admit I was nervous. I was definitely a fish out of water. Put me in Hollywood, introduce me to the biggest stars in the world, and I'm fine...but Washington...the White House...the presidential couple, that was a different fishbowl. My dreams of being in the White House were suddenly a reality.

Kelly escorted us into the Gold Room. The room, aptly named, was decorated all in gold tones. Two magnificent chandeliers hung from the ceiling. There were a lot of younger people there, friends of Kelly's and her fiancé, I assumed. Except for us, everyone seemed to know everyone else.

Kelly introduced us to her friends, including some prominent Washington attorneys. Suddenly I remembered the "no camera" sign. I pulled Kelly aside and admitted my transgression. "Kelly, I do have a camera with me. Would it be all right if I take a few pictures tonight?"

"Have at it." She giggled.

Bobby and I observed the presidential portraits hanging on the walls. In the dining room, I placed Bobby in front of Abraham Lincoln and snapped his picture. Then I stepped in front of Lincoln, and Bobby took one of me. When we got home I had a frame made with two sides so we could both be together with our country's sixteenth president. I took some other photos, but I didn't want to abuse the privilege. We were the only ones with a camera and I wanted to be discreet.

It was probably close to five o'clock when Kelly introduced us to one of Hillary's closest friends, Suzie Buell from San Francisco. Suzie had a very outgoing personality and the vibrant red of her blazer matched her persona.

"Are you friends of the bride or groom?" she asked.

"Neither. Actually, we're here for the Inauguration," I answered, not thinking I was saying anything wrong.

Suzie sucked air and looked like a deer in the headlights. She leaned forward and whispered, "Um...don't say that out loud."

With that settled, her eyes lit up with a twinkle and she offered a little smile. "Besides, I think you'll find out the Democrats are much more fun than the Republicans."

I hadn't forgotten the way I'd been treated by the Republican Party, so I concurred with my new acquaintance. "As of this moment, I would have to say you're probably right."

After Kelly introduced us to her mother and father, I looked at my watch. It was well past five o'clock and I was getting anxious. For all I knew, the Clinton's might not show up for another hour or two. I whispered to Kelly in a confidential tone that we couldn't wait much longer because we were due at the Library of Congress for the Bush meet-and-greet cocktail party at six.

"You can't leave," Kelly insisted. "You simply cannot leave. The Clintons want to meet you." She quickly scanned the room as if devising a plan, then linked her arm through mine. "Come with me," she said.

Moving quickly through the crowd, Kelly led us out of the Gold Room, back into the main hallway, and into the Blue Room right next door. The room was all blue, of course, and there were fifteen or twenty people already there, including Kelly's fiancé, Eric, and their respective families. Kelly introduced us to Eric and disappeared again. It was beginning to feel like going to the doctor's office, where each room you go into moves you steadily closer to actually seeing the doctor.

At this point, it was nearly six o'clock. My stomach was in knots. Bobby could sense my anxiety and tried to calm my nerves. What to do? Stay and meet the outgoing president, or say "thank you" and leave to meet the incoming president? After a brief discussion we knew we had to do both. There was just no choice. I found out later that President Clinton is *always* late. Had I known, it wouldn't have changed my decision. I was determined to stick it out.

But that didn't stop me from cornering Kelly again. By this time, she must have thought I was completely neurotic or some high-maintenance broad from La La Land. I know I sounded like a broken record.

"Kelly, I don't know what to do. I'm really getting nervous. How much longer is it going to be before the Clintons arrive?"

"Just another minute or two," she insisted. I had to hand it to her—her patience was astounding. I probably would have punched me in the nose by then, but Kelly maintained her cool. Then came the magic words. "Come with me."

As if Kelly was the Pied Piper—and maybe she was—we followed her through a door that connected to the adjoining room. This room was smaller than the others, and it was all in red. "Wait. They'll be right here." Kelly flitted back into the Blue Room, closing the door behind her.

Now Bobby and I were alone. Just the two of us and a lot of red. "Wanna guess what *this* room is called?" I cracked, trying to break the tension.

All of a sudden it hit me and I got very nervous. I was actually in the White House *and* I was about to meet the president of the United States—at least he would be president for another few hours—and his wife, the newly elected senator from New York. There I was, Miss Calm, Cool, and Sophisticated, the same person who had interviewed hundreds and hundreds of important celebrities, and I was on the verge of an anxiety attack. Where's the Xanax when you need it?

The door to the center hallway suddenly burst open and two photographers scurried into the room. Neither one looked at us as they took their positions like commandos on a raid, crouching down behind the door as it slowly closed again. Every muscle in my body tightened and my mind swirled with all kinds of thoughts: Why did the Clintons want to meet us? How did they even know we exist? Was the universe making up for the lousy way the Republicans treated us? *What the hell am I doing here?*

The thoughts raced through my mind as milliseconds passed. I squeezed Bobby's hand, trying to stay centered. While I was flying a mile a minute, he was calm as can be.

He tried to settle me down by saying chit-chatty things as if he were talking to a three-year-old. "Nice room. Gee, we also have a red room in our house—the pool house. Remember how the painters thought you were crazy when you wanted to paint that room red? You see! You were very much in fashion."

Bobby gestured around the room to confirm his observation, but I was barely paying attention to him. My gut was telling me something important was about to happen in my life. When my gut speaks, I block out anything and everything that might distract me.

The hallway door swung open and there was Hillary Rodham Clinton. She was alone and she paused for a split second in the doorway before walking briskly into the room with a smile from ear to ear. The first thing I noticed about her were her eyes. They were wonderful—alive and sparkling, and filled to the brim with joy. She was wearing a navy-blue pants suit, a fuchsia blouse, and Ferragamo pumps with a three-inch square elevation, like flats only with a little lift to them—the same kind of shoes my mother loved to wear. They even had a little bow or doodad of some sort across the top. To be honest, I hated them. The flat heel made the shoes easier to walk in, especially in Washington, which is filled with steps that lead to gridlock.

I was totally mesmerized by the soon-to-be former First Lady. With the photographers clicking away at us, I went completely blank. For the first time in my entire life, I had nothing to say. The only thing that came out of my mouth was air. Hillary must have thought I was a mute.

"Congratulations, Senator," Bobby said, shaking her hand. "Toni is a big fan of yours. She's so excited to meet you."

Ah Bobby, always my hero. Thanks to him, I had the few seconds I needed to pull myself together and find my voice. "Yes, Senator, my girlfriends are very impressed with you. They think it's wonderful what you've been able to accomplish…and how you've gone from First Lady to become the junior senator from New York."

Hillary took my hand in hers, and I could feel the warmth and sincerity in her touch. "Toni, I'm so happy to meet you. I've heard the nicest things about you."

"Well, thank you," I said. Not a sterling response, I know, but it was all I could muster at the moment as I was still overwhelmed by her smile and charisma. I'd never been in a room with anybody whose presence had such an effect on me.

"No, I really mean it," she added. "I hope we're going to see a lot more of each other in the future."

"We'd be thrilled," I bubbled.

After a few minutes of chitchat, Hillary excused herself. "I really have to go into the Blue Room to see Kelly's family. I know my husband wants to come in and meet you." With that, she grabbed both my hands and shook them. She was so warm you would have thought we'd been best friends forever. She hurried through the connecting door into the Blue Room, leaving the two photographers behind. By this time, they were all but invisible to me.

Once Hillary was gone I said to myself, *Take a deep breath…breathe in…breathe out.* A few breaths later I was fine, back in control.

A second later President William Jefferson Clinton opened the door to the room. Unlike Hillary, Bill stood in the opening long enough to either warm the cockles of your heart…or terrorize you. The photographers clicked away at the imposing figure in the doorway. The saying "larger than life" was never truer than at that very moment. At six-foot-three, Bill Clinton was definitely larger than life.

He walked toward us with a wonderful smile and extended his hand. "I'm so happy you came here today Toni…Robert," he said with his Arkansas drawl.

I looked up at him and said something I've always wanted to say. "Oh, Mr. President." The words escaped from my lips as if I'd channeled Marilyn Monroe herself. "What a bittersweet day this must be for you."

Believe me, I don't know where that line came from, but that's my third eye. That's what happens when I interview people—it's my instant connection to the other person's feelings. The president's smile faded, and he looked at me as if I'd struck a raw nerve. I could almost feel his inner struggle as he spoke, his words just above a whisper. "I've just recorded my last radio aaa-dress."

I couldn't believe what happened next. Tears began to stream down his cheeks, real, honest-to-goodness tears. My "bittersweet" comment acted as the final drop of water overflowing the dam, bringing his emotions to a pitch and causing them to spill out. I couldn't believe what I'd done—I had actually made the president of the United States cry. Me, a kid from Brooklyn. I just stood there, paralyzed, thinking, *What do I do now?*

As usual, I just kept talking. "Oh, Mr. President…it's so wonderful of you to have invited us here. This is really the most special moment that's ever happened to us. We'll probably be the last civilians to meet you in this room." The president just smiled and nodded, but as I kept talking, I felt the awkwardness between us completely evaporate.

"I know we'll be seeing each other again," he said.

He told us they would be leaving Washington the next day. I asked about Hillary...if she was excited about being senator.

"Oh, yes, she is. And so am I," he answered. "You know how much she loves New York...and she felt she could do a good job for the people. Now, if you'll excuse me, I really have to go join her."

I wasn't about to let that once-in-a-lifetime moment slip through my fingers without at least a chance to record it for posterity. "Mr. President, just one more thing. May I take a photograph with you?"

Toni and President Bill Clinton in the Red Room at the White House.

To my surprise, he didn't resist. I moved to the president's side, and Bobby snapped a picture of the two of us. The president gave me a kiss on the cheek and started through the door into the adjoining room. I watched him go…and at that very same moment, he turned back to look at me. "God bless you, Toni," he said. He turned on his heels and walked into the Blue Room. The photographers scampered out behind him.

The drama of that moment for me was truly palpable. The way he had said "God bless" was so genuine and so real that it felt like a Sunday sermon. I was rooted on the spot, caught in a haze of awe.

"Toni, it's six-fifteen," Bobby said urgently, grabbing my hand. "We were due at the Library of Congress at six."

"Okay, honey," I said. "What are we waiting for?"

CHAPTER FORTY-THREE

President George W. Bush

Bobby's touch snapped me out of the moment. We ran out of the Red Room like two fugitives on the run into the center hallway of the White House. We kept running until we reached a wide stairwell and almost collided with Betty Currie, Bill Clinton's longtime secretary. I recognized her from pictures in the newspapers and television. "Aren't you Betty Currie?" I asked, pointing my finger at her.

She acknowledged the identification and said "hi" as if she figured she must know us. "We're really late," I said, trying to catch my breath. "Can you please get us out of here? Our driver is waiting."

I told her where the car left us off. All of a sudden the three of us were running through the White House. Betty took us through some back corridors and stairwells, and the next thing we knew we were outside. It was colder than before. Sleet was coming down like razor blades. I kissed Betty on the cheek, and we slid into the limo.

"Library of Congress...and step on it!" I'm sure I sounded like Humphrey Bogart in a bad cops and robbers flick, but it didn't matter. Our driver "stepped on it" and a few minutes later we skidded to a stop outside the Library of Congress. We didn't even let the driver park the car. We climbed out, jumped over a puddle, and ran up the pathway into the building. As we ascended the steps, we were horrified to see a mass of people coming toward us. Obviously the event was over and we had missed it. We were too late.

"Bobby, grab onto my belt. You're going to lose me if you don't."

Bobby grabbed hold of me and I took off. Like salmon swimming upstream, we pushed our way through the oncoming crowd. "Excuse me...excuse me...sorry... whoops...sorry..." until we finally got inside.

Between the rain and the people and the running, we really had no idea where we were, then suddenly I looked up and there was President-elect George W. Bush, standing directly in front of me. The only thing separating me from the next president of the United States was a red velvet rope hanging between two gold stanchions.

I stopped dead in my tracks and Bobby piled into me like one of the Three Stooges. It was truly comical. I glanced around and discovered we were the only people in the hall other than George Bush, his staff, and the Secret Service. Everyone else had already said hello and good-bye. I put my hand out and said, "Oh, Mr. President." (I was getting good at saying that.)

We introduced ourselves as we shook hands and I suddenly realized my hands were ice cold from being outside. It must have felt like my hand had been left in the freezer overnight. I was so embarrassed I had to say something. "I'm so sorry, my hands are like ice."

He looked back at me and grinned. "Hopefully it's nothing I said," he responded with a twinkle.

When I reflect back on that moment, I feel I saw a side of George Bush that was rarely if ever seen by the general public. He was like a little boy with a wonderful smile and warm, warm eyes, just trying to relax me. There was an unexpected humor and sweetness to the man.

He asked us if we were having a good time in Washington. "Oh, yes. We're having a wonderful time. It's all very exciting. This is our first Inauguration. It's a really moving moment." I added that I liked the Lincoln Memorial, which didn't get much of a reaction…but then again, I don't know what I expected him to say.

"Well, I'll see you again this weekend," he ventured. We said our goodbyes rather awkwardly, and the soon-to-be forty-third president was hustled off by his aides. His footsteps reverberated on the marble floor as he walked away.

Bobby and I stood alone for a moment in the vast lobby of the Library of Congress, and I realized we should have been inducted into the Guinness Book of Records right then and there. For I, Toni Holt Kramer, along with my husband Robert Kramer, had just shaken hands with the outgoing and incoming presidents within minutes of each other—and we hadn't even washed our hands in between.

* * * * *

The day of the Inauguration was a cold thirty degrees. A light snow fell early in the morning and gave way to rain and fog. Despite the dreary weather we were excited to go to the ceremony. It was a piece of history and Bobby and I were elated to be there.

We dressed warm, and I couldn't resist wearing my brown, gold, and cream-colored cowboy boots—a Texas fashion statement that seemed appropriate for the incoming president and his family. Of course, the five-inch heels were not very practical for walking in the soft, mushy ground outside the nation's capital, but hey, who hasn't sacrificed convenience for fashion?

The crowd was already enormous by the time we arrived, stretching back from the podium as far as the eye could see. We didn't have preferred seating up close, so we joined the crowd wherever we could find a spot. Between the friends and family of George Bush, plus all of his political allies, it was impossible for us to expect or even attempt to get special treatment. Even *I* had to be realistic.

We were so far away it was like watching the ceremony from another zip code. Still, it was a thrill to be there in person. As we listened to Bush get sworn in, I realized how seldom in my lifetime somebody becomes president. To be standing in the same area where he was actually taking his oath of office was pretty darn amazing. Sure, you can see it much better on television, but it's like the difference between seeing your favorite band live versus listening to them on your car radio. The former is far more spine tingling. Even through the cold Washington air, I felt electric with excitement.

A few minutes later, George W. Bush was no longer the president-elect; he was the new president of the United States.

After the ceremony there was the traditional parade down Pennsylvania Avenue to the White House, followed by an array of concerts, parties, and luncheons all around D.C. Our ticket package included a Texas barbeque at a local restaurant, so off we went.

There were red-and-white checkered linens on the tables, and each room in the restaurant featured something different to eat, from ribs to steak to chicken. The food was fabulous, probably the best meal we had during our stay. My guess is the spread was hot off the Texas ranch of a George Bush supporter.

Toni and Bobby at the Bush inaugural. Her political life begins.

During that lunch, President and Mrs. Clinton left Washington for their home in Chappaqua, New York. Their departure was captured on TV screens spotted all around the restaurant. As the plane flew overhead, the place erupted with ecstatic screams of elation. Everyone there was overjoyed to see the former president and first lady leave town. The people, all Republicans of course, carried on like it was the end of a war, and for some, it probably was. It felt like the evacuation of the enemy rather than the ceremonial leaving of an ex-president.

The dancing around and disrespect had a tribal quality to it that made my stomach churn as I stood there in the restaurant. It was almost grotesque to see such a violent reaction from what I assumed were civilized people. Yes, I understood their happiness, but my God, the event could have been met with a lot more dignity than was shown that day. Some applause and a few cheers would have been more appropriate than the carrying on that occurred. For the first time, I saw the truly ugly side of politics—and it wouldn't be the last.

It was evident from my emotions that I'd been taken by the Clintons the night before, but I was also taken with Bush. I really liked them both. I saw great strength and humanity in the Clintons, even though they put Bill's head at the end of a pole and mopped up Washington with him as his term expired. I simply couldn't erase the image of bringing him to tears in the Red Room the night we met. His reaction was so real that it struck a chord somewhere deep in my soul.

In President Bush I saw a man of tremendous character and principle. Whether you supported the decisions he made during his eight years in office, whether you felt he did everything right or wrong, you have to acknowledge that he stood by his word, maybe to a fault sometimes. His response to me at the Library of Congress showed me a side of the man that most others would never see. It was clear to me that he had a wonderful sense of humor. The warmth he exuded was genuine, and not just because my hands were so cold during our introduction!

The Inaugural Balls spread glamour and music throughout the city. My magnificent Nolan Miller brocaded gown with a big trumpet bottom made a worthy contribution to the razzle and dazzle of the affair.

I don't know exactly how many balls and galas were going on that night, but the routine was...well, routine. The president and vice president, and their respective wives, would make a stop at each and every ball. They would go up on stage, greet their supporters, say a word of thanks, make a few promises for the future, and maybe share a dance with the crowd before whirling off to the next event.

Bobby and I had tickets to the California Ball, and that's the one we went to. Our excitement and anticipation at going, however, quickly turned to dismay. Instead of numbered tables with fine linens, crystal glasses, and exquisite silverware, there were rows of folding chairs spread throughout the room like a get-together at the local American Legion Hall. There were no waiters with white gloves serving expensive wine and meals by Wolfgang Puck. Instead, there was a long buffet table against one wall where—if you were really hungry—you could pluck your dinner from a sea of white and green cardboard boxes.

Are you shocked? Well, I was! Not only shocked, but incredibly disappointed and yes, even angry.

What a waste of a gorgeous dress. Nolan Miller would have been mortified. Bobby and I snatched our box dinners from the table, plopped unhappily down onto a couple of uncomfortable fold-up chairs, and ate on our laps with plastic knives and forks, the ultimate insult. Hardly presidential, I thought. And hardly worth the $$$$$$ we sent them.

There must have been a thousand people, jammed shoulder to shoulder, all doing the exact same thing we were. If I had to go to the ladies' room—and thankfully I didn't—God knows how long the wait might have been. To sum it up, the California Ball was a happening that didn't happen.

The next day we left for California. My mind was filled with all sorts of thoughts and recollections. I bought a yellow legal pad at the airport so I could jot down my feelings on the flight home. As I wrote, I had an almost psychic premonition that there would be really difficult times ahead, and I couldn't rid myself of the negative feelings about Vice President Cheney.

I saw Cheney earlier that weekend and was able to get a good look at him as he came up the stairs at the Watergate Hotel. I recall how tough he looked. As we all learned soon enough, he *was* tough, and that was probably a good thing. Cheney could never be accused of not standing up for our country. After Cheney left office—and in comparison to the administration that followed—I truly began to miss him desperately.

The reaction to Bill Clinton's departure from office also weighed on my mind. I'd always felt that Washington overreacted to the Monica Lewinsky affair, that they tried to impeach Clinton more to demean him than to punish him for his infidelity. In France, it would not be shocking for the president to have a mistress, or even a child out of wedlock. Does that make what Clinton did okay? Absolutely not. But I was more upset with the message Hillary was sending to women.

Now, these many years later, I look back at Clinton's sexual escapades—and all the embarrassment it must have caused—and wonder if his behavior was partially responsible for changing Hillary from the warm-hearted woman I knew and liked so much then into the harsh and stern woman she appears to be today.

CHAPTER FORTY-FOUR

Hillary Rodham Clinton

Back in California, I felt my foray into politics was off to a good start. A few months later, I received a phone call from Kelly Craighead, asking if we could come to Washington in June. "Senator Clinton would like to invite you to her home for a dinner party."

An artist friend, Sharon Whisnand, who worked on my Palm Springs estate, was an avid reader of political literature. I asked her if she had a book about Hillary that I could read before the dinner party, a book that would tell me all about her from the time she was a child up to the time she became first lady. If I was going to have dinner with Hillary, I wanted to know what made her tick, where she came from, and what she was like. I wanted a better understanding of what she was really saying and why she was saying it.

Sharon gave me a book and I started reading it on the plane to New York. I underlined the key facts and finished the book under my hair dryer in our seventh-floor suite at the Watergate. The more I read about Hillary, the more I was able to get a sense of her as a person. At the same time, I realized it would take a friendship over a long period of time to truly understand a woman of such vast complexities.

According to the book, Hillary came from a good suburban family outside of Chicago. Her father was a staunch Republican, while her mother was said to be a closet Democrat. Hillary went to Wellesley College, where she made her own transformation from a Goldwater Republican to a liberal Democrat. Then she went to Yale. She was passionate about the causes she believed in, but she wasn't a rabble-rouser. She didn't participate in protest marches and campus demonstrations.

Her heroine was—and is to this day—Eleanor Roosevelt. Whatever Hillary did she conducted herself with ultimate dignity. She had a strong sense of where she was going. The impression I got from the book was that she had serious political intentions from an early age.

When Bill arrived at Yale, Hillary had already been there for a year. Bill wore denim overalls and spoke with a country drawl, telling anyone who would listen that he was going to be president one day. Hillary and Bill met in the school library, and she immediately took him under her wing. She was highly respected at Yale, and it was evident that Bill was attracted to her brains and power. The story goes that once Bill was connected to Hillary, he was accepted too.

Something that struck me in my reading was a discussion of Hillary's fashion sense. From what I could gather, Hillary's hair wasn't styled in any particular way. She often wore flip-flops and parachute pants to school. It was obvious Hillary was more interested in social and political issues than fashion.

Despite being a fashion girl myself, I deeply admired Hillary's lack of obsession in her appearance. It seemed that those who knew Hillary at the time were much more interested in her mind and what she had to say than what she looked like and what she wore. She was recognized for her intelligence and wit.

By the time we arrived at Hillary's home on Ambassador Row for dinner, I knew as much about her as I possibly could. I was filled with excitement and more at ease, knowing I had done my homework. Hillary, wearing a yellow pants suit, greeted us with a big smile.

I soon discovered that when Hillary is happy, her eyes light up and she becomes totally in tune with the person she's talking to. She never looks off to the side—never looks this way or that to see what else is happening or who else is in the room. Then there is her laugh. She has the most fabulous laugh. It seems to rumble up from somewhere deep inside and escape with unexpected spontaneity.

Hillary led us into the living room to meet the other guests and explained that Bill was unable to join us. The walls and fabrics throughout the room were all different shades of yellow, her favorite color. I noticed many loving pictures of Hillary and Bill on the walls and tables. That said to me that despite Bill's indiscretions, their relationship remained intact, or at least she wanted people to believe that.

We were glad to see a few people we already knew, people we had met when we were in D.C. and some we knew from LA. James Carville stopped in for a drink. I enjoyed his Arkansas charm and found him to be an interesting person who spoke with the knowledge of a true insider. After cocktails we moved into the dining room.

There were three tables of eight. I couldn't have been more pleased when Bobby and I were seated at Hillary's table. She served soup for the appetizer and lamb chops for our main course. The food was wonderful and everything was served with genteel elegance, no paper plates and plastic forks here. As we dined, Hillary moved from table to table, spending time with each and every guest.

My husband and I had just returned from another Volvo convention in Norway. I told Hillary about taking a tour bus through a town called Bergen, where they had a complex of condos for the elderly. And I do mean elderly. You couldn't move into one of them unless you were at least eighty-five years old. Many who lived there were well over a hundred.

Hillary asked why I thought they lived such long lives. I gave the answer as it had been explained to me. "The water they drank and used on their crops came from the fiords. Boats are allowed in the fiords for only a few hours each day, so the water is exceptionally clean and pure. Also, it's illegal to give cows or sheep or any other animals injections to make them fatter. Anyone caught injecting an animal with any additives is subject to a large fine, and a second offense could bring jail time. As a result, the meat is all natural. There was only a single doctor in the town of Bergen and one hospital. I was told neither was very busy."

Are you listening, Washington? Just maybe the little town of Bergen is on to something, as opposed to today where they don't have to disclose if the foods we buy are artificially created—a far cry from real food.

As Hillary and I spoke, I could tell she was hooked on what I had to say. I was providing information that was factual, something she didn't know—and she loved that. The evening wore on and gradually the guests began to leave. Hillary pulled me aside and said, "Stay…stay."

Maybe eight of us remained. Hillary's personality was so much warmer face-to-face than on television. I sensed a great heartiness about her that transcended politics, that set aside who she was and who I was. We were two girlfriends chatting away over a glass of wine.

About that time, Dorothy, Hillary's mother, came downstairs from her bedroom to join us. We drank a little more wine and I told Dorothy how close I was to my mother. She wanted to know all about her. Needless to say, we got along famously.

At the end of the evening, Hillary grabbed me and hugged me. She said to Bobby, "Toni and I are kindred spirits."

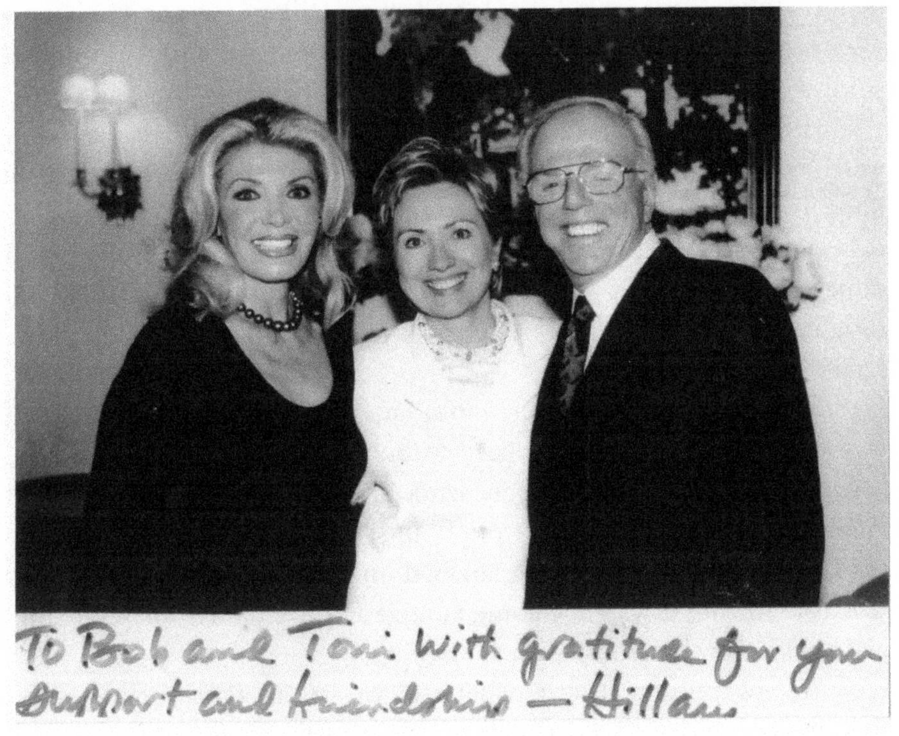

To Bob and Toni with gratitude for your
support and friendship — Hillary

Toni and Bobby at home with Hillary in Washington.

That comment had a profound effect on me. Some people have an education but no street smarts to go with it. As far as I could tell then, Hillary had both.

* * * * *

It was obvious at that point that fate had stepped in and shown me a new door into Washington.

Another invitation arrived from Hillary to come to Washington, and Bobby and I eagerly accepted. We took our usual suite at the Watergate. By now everybody at the hotel knew us. When we arrived I had a phone call from Hillary, who asked if we wanted a tour of her office.

The next day we hurried off to the Capitol. I knew from the book I read about Hillary that she idolized Eleanor Roosevelt. So it came as no surprise when we arrived at her yellow office to see photographs and memorabilia of the fabled first lady. I think Hillary surrounded herself with everything "Eleanor" as if to absorb the woman body, mind, and spirit. It was another inside look at the mind of Hillary Clinton.

Hillary had one more surprise for us. She invited us to the Senate to watch our government at work. We sat in the balcony above the Senate floor. We watched Hillary as she made an amazing presentation to her colleagues, complete with visual aids. There was little doubt that she'd done her homework, and the use of graphics provided clarity and insight as opposed to the boring speeches given by some of the other senators.

I remember Joe Biden's colorful entrance. He looked dapper and was Mr. Personality, working hard to be The Most Popular Kid in the Senate. You know the type; every school has one. He shook hands and laughed and hugged senators from both sides of the aisle as if they were his best friends, and everyone laughed and hugged him back. He just loved it. To me, it was like some strange mating dance, all very collegial...until they had to vote on something.

Ah, yes, politics. That is what senators are there for, right? When they are there.

CHAPTER FORTY-FIVE

9/11

It was September 10, 2001 at about 4:30 in the afternoon. For some inexplicable reason I began to cry. Bobby ran into our bedroom when he heard my sobs.

"Toni, what happened? What's wrong?"

"I don't know," I answered, tears rolling down my cheeks.

"Then why are you crying?" he asked.

"I just feel terrible...I can't stop. Call the doctor. Please, call Dr. Karpman right away. Maybe he'll give me some pills. Maybe I'm losing my mind."

Bobby knew I didn't like doctors and would never request one unless it was an emergency. The urgency in my voice frightened him. He called Dr. Karpman. I yelled into the phone over Bobby's shoulder. "Help me, Harold...do something! Help me! I don't know what's wrong with me."

I could hear the doctor's voice. "Bobby, Toni is always so up and so much fun. There's nothing wrong with her. What happened?"

Bobby held the phone up so the doctor could hear me crying. I grabbed it and pleaded with the doctor. "Harold, I don't know what's wrong. Just give me something to calm me down. Please!"

I don't pop pills. Never did, never will. I don't even take aspirin. For me to ask meant something really strange was going on.

Dr. Karpman agreed to phone a prescription to Bel Air Pharmacy to relieve my anxiety. Bobby drove me to Brentwood Village at the top of the hill near our home. We went to my favorite Italian restaurant, where Bobby sat me down and ordered a glass of red wine for me. Then he headed for the pharmacy to pick up the prescription.

I literally gulped the wine down, hoping the pain would go away. It didn't. I ordered a second glass, and gradually stopped crying. But I still felt the weight of the world sitting on my shoulders. I was about to down the second glass when Bobby returned with the prescription. He insisted I take a pill. I did and we ordered dinner.

"Honey, do you know what started it?" Bobby asked.

"No," I replied. "All of a sudden it just came on. It was like someone hit me with a baseball bat. I don't have a clue where it came from. Nothing like this has ever happened before."

The sense of heaviness I felt continued throughout dinner. We finished and went home, where I passed out on the bed from the combination of wine and the pill.

At 6:45 the next morning, LA time, my stockbroker phoned. I was in the habit of getting up early to watch the morning market action, but not that early. I was only half awake when I answered.

"Did you see what happened?" he shouted.

"What? The market tanked?" I was suddenly wide awake.

"Just turn on your television!" His voice was frantic. I told Bobby, resident king of the remote, to turn on the TV.

The very moment the TV picture came on, I saw a plane fly straight into one of the Twin Towers. I wasn't sure what was happening. After a few moments it suddenly became clear. "Oh my God!" I screamed.

The camera showed smoke and people running, a scene of absolute chaos. I heard people commenting on it. Like everyone else in the world, I was stunned and frozen in time. I couldn't pry myself away from the television set. I wanted to see and hear everything that was going on. It was just so shocking, so internally shattering...I couldn't believe it.

There are moments in history that forever burn in our minds. That day, the day those planes flew into the Twin Towers, is a day I'll remember the rest of my life.

"Now we know why you were so hysterical," said Bobby. "You had another one of your premonitions."

It took a moment for me to digest what Bobby had said, but I knew he was right. I knew something horrific was coming, and that was why my head was ready to burst the day before. "Oh, God. If only I had known what it was, I could have told somebody."

It was my psychic ability warning me a disaster was close by. I didn't know it was airplanes flying into buildings, killing three thousand people... including people I knew, which brought me even closer to it. There was a stockbroker in New York I watched on television named Fred Alger. I didn't know him personally, but I was crazy about him. I learned later that he was killed in the tragedy. I think I mourned him every Christmas for years, and felt sorry for his family.

I was terrified by my premonition, yet appreciated it nevertheless. It was a gift. At least I wanted to believe that. At the same time, I felt tremendous sadness. Since my premonition was a prelude to what was going to happen—why wasn't I given *all* the pieces to the puzzle?

CHAPTER FORTY-SIX

Nancy Pelosi

Because of my relationship with Hillary, we were invited to a lot of Democratic events in California. In the process, we met a number of prominent politicians, including Dick Gephardt, the minority leader in the House at the time. Nancy Pelosi, who was working her way up the ladder and wielded plenty of power, was his minority whip.

Dick Gephardt had boyish good looks, and I found him and his wife, Jane, to be remarkably unassuming for such public figures. Dick had run unsuccessfully for president in 1988. There were rumblings he might run again, and he did in 2004.

It was now the end of 2001. After spending some time with Dick, I said to Bobby, "Maybe we could do a dinner party to help raise money for his campaign."

Our house in Bel Air was a good size, but the backyard wasn't that big and the swimming pool took up a majority of the grounds off the patio. Bobby, ever practical, asked a key question. "Where are we going to put all the people? Hmmm?"

"Well, we don't really get much use out of the pool, right?" I said, a plan already unfolding in my brain. "The wind coming off the ocean makes it too cold. I can't even remember the last time we went for a swim. Besides, we have a pool in Palm Springs...we don't need one here too."

"Yes..." Bobby replied, waiting for the other shoe to drop.

"So...why don't we just throw dirt in there and cover it up?" Did I really suggest that? Yes, guilty as charged.

Bobby took an appropriate moment or two to digest my radical thought...then agreed it was a really good idea. And yes, we would get much more use out of the grounds if we didn't have a pool. Even the dogs would enjoy the backyard more. We both agreed and plans for the party went forward.

I called the politically connected Aaron Tonken, and he was more than happy to round up celebs who would want to show their support for Dick Gephardt. I got a list of people to invite from Gephardt's staff, and additional names from Sim and Debbie Farar, close friends of Hillary's. In the meantime, Bobby arranged to fill in the pool, and I began organizing my ideas for the food and décor.

After much internal debate, I decided not to have a special theme. Instead, I thought it would be more effective to simply mount a classy, understated party with good food and the right people unencumbered with splashy gimmicks. Once the pool was filled in, the backyard proved to be the perfect setting. The rear patio outside our house became a stage, and we set up tables where the pool used to be. There was plenty of room to seat the hundred or so invited guests, a group that included two Emmy award-winning actresses, Rosanne Barr and Camryn Manheim.

A couple of days before the party, I learned that Dick was bringing Nancy Pelosi, so I sat her at the same table as the Gephardts.

(left to right) Roseanne Barr, Camryn Manheim, Dick Gephardt, Toni, Chaka Kahn and Bobby.

As the big night unfolded and the guests began to arrive, the air was suddenly filled with the sound of sirens coming up the road to our house. I couldn't imagine what was going on until I saw a black SUV pull to a stop in front, complete with a police escort. Nancy Pelosi and her husband, Paul, a wealthy, good-looking guy, got out and joined the party. I thought her arrival was over the top, but then again, this was Nancy Pelosi. She obviously had her sights set on being a lot more than the minority whip.

After everyone was seated, I introduced the guest of honor. I offered a little of Dick's background so that my friends could get to know him better. I told everyone I thought Dick was a true American patriot. He said a few words and returned to his seat.

Next I introduced Nancy Pelosi, one of the best-dressed women in politics. She had great taste, a great fashion sense, and...great legs. I often wondered why she chose to wear pants suits when a skirt or dress would have been much more flattering. She had a Marilyn Monroe quality in the way she spoke and smiled at people with a wide-eyed innocence. She would tilt her head, like a lion or tiger sucking you into their lair. She had a sweetness about her that reeled you in, although to me it appeared to be a "trained" sweetness, as if she had rehearsed in front of a mirror.

Since I knew very little about Nancy Pelosi at the time, I did research on her prior to the party. I was prepared with an introduction that made her sit up and take notice.

It went something like this: "Also with us tonight is Nancy Pelosi. Maybe you don't know as much about Nancy as you'd like, so let me tell you a little about her. Nancy Pelosi has had an incredible life. Her father was the mayor of Baltimore, and from the time she was a little girl, every Sunday her mother would cook a big meal...and all the politicians in Baltimore would come by to see her father and his family. Nancy D'Alesandro would wear a little frou-frou dress and Mary Jane patent leather shoes, and she would curtsey to everyone who came in. Nancy's brother, Thomas, followed in his father's footsteps and eventually became mayor of Baltimore as well, so it's really no surprise that Nancy turned to politics. She met her husband, Paul, when they were both in college at Georgetown. After raising five daughters, Nancy got into politics because a close friend of hers in San Francisco, Sala Burton, became ill with cancer and was unable to run for re-election. Sala asked Nancy to run in her place, and after getting the nod of approval from her husband and children, Nancy threw her hat in the ring. She won, becoming a member of the House of Representatives, where she has risen to the rank of minority whip. Now that you know a little bit about her, I'd like you to meet Nancy Pelosi."

Well, Nancy got up from her table and gave me the biggest hug you can imagine. She was obviously overwhelmed and whispered in my ear, "In my entire life nobody has ever taken the time or made the effort to introduce me like that…to tell the people about me and my family. Thank you so much."

A few days later I received letters from Dick and Nancy telling me how much they enjoyed the party. I was proud and pleased that the party was a success, and soon we were flooded with invitations from all over.

My political star was definitely on the rise. Bobby was as thrilled. "What fun we are having," he would say.

He was right. We were having fun.

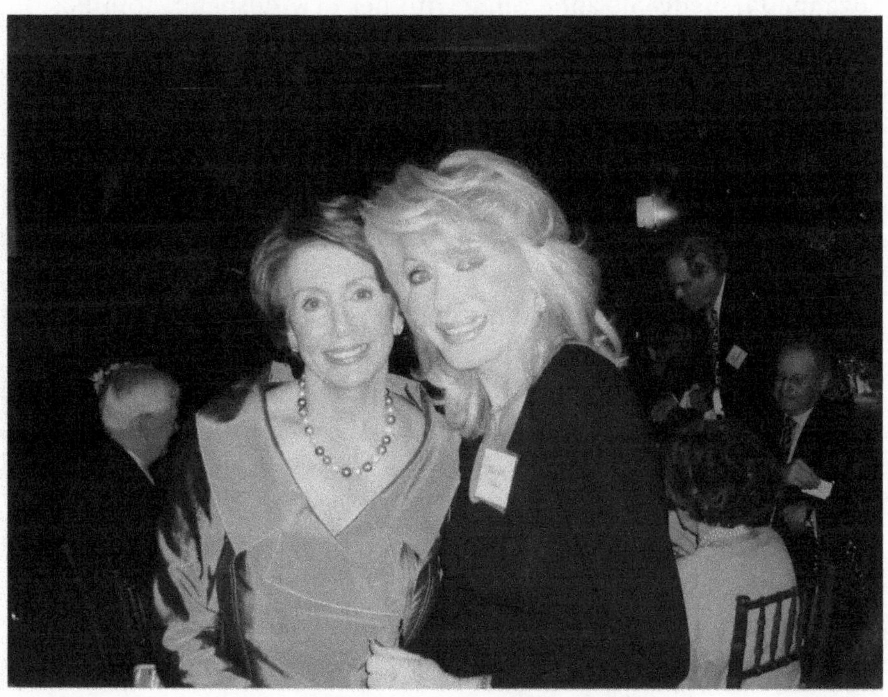

Toni with Nancy Pelosi.

CHAPTER FORTY-SEVEN

Lunch with Hillary

Like all members of Congress, Hillary had a PAC, a Political Action Committee formed to raise money through contributions.

In April of 2002, I offered to host a luncheon for Hillary at our Bel Air home for the express purpose of generating contributions to her PAC. I called on all my friends to come. "I don't care if you're a Democrat or a Republican," and most of my friends were Republicans like I was, "you're coming to meet Hillary."

The luncheon tables quickly filled up. Everyone wanted to meet Senator Hillary Rodham Clinton. All my friends came, including Warren Cowan, one of the all-time great Hollywood publicists. Warren arranged for many of his celebrity clients and friends to attend as well, including Suzanne Pleshette. Suzanne came with her new husband, Tom Poston. Each had co-starred with Bob Newhart at different times in his two long-running TV series, *The Bob Newhart Show* and *Newhart*.

I remember seeing Suzanne a number of years later in Beverly Hills. At the time it had been rumored she was having severe health problems and was forced to use a wheelchair to get around. Bobby and I were at Mickey Fine's coffee shop when we spotted Suzanne about to be wheeled into the elevator to go to a doctor's office in the same building. She caught sight of me and immediately got out of her chair, hoping I wouldn't see it, and made her way into the restaurant.

Suzanne put up a brave front through her illness, her bawdy sense of humor and smoky voice still intact. "They tell me I only have six weeks to live," she winked, "...so if you want to take me to dinner, you better do it soon."

That attitude was so typical of Suzanne. That was the last time I saw her. Not too long after, she passed away from lung cancer. Tragically, Tom Poston had passed away less than a year before Suzanne.

Warren Cowan died shortly after Suzanne. As they say in France: *Jamais, jamais, deux sans trois*...never, never two without three. *C'est triste*...how sad.

The celebrities at my party for Hillary mingled with the rest of the guests and everyone had a wonderful time. The décor was predominantly yellow, Hillary's favorite color.

Toni and Bobby with Hillary.

I made a short speech to welcome Hillary to our home. I made sure she was prepared when she met my guests for the first time. I stood right beside her as every person approached to say hello. I introduced each and every one of them to Hillary with a brief summary of who they were and what they did so she would have an immediate connection to them. I was her party liaison.

"Toni, nobody has ever stood by my side and done that," Hillary told me when the party was over. How often do we do little things for people that usually go unnoticed or unappreciated? Not so with Hillary. It was an absolute joy to stand with her at the luncheon, and she thanked me as though I had done her a huge favor. The day was a complete success for both of us.

After all the people left, Hillary asked if there was a place she could make a phone call. Thinking she wanted privacy, I walked her into our bedroom and gave her the phone. She sprawled across the bed and dialed a number. "Stay," she whispered.

The call was to Lew Wasserman, the retired chairman of MCA/Universal. Lew was ninety by that time, but not too many years earlier, he had been the most powerful executive in all of Hollywood. His clout in the world of politics was equally far-reaching. Hillary knew he wasn't well and told me she just wanted to see how he was doing. "I worry that next time I come back, he won't be here."

And she was right. A few months later Lew passed away. I was impressed with Hillary's act of kindness; it was really special given her time restraints. She had just flown in that morning, had all sorts of commitments, including my luncheon, and in between she made a stop at the home of Lew and Edie Wasserman to say hello.

I thought, *What a dame!*

* * * * *

A year or so later Bobby and I were in Florence, Italy, and we passed a quaint shop that had spectacular pillows in the windows. Two decorative throw pillows in particular—yellow silk with embroidered tigers on them—caught my eye. I couldn't pass them by and quickly pulled Bobby into the shop. The pillows looked like they belonged on the sofa in Hillary's living room. I bought them on the spot and had them shipped directly to Hillary's home in D.C.

When we returned to LA there was a personal thank-you note from Hillary telling us how much she adored the gift. "Come visit the tigers," she wrote. "They miss you."

CHAPTER FORTY-EIGHT

An Unexpected Standing Ovation

Bobby and I took another trip to Italy, this time to Lake Como to celebrate my birthday. I absolutely love Northern Italy. On a previous trip to Lake Como, we stayed at a world-famous hotel called the Villa D'este. I nicknamed it the Villa Dusty because it was so tired-looking at the time. Since then it was given a facelift, but this time around we made reservations at the Hotel Bellagio.

Toni enjoys her birthday in Italy.

We spent a fabulous day walking around and visiting the shops, followed by a divine dinner at the hotel restaurant overlooking the glittering lake. I was so exhausted from the time change and the day's activities that I slept well into the morning the next day.

It was eleven o'clock when the phone rang. Bobby answered it after one ring and told me it was somebody named Sarah, calling from Washington. "She needs to talk to you about Dick Gephardt."

I looked up from the bed with my sleepy eyes. "Now?"

Bobby covered the receiver with his hand. "She says it's important."

I couldn't imagine what was so urgent. "Sarah?"

"Toni, Mr. Gephardt wants you to come to Washington."

"But…we just got to Italy."

"I know," Sarah said apologetically. "But there's a big luncheon here in D.C., and Mr. Gephardt really wants you to be here."

I was flattered, of course, but not sure I wanted to leave Italy on such short notice. "Sarah, I'll call you back."

I hung up and turned to Bobby. "What do you think, honey?"

"I think we should go back. We've been waiting for something interesting to happen, and maybe this is it."

Since the event was a few days off, I figured we still had a little time to enjoy our trip. I phoned Sarah back and told her we'd be there.

How would I describe myself at that moment? Curious would be a good word. I would say that curiosity is one of my major traits. Curious, not nosy—there's a big difference. I'm curious about life. I'm curious about people. I'm curious about important things. And I'm always eager to learn.

I knew I couldn't show up at the Gephardt luncheon empty-handed. I needed to bring something of value along with me. So I went downstairs and spoke to the man at the desk. "How's business been since nine-eleven?"

He looked at me rather strangely, not sure what to say. So I asked him again. Finally, he answered. "A lot of people who stay here…they get food from the local market…they bring it back to the hotel and eat in their rooms. They don't use our restaurant as much as they used to."

His insinuation was clear. Times were lean. It wasn't business as usual.

I went back up to the room, pulled out my trusty yellow pad, asked Bobby to take the camera, and we went for a walk among the quaint shops that lined the main street. Ever the reporter, I went into a dress shop and asked for the lady who ran it. The sales girl went into the back, and a minute later a large woman wearing a black dress, her dark hair pulled back in a bun, emerged from the room.

"Good afternoon, Signora. Do you speak English?" I asked politely.

"Yes, I speak English," she said with a thick Italian accent.

I introduced myself and told her I was from California and then asked her the same question I asked the desk clerk at the hotel. "I'm just curious, how has business been since nine-eleven?"

The woman didn't even take time to blink. "Not very good," she said sadly. "But I'm very lucky because we own this building…and we live above the shop, thank God. At least I have a place to live…and we own the property here. But for me it is sad…I had to let so many people who work for me go."

I thanked her for talking to me, and we continued our walk. We went into every shop along the street. The stories were basically the same—all negative. All gloomy tales of bad times.

"Business is really bad…I had to let go of my assistant…there's not enough work…I can't afford to pay the people who work for me…I feel so badly …it's such a close family here…and now they don't have a job…and I am worried how are they going to support their children?"

I filled my yellow pad with story after story, and Bobby took pictures of the people I interviewed. I had no idea what I was going to do with the information. It was just data collected on a whim.

We briefly celebrated my birthday, then flew back to New York. We took a commuter plane to Washington and checked into the Four Seasons in Georgetown. We got a good night's sleep, and the next day we went to the office building in the Capitol where the luncheon was being held.

The room was set up for fifty people, five tables of ten. I was seated beside Ed Markey, the extremely liberal congressman from Massachusetts, whose most redeeming asset to me was that he resembled Gary Cooper. On my other side was Tom Daschle, the equally liberal senate majority leader from South Dakota. Dick Gephardt was seated across from me, and Ted Kennedy was at an adjacent table. Kennedy's son, Patrick, who was then the Democratic congressman from Rhode Island, sat at one of the other tables.

I suddenly realized that almost everybody there was either a senator or a congressman. I think the least important people in the room—other than Bobby and me—were a former ambassador and her husband. It was definitely a Who's Who or Who Was in Washington. As we say in show business, Bobby and I were the only civilians. Imagine going to an Academy Awards dinner and being the only one in the room who wasn't a Hollywood insider. But I didn't feel uncomfortable. In fact, I loved it. I felt flattered that, for some reason, Dick Gephardt felt it was important for us to be there. To this day I'll be damned if I know why.

As it turned out, I got along great with Tom Daschle, who gave a thirty-minute speech about the Iraq War and all the terrible things that had happened in our country since the invasion. Daschle was an outspoken critic of the war, but despite his reservations, he helped give George Bush the necessary votes in the Senate that the president needed to send our troops to the Middle East. It was evident from what he'd said that he wasn't happy he voted to support the war.

After everyone had spoken, including Dick Gephardt, someone asked if anybody wanted to add anything or had any questions. I raised my hand. I think Bobby almost fell off his chair when I did, but I figured I was an invited guest and I wanted to contribute, plus we had flown all the way across the ocean to get there.

As I stood up to speak, I could see out of the corner of my eye that Ted Kennedy was staring at me. So I nodded to him. "Good afternoon, Senator."

I was completely and totally awed to be in Kennedy's presence, even though his history was morally tainted. When he spoke earlier in the day, his voice boomed throughout the room with incredible authority and passion. There was no question he was Washington royalty, and I can just imagine the presence he was when he was younger and more vital. When I saw him that day, he was already overweight and red-faced with a big nose, but he came across as a gentle man with great strength. Without question, he commanded respect from everyone who attended that luncheon. Despite my ambivalence, I felt honored to have his complete attention while I spoke.

With the Lion of the Senate focused solely on me, I don't know how I had the courage to go on, but I did. Since nobody had spoken about the effect of nine-eleven on the people of Europe, I pulled out my yellow pad of notes and proceeded to share my experiences.

"It's even worse than you think," I began. "My husband and I were in Italy just a few days ago when Congressman Gephardt asked us to come here. Having been a reporter on television for most of my life, I went into the various restaurants and shops to take the temperature of the locals to see if they had been adversely affected by nine-eleven, not only economically but emotionally."

I hadn't rehearsed what I was going to say; it just seemed to pour out naturally. I'm always better like that anyway. I relayed how people were worried about their families, employees, friends, and neighbors. It was something I lived, something I experienced, and the emotion of my experience was evident in my story.

When I finished everyone broke into applause. I could see the smile on Bobby's face and I knew he was proud of me. Patrick Kennedy actually stood up and applauded, giving me a solid thumbs-up. Can you imagine? I got a standing O in Washington!

Patrick and I became friends after that, and he invited us to several parties over the next couple of years. In fact, the invitations began to flow in like water. Nancy Pelosi even invited us to her house in Northern California, but we couldn't go. Her husband, Paul, had reputedly made hundreds of millions in the business world, and they owned a vineyard in Napa Valley. Sometime later I met with Nancy about getting involved in Washington. I knew she was a chocoholic, and I brought her a glass container of candy Kisses almost three feet high.

In my humble opinion, Nancy Pelosi is a calculating, driven politician with a coquettish, theatrical flair who always has to win. And she is – and has been - a master of winning. Whenever it seems as though she's reached the end of the road, she comes back stronger. For that, I give her a wave of my hat. I'm guessing she took advantage of any and every opportunity to reach the top, but in truth, who wouldn't? Despite all the pros and cons that constantly surround her, Nancy has been nothing but nice to me along the way.

* * * * *

After returning from Washington, Bobby and I were invited to a small luncheon at the Regency Club in Los Angeles organized by Loreen Arbus. Loreen was the daughter of the late Leonard Goldenson, founder and former chairman of ABC Television Network. Rather than trade on her father's reputation, Loreen opted to drop her father's name and used her grandmother's maiden name as she navigated a very successful career, helping to launch what eventually became the Lifetime Television Network.

Loreen, who I consider a good friend, became committed to encouraging and mentoring women in television, film, and communications, and has been extremely active in a number of social, charitable, and political causes.

It was Loreen, along with Dana Goldinger, who proposed me for the Women's Leadership Board of Harvard University. The Board, made up of distinguished women from across the globe, was started to help women of all ages better their lives. After a year of being vetted, I was accepted onto the Board.

Bill Clinton was the guest speaker at Loreen's luncheon. He walked in with his great friend and political ally Terry McAuliffe, the former governor of Virginia.

"Hello, Toni," Bill said when he saw me. It was like he had just seen me the day before. His total recall for names is well-known, as is his incredible ability to speak extemporaneously.

It didn't matter that Bill was an hour late arriving, another trait he is well-known for. He spoke for two hours nonstop, without notes and in great detail, about all the major issues plaguing the world.

Slowly but surely I was getting noticed. I was meeting more and more people, and renewing friendships with those I had already met. At that point, there was no question in my mind I was going to have a place in Washington. Bobby and I even talked about living there part time. Even if I didn't become an ambassador, which might prove to be difficult, someone suggested that maybe I could be invited onto the Board of the Kennedy Center.

My dream was coming true.

CHAPTER FORTY-NINE

Click!

I was ecstatic to learn that Hillary Clinton was going to run for president in 2008. At the time there was no doubt in my mind that she was able and ready for the job.

I wanted to do everything I could to get her elected. I felt I could make a true contribution, something other than hosting parties and donating money. I wanted something more. I wanted something to do. I believed there was an opportunity to make a mark for myself. I just needed to seize it.

Toni with Bill Clinton and Whoopi Goldberg.

If somebody had asked me at the time what I wanted, my answer would have been to be an ambassador. I had complete faith and confidence in my ability to represent the United States on foreign soil.

I've always been an overachiever, the kind of person who refuses to settle for anything less than perfection. My extensive career in Hollywood allowed me to develop my outgoing personality into a forceful asset, while my years spent in the stock market have given me insight into world economics. I am well equipped to talk, entertain, and get the job done, no matter what it entails. I knew that Hillary, and the people who worked with her, liked and respected me, which gave me a huge amount of confidence. I felt primed and ready for the challenge.

Every so often you find yourself in the right place at the right time. As a result, good things happen. That's exactly how I felt then. I knew I wouldn't have been just a good ambassador; I would have been the best.

The deeper I got into the game, the more I realized that politics is a wolf's den for anyone involved. For women, the drama is magnified tenfold. For some reason or another, people still feel uncomfortable with women who achieve the same or more than their male counterparts. You would think as the world keeps progressing we would stop seeing one sex as inferior to another. Unfortunately, that's not the case—and it's often other women who act as the harshest critics. And that is a fact.

One day at a fund-raising barbecue, I couldn't help but notice that there was a ton of negative talk about women in politics. As conversation bubbled to a crescendo, I said, "Why is it that women will champion other women until that woman gets power—then those very same women will find anything and everything they can to undermine the woman who made it—and rejoice in her failure?" My comment was met with thunderous silence.

Ladies, we do need to stick together.

* * * * *

In the midst of Hillary's run, I was asked to join a conference call with Bill Clinton and ten or twelve other people across the country who wanted to see Hillary elected.

I, like the rest of the world, always considered Bill a brilliant politician. His ability to read his adversaries and maneuver any situation to his favor was a trait I admired and respected greatly. Bill struck me as a true thinker. He could sense which way the wind was blowing and use it to his advantage. But while politically savvy—he was incredibly unwise in his personal choices. Nothing to admire there.

It was 11:00 on a Saturday morning in Palm Springs when my phone rang in my office and they plugged me into the call. I knew some of the people on the line but not all. We went around the horn and introduced ourselves. I got to say my favorite phrase, "Good morning, Mister President."

Bill said a few words about Hillary and the campaign. As he spoke I detected a sense of anxiety in his voice, unusual for Bill Clinton. Was it just my imagination? I don't think so. Obama's presence was beginning to be felt, even if not acknowledged, and it had become clear that things weren't going as smoothly as we had expected. They asked all of us if we had any ideas or thoughts. They didn't say it exactly—but I'm sure they were looking for ideas to get the campaign back on track.

I knew there were people who thought Hillary was tough and cold, that she was manipulative and cunning but I didn't feel it then. I was with her when she tried to help the farmers in upstate New York when she was senator. They had a big affair in Washington where the farmers set up booths and presented different foods they were growing, as well as cheeses and wines. Hillary was dedicated. She went from booth to booth...farmer to farmer...to each and every one of them, offering her support and promises to do everything within her power to keep them productive and solvent. There was no coldness or manipulation. Instead, there was a caring woman who put her hand on every farmer's shoulder, smiled, and made human contact.

One of Hillary's strongest assets is her ability to talk *to* people rather than *at* them, and she listens carefully, anxious to give her input.

In truth it's just plain difficult for most women in politics. We even discussed this phenomenon at a forum at the Women's Leadership Board of Harvard. If women in politics appear too warm and friendly, they're perceived as being inexperienced to the point that foreign governments would run roughshod over them. To be president, conventional wisdom says a woman needs to be strong like a man, which is nonsense because a woman is often the great strength *behind* a man.

On the flipside, if a woman is too hard or too strong or too cold, people dislike her for it. It's a fine line all women must walk on the way to the top, whether in politics or the business world. Excelling at that balancing act is by no means an easy task.

When it came to my turn to speak on the conference call, I had a very different idea from what anybody else had said. I tried hard to be diplomatic. "Mr. President, maybe you should think about going on television as well as going around the country by train—like so many presidents before you—and talking to the men of America. You have to tell the men what an incredible fighter Hillary is. I know that *you* know that, but *they* need to know as well. We've already got the women's vote—we need you to get the men. Tell them how Hillary helped you, when all appeared lost, to get re-elected governor of Arkansas—and that perhaps you wouldn't have had the opportunity to be elected president if she hadn't done that. Share with the men how you know firsthand that Hillary is a hard-working woman who never says 'die' and—"

At that point I heard a CLICK and the line went silent for a moment. I could still hear the other voices but they couldn't hear mine. Did they cut me off because of what I said? Was it an accident? Was it intentional? All I know for sure is that the call ended soon after that.

I have no regrets about what I said. It made perfect sense at that time, and it turned out I was right. I think Bill needed to humanize Hillary and explain his relationship with her to the men in our country because they needed to be on her side. He needed to give her more credit and thus give her more credibility as a force capable of being president of the United States. Was it presumptuous of me to offer my opinion? I don't think so. After all, they asked for it.

Despite the glitch, I continued to work for Hillary. All of us who supported her at the time hoped the election was still hers to win. With Obama's lack of experience and all the tabloid-worthy gossip that was eking out about him and his past, none of us felt he posed any real threat.

Boy, were we wrong!

CHAPTER FIFTY

I Love You, Mother

Mother lived with us at our Palm Springs estate from 1996 right up until she passed away on March 22, 2007. The relationship that grew between my husband and her during that time was beautiful. Mother always harbored an incredible fondness for Bobby, but living together as we all did meant bonding on a closer level than most mother-in-law/son-in-law pairings.

Every night before dinner, Bobby and I would go to her bedroom and visit. She would call it her "fashion show." "Let me see what you're wearing tonight," she would say.

It gave her great pride to see the woman I had become, a sort of visual confirmation that she had done a very good job. Any mother watching their child decked out for a school dance or special event knows the feeling. It's universally wonderful, but for my mother it seemed something even more. For my entire life she'd stressed the importance of always looking my best, ingraining in me the value of putting forth a good outer image. She seldom criticized me. Instead, she might make a remark and let me find the answer on my own.

Despite her struggles with a variety of physical problems, she stayed upbeat and positive, just like she had her entire life—and the psychic connection between us remained as strong as ever.

For the last ten years of her life, I made a habit of tracking her blood work. I always asked the nurses and the doctors to give me a copy of the results. I knew that some readings were always high while some were always low. I wasn't overly concerned because the results were consistent over the years, and they matched her particular body chemistry.

But the results I received in January 2007 told a very different story. They showed her white blood count was much higher than usual. I asked her doctor about it and he soft-pedaled the change in numbers, saying he didn't think it was anything to worry about. "You know, at her age, blah-blah-blah..." That was not the answer I was looking for.

I was reminded of when I was in London working for *Playgirl* magazine, and I was fortunate to get an interview with Glynis Johns, the popular English actress with the quirky voice and pixie-like looks. She opened the door of her London townhouse wearing a black headband that held her hair back, a towel around her neck, and she was sweaty from doing exercises. I was surprised because I had recently read that she was very ill and presumably had only a few months to live.

As we sipped tea the conversation turned to her health. "I heard you were ill," I said as delicately as I could.

"Oh, that's quite true," she replied. "I was."

"But you look so great."

"Well, I figured it out one day. I wasn't feeling very well and I asked myself, 'What is the problem—how did this happen—how did I get like this?' I thought about the word 'disease' and I hyphenated it into two words…'dis' and 'ease.' Once I did that I suddenly realized that, yes, my life was at 'DIS-EASE.' So I decided to change it. I changed everything. I changed who I was…what I was eating…what I was drinking …everything, absolutely everything about myself…until I got to feeling that I wasn't at 'dis-ease' anymore. And guess what? I wasn't ill anymore, either."

I never, ever forgot what Glynis told me that day. I thought it was powerful advice, and it has stayed with me as if I had just heard it yesterday.

If only it had been that easy for my mother.

Mother suffered from bladder infections and a problem knee from playing golf. Eventually we arranged for round-the-clock caregivers rather than nurses because she really wasn't ill. As time went on other maladies began to manifest, and a nurse came a couple of times a week. One nurse in particular was responsible for changing Mother's catheter every thirty to forty-five days.

Mother had been bothered by a nagging cough, but the doctor didn't think it was anything serious. At one point, a few years earlier, the same doctor thought she was going to die. He sat us down in our living room and told us that we had to come to grips with the fact that she might go. The doctor was so stressed about it that he suffered terrible stomach pains while at our house and wound up in the hospital himself that night. In the meantime, Mother recovered.

On Wednesday, March 21st, the night before she died, Bobby and I were going out to meet some friends for dinner. As usual, we visited

Mother in her suite and I gave her a fashion show. She loved what I was wearing. "Oh, darling, you look so beautiful."

Over the years, there were instances where we didn't think my mother was going to make it, so many in fact that I didn't connect the dots that night. Bobby and I went out, had dinner, and came home early. Everything was fine.

The next morning I had scheduled a doctor's appointment in LA for some facial injections, and I didn't feel it necessary to cancel it. I felt secure that Mother was in good hands with the parade of caregivers who took care of her around the clock. Bobby and I called it the "changing of the guard."

Before we left that fateful morning, Bobby and I went into my mother's room to check on her. I asked her if it was all right if we went to LA for a couple of days. "Fine, go," she said.

"Will you be okay?" I asked.

"I hope so," she replied.

That should have been my signal. Mother never said that. Normally, she'd reply, "Of course I'll be okay. You go."

For some reason that morning, I didn't pick up the subtle difference. I called her doctor before we left just to make sure. "Toni, if we need you, we'll call you. Just go." He didn't think it was anything serious. He was the same doctor who didn't think her elevated white count was that serious either.

So Bobby and I drove to LA and I went to my doctor's appointment. Late that afternoon, around five o'clock, one of the caregivers called. "Your mother didn't want me to call you...but I don't like how she's doing."

"Do you think I should come home?" I asked. "I'll come home now."

"Well, let me see how she's doing in a little while and I'll call you back."

Satisfied that it wasn't an emergency, Bobby and I had an early dinner. Less than an hour later, the caregiver called again. "You better come home now."

Five minutes later we were in the car on the way back to Palm Springs. It was about a two-hour drive, but before we got halfway there my cell phone rang. It was the caregiver. Mother had died. Just like Zvia had predicted, I wouldn't be there when it happened.

"No! No! It can't be!" I screamed.

I began to weep uncontrollably as Bobby pulled the car over to the side of the road. Between tears of his own, Bobby tried to console me, but my loss and my guilt were overwhelming. I was angry and blamed myself completely for what had happened. Why didn't I stay home? Why didn't I realize what was happening? All because I was so stupid, so selfish, I just had to have my injections. How much beauty do you need, for God's sake?

When Bobby and I arrived home, my son Adam and his partner Doug were waiting for us. Adam insisted we sit around my mother's bed, explaining that for the first three hours after a person passes, theit spirit stays around, hovering over their physical body. So we sat there: me, Bobby, Adam, Doug, our staff, and our dogs, all keeping my mother company.

At approximately eight o'clock on the evening of Thursday, March 22, 2007, my life changed forever.

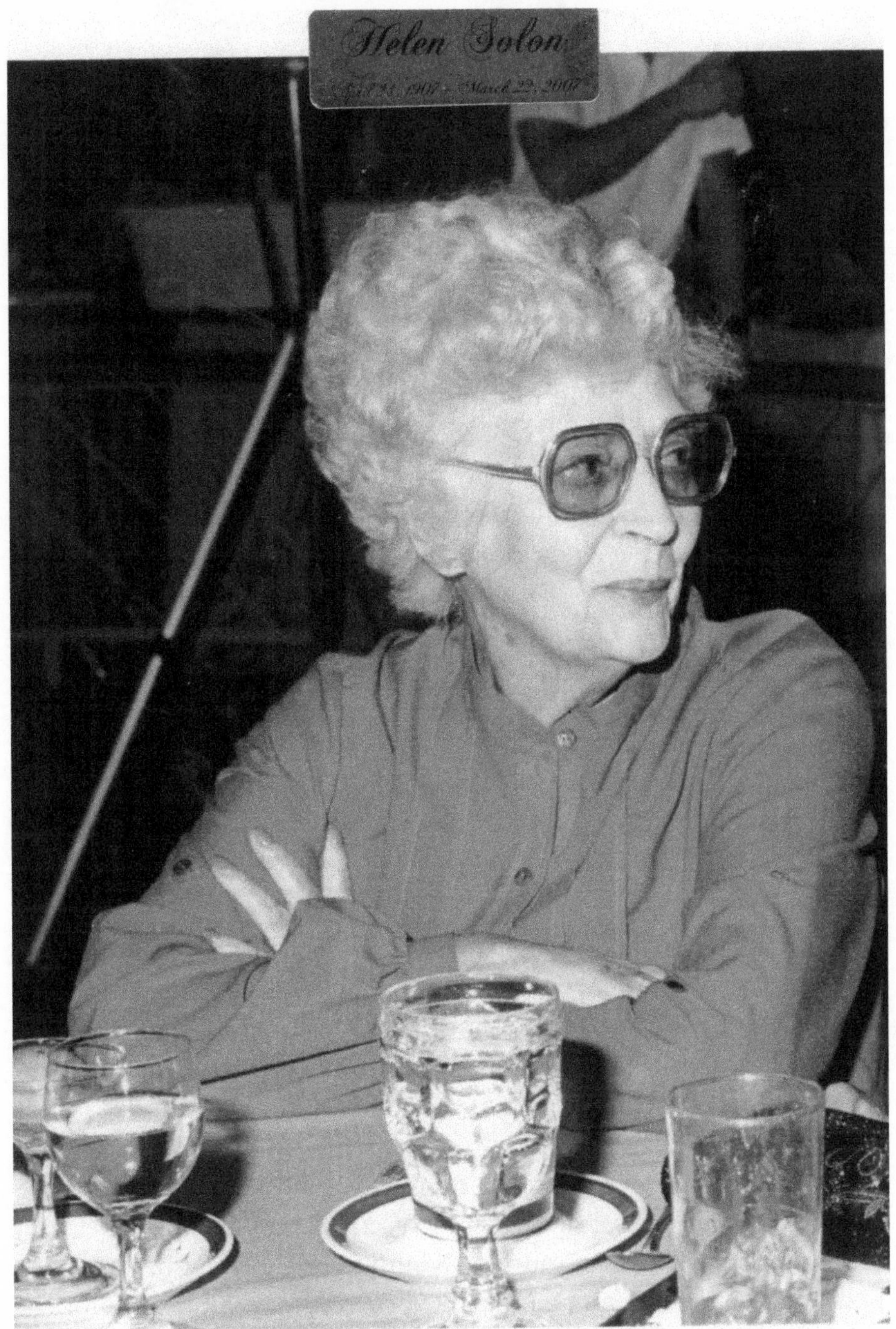

A CELEBRATION OF THE LIFE OF HELEN SOLON

BELOVED MOTHER, GRANDMOTHER AND BEST FRIEND

CHAPTER FIFTY-ONE

A Phone Call from Hillary

As I searched for answers the day after Mother passed, I called a friend who owned a horse named Whiskey. I love horses and thought it might be a good idea to take a ride to clear my mind. My plan was to go up to the mountains that overlook the desert and ride along the trails I had walked and ridden many times before. I knew the trails were dangerous. On occasion a horse might lose its footing and slip, but that was the farthest thing from my mind.

It was early Saturday morning. I was getting dressed to go riding when my housekeeper, Francesca, came running into our bedroom as if she had just seen a ghost. "Mrs. Kramer, Mrs. Kramer...come quickly!" I hurriedly followed her into the family room.

The room had an incredible view through a huge picture window that looked out at the distant mountains, a source of great strength for me. When you see them in the morning, they are one color, in the afternoon a different color. There's nothing more energizing, more amazing than those big gorgeous mountains and the blue sky above them. If only you could put an ocean at the foot of those mountains, you'd really have paradise.

Along the inside of the picture window is an extra-wide sill upon which we displayed framed photos of our family and friends, along with mementos of our time in the desert. A fur-covered miniature stuffed horse that Ruta Lee had given me sat for years between the photos and the window at the deepest part of the sill. But not that Saturday morning.

Instead, the horse was lying on the floor upside down. Only one photo had fallen off the sill: a picture of my mother, Phyllis Diller, and me. Everything else was untouched. Nothing else had moved. It was all a bone-chilling mystery to me how the horse could have fallen off the sill without knocking down the photos in front of it. After an experiment or two, it became clear that the only way the horse could have wound up on the floor was if someone—or some force—had lifted it up and over the photos. I knew then what had happened.

Being psychic, Mother had the ability to reach out to the other side. That morning, I realized she also had the power to reach out from the other side back to the living. Her message was clear: "Toni, do not go horseback riding today."

I didn't.

* * * * *

My psychic, Zvia Holmes, had told me years earlier that when my mother's time came, I wouldn't be with her because she didn't want me there. Leave it to Mother, always worried about me first.

Her funeral was scheduled to be held at Hillside Memorial Cemetery in Los Angeles, the final resting place for some of Hollywood's brightest stars, from Al Jolson to Michael Landon to Leonard Nimoy. Mother would have approved of the company.

My television partner and best gal pal, Ruta Lee, had promised from the start of Mother's health issues that she would deliver the eulogy. Ruta could have made a career of giving eulogies, whether she knew the deceased or not, and I'm not kidding. There was just one problem: six thousand miles. Ruta was in the middle of the Mediterranean on a private yacht, and it was impossible for her to get back in time. The eulogy was up to me.

To say I struggled to put my words on paper is an understatement. How do you say a final good-bye to your best friend, to the woman who single-handedly raised you to be everything you had become, who shared your laughter, held you when you cried, cared for you when you were sick, convinced you there was nothing in the world you couldn't do, and who was the backbone of your very existence? How was I supposed to find the strength to carry myself through the ultimate farewell when the grief and the thousands of other emotions I was feeling were all-consuming?

It was 11:25 a.m. on the Monday before the funeral. I was locked in my office at our Bel Air home, attempting to steady my nerves and find the right words to say good-bye. I told my husband, Bobby, not to disturb me. I needed quiet time to reflect and create the eulogy. That's when I heard the light knock on my office door.

"Bobby, I really can't stop right now. I'm a mess," I cried, fighting to control my emotions.

"I'm sorry, honey, but there's a call for you. I think you'll want to take it." He paused. "It's Hillary."

Hillary and I spoke to each other like girlfriends. Bobby and I had been invited to a fund-raiser for her the weekend of Mother's passing. Hillary said she asked my friends at the party why we weren't there, and they told her about my mother.

"When I heard the news I recalled a conversation you had with my mother, Dorothy," said Hillary. "You once told me how inseparable you and Helen were. I knew you had to be devastated."

Hillary knew a lot about my life and my interests from the many conversations we had over the years. We always enjoyed sharing thoughts and ideas about a variety of subjects, including health and longevity.

"Toni, I think your mother would agree that the world needs to know you and your story. You should write a book. It will help you heal while you help others."

Mother always told me I should write my story, but until I heard Hillary echo her advice, it hadn't really sunk in.

"You've led a remarkable life. You've met and interviewed so many important and powerful people. More than that, Toni, you've faced some incredible odds and climbed each mountain that stood in your way. Your story will be an inspiration, especially to women who have faced their own share of hardships with their husbands, children, or careers. Do you understand how much hope you can give them just by sharing the details of your life?"

"But what would I write? How could I begin?"

"You tell them everything. The things you've done, the things you've seen, the troubles you've had. Tell the world all of it. Let women everywhere see that there is a light at the end of the tunnel. Even if everything seems doomed, there is always a way to make things better. We are all born with the burden of making our lives count for something, and this can be your way to make yours count even more. Toni, promise me you'll share your story."

"You have my word," I replied.

I glanced at the clock and realized we had been talking for half an hour. Reality came flooding back in. I had a eulogy to write.

"Hillary, did you forget you're running for president?"

"I didn't forget." She laughed. "But you're my friend. I wanted to make sure you were all right."

After we hung up I was in a far different place. The simple act of her reaching out, despite the intensity of her work schedule, to check on me, that one gesture of friendship helped to put me back in control.

I suddenly felt my scattered thoughts shift together like puzzle pieces being pressed into place.

CHAPTER FIFTY-TWO

A Tribute to the Pink Queen

Fighting back my grief and the guilt that somehow Mother's death was my fault, I set about making the arrangements for the funeral. I had her taken to a mortuary in Palm Springs. "I don't want that yellow, early Egyptian makeup on her," I told them. "I want her skin to be the color it always is. I want her to look beautiful. I want her to have pink lipstick. And I want to see her before you're finished."

I gave the makeup person an extra hundred dollars to make sure Mother went to heaven looking pretty. And she did.

On the day of the funeral in LA, I dressed in pink, my mother's favorite color. My two sons wore pink ties with their suits, as did Bobby. Marlin, our assistant at the time, brought pink balloons. All the flowers were pink. Bobby had gone himself to pick out the casket—white with pink flowers on it.

I dressed Mother in pink too. For two days prior I had gone back and forth to the mortuary to make sure she looked like Lana Turner, the movie star she had often been compared to. Her hair, her makeup, her dress...everything was perfect. Even her pink lipstick.

Bobby's son Stephen, his wife, Wendy, and all of their children were there to support me, and their presence meant so very much to me. Many of my closest friends came as well, including my one-time assistant Sammi and her husband, Robert Vudgrovic. Sammi, who knew my mother very well, said a few loving words about their relationship.

"No one is to cry," I said. "This is to be a celebration. Mother would want it that way. She would want people to look beautiful and be happy. Be sad in your hearts...but carry on with dignity."

At the end of the service, Marlin released all the pink balloons, and they floated skyward like puffs of cotton candy. Although we were all fighting back our emotions, everyone except my son Adam kept their tears in check.

When we arrived home, we found a huge white orchid plant from Nancy Pelosi, along with a note expressing her regrets. When Ruta returned from Europe, she gave me a pink rose tree that I planted outside Mother's window. Every time I look at it, I feel as though my mother is seeing it too.

A tribute to the Pink Queen.

* * * * *

In the days that followed, I tried to piece together exactly why my mother had died. About a week before her death, I was in LA and received a call from Lydia, one of her caregivers. Because mother had a chronic bladder condition she had to be monitored daily. Lydia told me that the nurse who was supposed to change my mother's catheter hadn't changed it for over eighty days. The recommended schedule was every 30 to 45 days.

I nearly jumped through the phone. "Why didn't you tell me? If you don't tell me, how can I know?"

Lydia was obviously shaken. "The nurse warned us not to tell you. She ordered us to write in our logs that she changed it. She said if we told you the truth, she'd make sure we never worked again."

I couldn't believe it. My next call was to the nurse.

"I understand you haven't been changing my mother's catheter. What are you doing? Get over there and change it now!"

The nurse made all kinds of excuses. "Well, she didn't need it….it was too hard to do… she always gets an infection when I change it…" She insisted it was better not to disrupt the way things were than to change the catheter. Under pressure, she agreed to change it the next day.

In hindsight, I realized she was an irresponsible liar. As a nurse, she had an obligation to protect the life of her patient. I'm sure she was aware of the impending danger to my mother's life. One could easily say she had murdered my mother with her negligence.

Here's what I believe happened: When the nurse finally changed the catheter, all the bacteria that had been growing for more than eighty days was released into my mother's body. The nurse changed it on Saturday, March 17th. Mother died on Thursday, March 22nd.

When I researched how she died, I learned that you can die from a bladder infection if it has time to poison the entire body. It's called septicemia. That's why she had the cough, although the doctor wouldn't admit that.

I don't care what it said on the death certificate—I know what happened. She wasn't ill with anything else. Sometime later the doctor admitted to me that my mother did die from septicemia.

In the days surrounding Mother's death and funeral, I was obsessed with bringing her death to justice. It was obvious even to me that my mother's white blood cell count in January should have been investigated further.

My relentless research and focus on the circumstances of her passing were no doubt coping mechanisms for the sadness and loss I was feeling. I was overwhelmed—my mother, my best friend for my entire life, was gone because of lies, incompetence, threats, and stupidity.

The hospital defended the nurse who had lied about changing my mother's catheter, but after much prodding on my part—and a little push from some lawyers—they agreed to change the rules so that what happened to my mother would hopefully never happen to anyone else.

The rule change didn't bring back my mother, nor dissipate my grief and guilt, but I felt vindicated for pursuing what I thought was a just cause.

CHAPTER FIFTY-THREE

The Boat Begins to Sink

It was the spring of 2008, a few months before the primary election. At this point I had spent enough time in Washington to grow comfortable in the political environment. I was now as much at ease in D.C. as I was in Hollywood, and I liked it even more. I felt I belonged in Washington.

Despite the Obama factor, I felt sure that Hillary—one way or another—was going to be the next president of the United States. She'd been preparing for it her entire life. I was happy for her and optimistic about my own future. It was a euphoric time. I had a smile on my face and in my heart.

But alas, isn't this the most classic storyline we know? It's the great rise before the fall, the smooth sailing before the boat begins to sink. As the primaries grew closer, we all began to realize it wasn't going to turn out the way we had hoped. We didn't really speak about it openly, but I began to feel there wasn't going to be a happy ending.

Much of my anger was aimed at Nancy Pelosi. She had deserted Hillary and taken up with Obama. Even worse, as a woman, I believed Nancy *betrayed* Hillary. Why would the woman who broke the glass ceiling—the first woman in history to be elected Speaker of the House—not want another woman to join her at the top of the ladder? Maybe it's the combination of her sweet smile and pit bull mentality, but I can only surmise that Nancy preferred to be the most powerful woman in Washington.

There is little doubt in my mind that when Nancy threw her support to Obama, she used her leverage as Speaker of the House to persuade many of the super delegates not to endorse Hillary at a time when she needed them the most. Had Hillary gotten their endorsements early on, it might have changed the course of the election.

June 7, 2008. The boat sank. Hillary suspended her campaign and endorsed Barack Obama.

Shortly thereafter, Debbie and Sim Farar phoned to invite Bobby and me to a small buffet they were having for Hillary. As depressed as I was about the situation, I was determined to show support for my friend as best I could.

As I got ready for the party, my spirits were truly at their lowest. The reality of what was happening had sunk in. In my sad state, I recalled Mama Gabor's advice, "If you look good, you feel good."

I decided to wear a bright color to lighten my mood. Orange is one of my favorites, and I needed all the help I could get. So I wore bright orange from head to toe.

I walked into Deb's party with a big smile, trying to be as cheerful as possible. Bobby and I scanned the room, and I spotted Hillary saying hello to some of the guests. Hillary always greets people individually. As I watched her, I was saddened to see how tired she looked, how unhappy and beaten she seemed to be. And yet there she was, trying to be nice to everyone through her own doleful time.

Hillary caught sight of me through the crowd, and her eyes opened wide. For just that split second the twinkle came back. "Toni," she called.

We hugged like old friends. I don't recall exactly what I said, but I know I didn't say "I'm sorry." That would have been saying the obvious. We chatted for a few minutes before it was time for the buffet out by the pool.

With everyone seated after the dinner, Hillary got up and spoke. It was clear she wasn't happy, but still, she was gracious. Despite being the one who needed consoling, her speech was all about comforting us. She thanked each and every one of the guests by name. I'm sure there were hundreds of other luncheons and dinners all over the country where she did the exact same thing, but she managed to make us feel like *we* were the special ones.

I glanced over at Bobby and saw tears in his eyes. He was clearly just as upset as I was. For the second time, Hillary's words caused me to realize something about my own life. Just as she had helped me to recognize my mother's wish for me to share my story, she helped me see how absolutely amazing my husband is to me. I'd always known, of course, but sitting there at dinner and seeing how invested Bobby had become in the affair truly immersed me in a feeling of wonder for a few moments. Bobby had been by my side through it all, pushing us forward with my dreams of Washington and becoming just as emotionally attached to Hillary's campaign as I had.

A true partner is one who helps you become the best person you can possibly be. Bobby has done that for me since day one, and my heart filled with a mixture of gratitude, adoration, and pure love when I saw his reaction.

As Hillary's words washed over us, I took Bobby's hand. We were angry and upset over what had happened, but we were in it together, for better or worse as always.

* * * * *

I saw Hillary one more time before the election. Haim Saban, an Israeli-American producer and media mogul who gave the world *Power Rangers* among other children's television programs, threw a party for Hillary at his hilltop estate in Beverly Hills. I'd been there several times before for other political events. There were about forty people in attendance that night, and I was overjoyed to see my place card right beside Hillary's. Haim was seated on her right and I was seated on her left.

I could also tell something was different about Hillary from when I'd seen her last at the Farars' house…different in a good way. The excitement in her eyes was back. Bobby and I both noticed it, and we thought for sure something was afoot.

It wasn't long after that she accepted the position of Secretary of State.

CHAPTER FIFTY-FOUR

Phyllis Diller

I loved Phyllis Diller. I met Phyllis in the late seventies when I interviewed her for my column with the *National Tattler*. We immediately bonded and became great friends.

Phyllis loved to laugh, and what a laugh she had. It seemed to start somewhere in her toes and explode like an erupting volcano. It swept up anyone within earshot into the moment with laughter of their own. While Phyllis's comedic image dominated her persona, most people didn't have a clue how bright she really was. She was a refreshing mix of brains and humor that drew people in like "friends" to Facebook.

Phyllis lived in great style. She had one of the most gorgeous homes in Brentwood, brimming with life and a constant array of fresh roses in a variety of colors. A mega-sized portrait of Bob Hope hung in her living room. The tribute understandable since Bob gave Phyllis her first real break on big-time television, nudging her early TV weather girl days into the past.

I knew Bob very well in Palm Springs. He was a humble and friendly man who appreciated beautiful women and always had time for yours truly. I interviewed him several times, including a TV special with him celebrating his birthday on the NBC affiliate in Cleveland, Ohio, Bob's hometown. Bob Hope, another spectacular Gemini.

The first interview I conducted with Phyllis became a hilarious comedy skit. I remember she took me into her giant-sized closet, and we did the entire interview right there. She put on all her funny wigs and showed me her outrageous clothes, dropping into character with each new outfit. Too bad we weren't filming. It would have made great television history.

Toni with Bob Hope.

Toni interviews Phyllis Diller in her closet.

Years later, Toni with Phyllis Diller at the home of
Sherry Hackett, Buddy's widow.

Somewhere in 2004, I took my mother to a luncheon at the Beverly Hills Hotel. Phyllis was there and came over to our table. She made a big fuss over Mother, and the three of us took a photo together.

When we got back to Palm Springs, my mother tucked that photo onto the edge of the mirror in her bedroom. Every week after that, Phyllis sent her a funny card with something silly written on it. One time the card read: "Helen, don't ever hire a housekeeper named Dusty."

If she didn't send a card, Phyllis would send a short note or a maybe a little trinket of jewelry. Whatever it was, it was always funny, thoughtful, and good for a laugh. She never missed a week up until my mother passed away in 2007. Phyllis was an amazing human being.

My husband Bobby and I had dinner with Phyllis one night and told her our plans to move to Palm Beach. Phyllis lit up like a Christmas tree. "There's somebody I want you to meet. Her name is Terry Ebert and we've been friends for thirty years. You're two of a kind...and you're going to love each other."

A couple of weeks later, Terry arrived in LA with her future husband, Joe Mendozza. Bobby and I took them and Phyllis to dinner at Hillcrest Country Club. Terry and I instantly felt as if we'd known each other forever.

"The next time you come to Palm Beach, you have to call me," Terry said. "We'll get together and I'll show you around."

Not too long after that, Bobby and I returned to Florida and we met up with Terry and Joe. They took us to all the good restaurants and filled us in on what it was like to live in Palm Beach. Nobody could have been more loving and gracious, and though it was only our second time together, it didn't take long for Terry and me to realize we had a lot in common. It was a match made in heaven, soul sisters, a relationship that has only grown closer over the years.

Toni with Terry Ebert Mendozza, known as 'Twinnie'.

At the time, Terry and Joe, a talented builder/designer, lived in an oceanfront mansion in an area a stone's throw from Palm Beach called Manalapan. The fabulous property ran between the ocean and the Intracoastal, with a man-made lake in between—complete with a few mean-spirited swans.

After Terry and Joe got married at Mar-a-Lago in December 2009, she sold the house in Manalapan and they bought a new one. There, Terry's fascination with Cleopatra was brought to life by Joe, who created a Romanesque ambiance throughout their new home. He also built a home theater that included an ornate bed so Terry could recline and watch her favorite movies, especially *Cleopatra*, which she does daily. To complete the picture and make the scene even more authentic, there is an open coffin at the foot of the movie screen that contains a manikin that Terry made up to look like Cleopatra, complete with heavy eye makeup, dark wig, and gold lamé gown from Terry's own closet.

The last time I saw Phyllis was June 12, 2012 when Bobby and I renewed our vows for the twentieth anniversary of our marriage. We held the elaborate ceremony at the Bel Air Hotel. Phyllis was one of my eleven matrons of honor. Like our original wedding, the event was a Las Vegas extravaganza.

Ruta Lee emceed the festivities that followed the ceremony in the hotel ballroom. Jack Carter told jokes, the incredible Helen Greco, former wife of Spike Jones, sang, and actors Michael Dante and Anne Jeffries spoke.

Also there was my long-time friend Carol Connors, who wrote the theme song for the movie *Rocky* (Kim Jung Un's favorite song). Among other songs, Carol wrote the theme for our TV show, *Talk of the Town*. I exchange emails and texts almost daily with her, and years ago she gave me the nickname BTL, which stands for "bigger than life."

Just prior to the party, Phyllis suffered a stroke. I was told her condition was getting worse and her eyesight was failing. Still, she showed up for the ceremony in a wheelchair, obviously not well, but all smiles and laughter.

That was probably the last night Phyllis was seen in public. She passed away two months later.

So much goodness has come from my relationship with Terry that we refer to Phyllis as our guiding angel. And each other as "Twinnie."

Toni and guests at her 20th wedding anniversary celebration.

Phyllis Diller at Toni's 20th wedding anniversary celebration, ever the trouper.

Phyllis lives on in my memories and through the photos of her on my piano as well as some of her special artwork. Not many know this, but she was a great artist on top of all her other talents, including being a symphony conductor. I will always be thankful for my special time with Phyllis. She meant so much to me and my mother.

* * * * *

With the wound of Washington still throbbing freshly in our minds, Bobby and I were in desperate need of a pick-me-up. Between LA and Palm Springs, we still had a lot of friends. Unfortunately, when you have a lot of the *same* friends for a long time, the conversation can become a little stale. Lives sometimes become intertwined in ways that aren't really healthy. We wanted a shot of new blood, a new experience, a new challenge.

And so, with Terry on one arm and my cousin Enid on the other, I was ready to move to Florida. But the move wouldn't happen overnight.

By this time, my cousin Enid and her husband, Louis, were living in West Palm Beach, Florida. We spoke on the phone daily, and still do. I found Enid to be an incredibly grounded person, a sharp contrast to yours truly, who has a tendency to be "on" a lot of the time. I'm an air sign, I can't help it. Maybe it's because of all my years in Hollywood, but when I'm on… I'm *on*! I always think it's my responsibility to entertain everyone in the room, even if I don't know them.

Enid is a breath of fresh air. She's patient, loving, and has broadened my horizons in ways I never thought about. She encouraged me to work with a personal trainer, introduced me to a life coach, and even taught me to meditate.

Enid was a truly positive influence on me at a time when I needed it most. I credit her with my development as a spiritual person, and I have become more in tune with myself, more in sync with the universe.

After returning home from one of our frequent trips to Florida, Bobby was reviewing our bills, and joked, "You know, you might as well just pick out a house there, because these hotel bills are killing me."

So I took him up on the offer and we found the perfect Palm Beach home, nestled comfortably amidst my star-studded neighbors. Never a dull moment

CHAPTER FIFTY-FIVE

Adam and David

My youngest son, Adam, lives in Northern California. When he was in his late teens, his older brother David confided in me, "Mom, I think Adam is gay."

My first reaction was disbelief. Maybe I was naïve at the time, but the possibility that Adam might be gay never crossed my mind. He eventually revealed to me that he had told my mother he was gay long before he told me. True to Mother's character, she never betrayed his confidence. Adam admitted he knew he was gay when he was only eleven or twelve, when he went to military school. He said he felt a much stronger attraction to boys than girls, a lifestyle he maintained as he grew into a fine adult.

Adam has lived with his partner, Douglas, for more than twenty years. They found each other on an online dating service, and met face-to-face for the first time at a coffee shop in Hollywood. Douglas was in college at the time. They dated for about a year before they moved in together.

Douglas is very artistic and has a degree from Cal Arts. Bobby and I went to his graduation. He is a talented set designer and has worked on many theater shows. He also taught classes at The College of the Desert, a community college in Palm Desert, California. He's presently teaching at a college in Northern California where they live.

Adam has a great job with an automotive company, and has won a number of awards for his work, including one from Honda Motors. He's also a computer guru and proficient at creating websites.

While Adam's revelation took me by surprise, I certainly wasn't angry or upset. My reaction was probably influenced by my years in Hollywood, where I have many friends and associates who are gay or bisexual.

When I write about my children, I feel a number of emotions. Among them is a sense of unease. It's hard for me to look back and say that I was the best mother I could have been, because being a mother was a role that didn't come easy to me. To steal a Hollywood term, I was hopelessly miscast.

Don't get me wrong. I love my children, but I was never as close to them as I should have been. I made a difficult choice, one I felt I had to make. I sacrificed my time with them for a career that could support us all financially. As a result, I have a distance from my children that is utterly alien to me given my own close relationship with my mother.

Toni's mother with her grandsons, David (left) and Adam (right).

Despite the distance, I've always been there for Adam and David for whatever they needed, and more. Even so, I know I've come up short as their mom in many ways. It fills me with sadness to think about it.

* * * * *

After many, many years of a long and very painful struggle, Bobby and I thought my son David had finally conquered his drug addiction. He became a missionary, an ordained minister in the State of Florida, as well as a Scientologist.

I know that people have negative things to say about Scientology, but at the time it appeared to save David's life. While David moved fairly high up the Scientology scale, he never reached the level of "being clear," like Tom Cruise, John Travolta, and Kirstie Alley. Attaining this level means all of the bad memories have been removed from the reactive mind through a process known as auditing. This was the reason we sent David to the main Scientology Center in Clearwater, Florida, hoping it would end his dependency on drugs. Unfortunately, it did not.

David is and always has been a fabulous, self-taught musician. He plays the guitar in the style of Carlos Santana. His band played professional gigs and he performed at Scientology events where the crowds loved his music.

A little while before David joined Scientology, he met a girl named Poppy. "Mom, she's just like you," he said. "She's so beautiful. She just reminds me of you, and I know you're going to like her."

For some reason, David was hesitant to have us meet Poppy in person. He'd make excuses as to why we couldn't meet, always acting very elusive. He finally gave in, and we invited them to our country club in Palm Springs for dinner. When I saw her walk into the dining room, I thought, *Oh, my…she really is beautiful.* More importantly, I saw a warm smile and a light in her face that I instantly fell in love with.

Poppy was in her late twenties, about the same age as David. I could see she was a bit apprehensive at meeting us, so I insisted she sit next to me. Within minutes she relaxed. She was a truly lovely girl, and everything David had said about her was right on. She had a great chuckle, a great voice, and a great big heart you could see across the room. I felt that David had finally found the perfect mate. It warmed me to see such a positive relationship forming in my son's life after so many negatives had taken root.

"You know, Poppy, you're about my size," I said to her at the end of dinner. "Why don't you come over to the house? I have some clothes I want you to try on. In fact, you resemble me enough to be my daughter…so right here and now I'm adopting you!"

Poppy giggled. All traces of apprehension had vanished. It was a wonderful moment, but after dinner, David told me Poppy's story, breaking my heart in two.

I learned that Poppy's mother had abandoned her at a young age, while her father remained close. According to David, Poppy got into drugs and did some really bad things. She sold her body, just like Julia Roberts' prostitute character in *Pretty Woman*. My eyes filled with tears as David told me the story. What had this beautiful girl done to herself? Regardless of her past, I knew Poppy was someone worth saving. Selfishly, I suppose, I thought maybe Poppy could help save my son.

Poppy and David saw each other for a while after that, but David continued using drugs, which eventually caused their permanent breakup. I was always encouraging Poppy to stay on the right path despite what David was doing. "Poppy, you have to get your life together...whether it includes David or not. I really wish you two would marry, but if David doesn't stay sober, you can't stay with him. I'd love to have you as my daughter, but it might cost you dearly."

Unfortunately, as with most girls in David's life, Poppy just seemed to fade away.

A summer or two later, Bobby and I were out to dinner in Palm Springs. It was an unusually warm night. We left the restaurant around ten o'clock and walked to our car when Poppy suddenly appeared out of the night like an apparition. Seeing her right there in my face after two years shocked the hell out of me. I took a step back and my heart sank. She was barely recognizable, a mere shadow of the beautiful young woman I had met that night at our country club. Now, she looked bedraggled and wasted.

"Poppy," I cried, "what are you doing here?"

She could barely look me in the eye. "I don't have any money...and I need money for a room to stay in tonight. I need a room to stay in."

As much as I liked Poppy and wanted to help her, I knew it would be a mistake to give her money. I pointed to the small hotel across the street. I think it was called the Stardust. "Fine," I said. "Let's go over to the hotel and I'll get you a room."

"No, no...I can do it," she said, but I remained firm.

"No, you can't. I won't let you."

Bobby stayed in the car and I walked across the street to the hotel with Poppy. "This is my mom," Poppy said to the clerk behind the desk. Was I being manipulated? Was she trying to con the desk clerk? Probably both, but I still felt something for Poppy and I wanted to help.

"Do you have a room for her," I asked, cutting in. "I want to pay cash."

As we checked in, two other girls joined us, friends of Poppy's. I assumed they were hookers or addicts as well. One was tall, Cajun-looking, a beautiful, light-skinned black girl. The other was a slender redhead. It was a bad situation and getting worse by the minute, and I decided to take charge.

"Come on, girls, let's go outside. Let's visit for a while."

The girls went outside with me, and we stood at the corner of the hotel on Palm Canyon Drive. Bobby was well in view and could see us from his car across the street. Whether it would do any good or not, I needed to have my say.

"Girls, you're wasting your time. Each of you is beautiful. Each of you can do something better with your life than worrying about the next hit...your next smoke...your next trick. Don't you realize what you're doing with your lives? Don't you see the risks you're taking? Someone is going to kill you—or you're going to kill yourself. You're going to overdose...or something awful is going to happen if you don't straighten out. Look at you...you're all gorgeous now...but you're not going to be young forever...and you won't remain beautiful because of what you're doing to yourselves. Let's talk about it. Please, let's talk about how you came to be on this street corner."

We stood there and talked until one o'clock in the morning. By the time we were done, I knew everything about their lives...their childhood...their education or lack of it...and why they did what they did. For three hours we talked and never once did my husband, God bless him, get out of the car and urge me to leave. When we finally stopped talking, I hugged them and they promised they would try to get straight. I had no idea if they would, but I had hope.

I learned a short time after that Poppy had gotten pregnant and made a complete exit from "the life." Because of the pregnancy she had given up drugs and decided to become a nurse, the very best nurse she could be. She had the baby, a gorgeous boy with dark hair and dark eyes, and she seemed to be on the right path.

A short time later Poppy was diagnosed with cervical cancer. She was treated, told she was okay, and continued going to nursing school. Poppy and David were just friends at this point, and I would only hear bits and pieces of what was going on with her, but it made me beyond happy to know she was trying to get her life in order.

A year later, Poppy stopped by our house in Palm Springs with her son. He was an adorable little boy, and I could see she was the most devoted, doting mother. She had managed to get straight and was working part time at a Starbucks, dedicating herself to her son, her sobriety, and her nursing profession.

David, unfortunately, was still fighting his demons.

CHAPTER FIFTY-SIX

Connections

I love Europe, especially anyplace where I can speak French. So I was delighted when our friend Palm Beach philanthropist Lois Pope invited Bobby and me to go to Monaco with her.

A G5 and a few hours later we arrived in the South of France. It had been a few years since I'd been to Monaco, and if anything, it was even more expensive than I remembered.

Only one square mile in size, there are more jewelry stores, fashion boutiques, and private wealth banks per square inch than anywhere else on the planet. The real estate is some of the most expensive in the world, and the apartment buildings climb the mountainsides like cement and glass vines. It's nothing to spend ten or eleven million euros on a two- or three-bedroom apartment. According to a recent survey of places where people live the longest, Monaco is number one. Hmm…and they say money can't buy happiness and longevity.

I noticed that photographs of the late Prince Rainier and his late movie-star wife, Grace Kelly, were still everywhere. Also plentiful were photos of their son, Prince Albert, and his bride, Charlene Wittstock. The current princess may not be as beautiful as Grace Kelly, but her figure is outstanding. In one photo on the cover of *Monaco Magazine*, her hair was swept up to give her that memorable Kelly-esque look.

No image captured the attitude of Monaco as perfectly as the one I saw as I strolled along the street with Bobby. A chauffeur-driven Mercedes pulled up ahead of us, and my eye was drawn to the license plate: "PRIVILEGED." That really sums it up.

One night we had dinner on the terrace at Hotel L'Hermitage, where we were staying. We had a panoramic view that overlooked Monaco's main harbor, Port Hercules, below. I was in awe at the size and scope of the yachts moored there, many well over two hundred feet in length.

Toni and Bobby, a night in Monaco.

"Almost every yacht down there is for sale," said Alexi Mercentes, a sophisticated Greek jet-setter. He and his then-wife, Veronica, the widow of Dr. Robert Atkins of the famed Atkins Diet, were hosting our dinner group. Alexi owns a residence in Monte Carlo, and I knew them from Palm Beach, where they were very active in society as well.

I gestured to another boat moored not too far away. "Whose yacht is that?"

"That boat belonged to Stavros Niarchos."

"Wasn't he married to Tina Onassis?" I asked.

"Yes." Alexi nodded.

My gaze shifted to an older boat in the next slip. The name emblazoned on the bow read: "CHRISTINA." It was Aristotle Onassis' yacht, named after his late daughter and now available for charters and dinners at sea. *This is so strange,* I thought. Even after death, Onassis and Niarchos sat side by side. They may be gone, but their boats were still there to tell stories. How eerie.

As a little background, the web of intrigue that embraced the intertwining lives of shipping rivals Onassis and Niarchos is truly a Greek tragedy. The CliffsNotes version of the story goes something like this: Athina was the daughter of shipping magnate Stavros Livanos and the first wife of Aristotle Onassis. Athina is the mother of Christina Onassis, and she divorced Aristotle when she allegedly caught him in bed with his lover, opera singer Maria Callas. Athina's sister, Eugenia, was married to Stavros Niarchos, who was known as the Golden Greek and who had a reputation for being rough on women. Eugenia divorced Niarchos after nearly twenty years of marriage, and she died a few years later from an overdose of barbiturates. Shortly after Eugenia's death, her sister Tina, then divorced from John Spencer-Churchill, a nephew of Sir Winston Churchill, married Niarchos, and three years later she, too, died from a drug overdose in Paris. Phew!

But wait, there's more. Onassis lost his son Alexander in a plane crash at the age of twenty-four, and two years later Onassis himself died while still married to Jackie Kennedy. Many said that Alexander's death was the beginning of the end for Onassis.

I met Christina in California when she had just married an American, Joe Bolker, who lived in Century City. Christina and I took an instant liking to one another. She was married three more times after Bolker, the last time to Thierry Roussel, with whom she had her only child, Athina. Christina died pathetically at the age of thirty-seven in Buenos Aires, and Athina became the richest child in the world. Now thirty-three, and an accomplished horse jumper, Athina is still one of the wealthiest women in the world.

The experience in Monaco made me realize that people with real money form a very small circle in a very small world, and they're no more than a G5 apart. It's all very cozy. Not six degrees of separation—more like an omelet, with everyone in their world right in the middle of it. And that's the absolute reality.

If I needed more evidence, I found it just recently when my friend and neighbor Ava Roosevelt invited me to a dinner she was hosting at the Beach Club, a private club at the North End of Palm Beach.

Ava Roosevelt with Christopher Twardy

I know the club well and even gave a talk there a couple of years earlier for the elite Roundtable Group, one of the oldest organizations in Palm Beach. My talk was about Hollywood and Washington.

At the Beach Club Ava introduced us to Paola Bacchini-Rosenshein and her husband, Arnold. Paola was born in Rome. She's beautiful, and reminded me of the late Italian movie star Virna Lisi.

At the end of dinner, I found myself at the dessert table with Paola. "Were you ever married before?" she asked in her charming Italian accent.

"Yes," I said. "Do you happen to know a man by the name of Tony Murray?"

Paola's mouth dropped open in shock. "He is our best friend!"

Tony's ears must have been burning as we spoke about him and his family. I realized then that the omelet of association had just gotten smaller.

Meanwhile, back in the south of France, anyone who wants to see or be seen in Monte Carlo dines on the terrace of Hotel de Paris. In a very, very small way it reminds me of where I lived in Brooklyn and the ice cream store Cookies on 16th Street and Avenue J. It was the place to hang out, where all the kids from school would gather. Okay, so it wasn't the Hotel de Paris, but you get the picture.

The conversation at dinner was lively and very telling, with Alexi, Veronica, Lois, Bobby, and I all sharing stories from our lives. At one point, I remember someone asked me how I became a model. I told them the story of how I went to the Huntington Hartford Modeling Agency when I was fourteen. There I met a stunningly beautiful woman named Blanche who told me I was too fat to be a model.

Everyone had a healthy laugh at that tidbit.

"It's true, she said I was too chubby. But she did concede that I had a photogenic face, and she thought I might do well in head shots for magazine covers. Before she could sign me to the agency, I had to meet Huntington Hartford himself. I tried not to seem nervous when I went into his office. He was middle-aged at the time and spoke like no one I had ever met before. His cadence was like a man from a different era. Very proper, very refined, probably due to his wealthy upbringing and upper-crust schooling. In some ways he was sort of feminine, but I knew he wasn't. After all, he was married five times and had an eye for a pretty face."

"And what happened?" asked Alexi.

"Well, Mr. Hartford said, 'Toni, do you want to be a model?' And fourteen-year-old me said in all earnestness, 'Yes, I do.' Mr. Hartford eyed me up and down, shook my hand firmly, and said, 'I think you're just perfect.' And that was it, I was suddenly a model."

Of course, there was some hard work put into my modeling career, but the concept of me at fourteen going out and simply *doing it,* seemed to amaze my friends. But for me, it was just another "if you can think it, you can do it" situation. I could hear my mother's words ringing in my ears.

I was shocked when one of my friends told me that Huntington Hartford died broke on New York's Bowery. Hartford's grandfather was the principal founder of The Great Atlantic and Pacific Tea Company, which later became the A & P grocery store chain. He had inherited a ton of money, and it seemed impossible to me that such a kind and gracious man would meet such an unbelievable end. Curious, I checked it out and learned that, yes, Hartford did blow through most of the fortune he inherited, but he died at age ninety-seven at his home in the Bahamas, not on New York's Bowery.

As much as I love Monaco, I think my heart truly resides in Sardinia. The island has maintained a certain mystique and glamour over the years, and has become a very popular destination for wealthy Russians who own multimillion-dollar homes there. It should come as no surprise that Vladimir Putin, the Russian president, has the largest estate of all. But then, it's just one of the twenty residences it is believed he has all over the world.

My favorite place there is Hotel Cali di Volpe, where you can have the most fabulous brunch in the world (and one of the most expensive) while people-watching, especially on Sundays. The hotel was built by Aga Kahn III, and the romantic setting is where his son Aly Kahn married actress Rita Hayworth, an unbelievable number of years ago.

For me, Sardinia has some of the best shops, best food, and lots of interesting people. I don't know this for a fact, but I wonder sometimes if I'm drawn to Sardinia not only because it is a spectacular place to visit but because of my Russian heritage. My great-grandfather was the best friend and financial advisor to Czar Alexander III of Russia, known as "The Bear."

Prince Aly Kahn and Rita Hayworth's daughter, Princess Yasmin, who bears a striking resemblance to her mother, supervised her mother's care until she died from Alzheimer's in 1987. Not many know this, but Rita Hayworth became an accomplished artist in her later years as she battled the inevitable.

I did three TV specials on Alzheimer's for my *Talk of the Town* TV series, one with Princess Yasmin. I'm very proud of the specials, and they were very well received. I learned from the people I interviewed how heartbreaking the disease is, not only for the patient but for the families.

I had lunch with Princess Yasmin in Palm Beach before completing my book. Since her mother's death she has devoted her life to finding a cure for the disease, and she is president of Alzheimer's Disease International.

Seeing Princess Yasmin again after so many years assured me that the omelet has no geographical boundries.

CHAPTER FIFTY-SEVEN

Poppy

As Bobby and I were about to leave Monaco, my cell phone rang. "Hello, Toni? This is Sky."

At first the name didn't register. "Sky?"

"Poppy's father."

"Oh, of course. How are you?"

I had never met Sky, but we had spoken on the phone once or twice before. David adored Sky and told me so much about him that I felt I knew him. He was a straight shooter, a kind person. No matter what trouble Poppy had gotten into—he was always there for her.

"Toni, I have something to tell you. Poppy has left us," he said, his voice cracked.

"What? What do you mean?" I asked, confused.

"She's gone," he replied.

"What happened? When?"

"A few days ago, the cancer…it came back with a vengeance."

It was as if someone had punched me in the stomach. "Sky, that can't be. That just can't be," I said, unable to grasp the truth. My mind was a jumble of thoughts and the words just tumbled out. "She finally got her life together…her beautiful son…such a great mother…she became a nurse…she gave up drugs...she did everything right. She worked so hard, Sky…how could she be gone?"

"I know," he said. There was a long pause before he spoke again. "I picked up her ashes this morning."

By then I was shaking from head to toe. Bobby helped me as I slumped into a chair in the lobby "How did you know how to reach me?"

His answer moved me beyond words. "I was going through her personal effects and I found a note: 'Dad, please call Toni. Her number is in my book. Please tell her I love her…and I'm sorry things didn't work out differently.'"

I thanked Sky for calling and hung up. Bobby put his arms around my shoulders. I was totally crushed. This was the one and only girl David was involved with who I truly liked. She had something special, some light inside of her, and despite her life and the mess she had made of it, I knew she was innately good. She had come out of it, beaten cancer for a time, got herself into school, and turned into a loving and devoted mother with the most adorable little boy. It didn't make sense for her life to be cut short—especially not now that she had finally managed to create one worth living. It completely devastated me.

Poppy's presence in my life had given me a different perspective on David. I saw what was possible for him. I saw that it wasn't foolish to have hope, because people can beat their addictions. Make that *some* people.

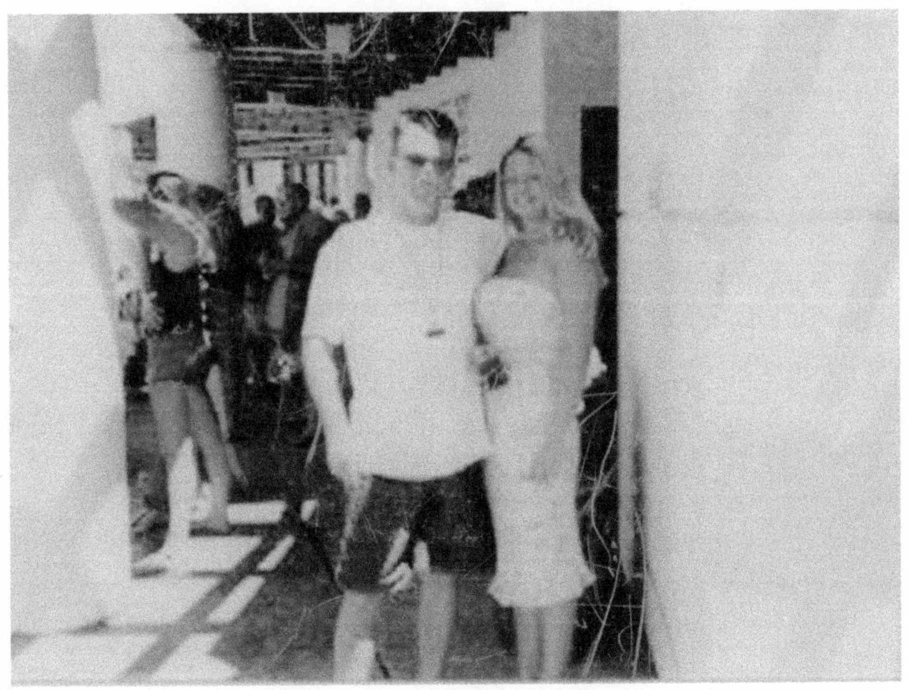

David and his girlfriend, Poppy.

At the time of Poppy's passing, David was back in rehab after another relapse. He was in a place in Indiana in the hands of a life coach named Criss. David had been steered her way by Cookie, a woman in David's band in Clearwater, Florida. Criss felt the auditors at Scientology had missed an important key to his problem, that the reason he kept going back to drugs was never addressed. She spent many hours talking with David and sent me an email telling me that he was desperate, that he really wanted to get over his addiction this time. It was Criss's opinion from what David had told them that his drug use was connected to sex, that he couldn't have sex without drugs. Armed with this new information, Criss went to work with David in Indiana. Criss and I believed that if David didn't kick his habit now, he'd either OD or just die from being worn out.

I phoned David from Monaco and gave him the bad news about Poppy. The following is an excerpt from an email I received from Criss when I got home, dealing with David's reaction to Poppy's death:

> Dear Toni...
>
> David is in and out of tears over Poppy. He can't believe she's gone, tremendous upset on this & a lot of regret, blame. She sounds like a really good person after she changed.
>
> I've been helping David every day, getting him to line up work, make phone calls, answer his mail. Life coach type things. He's slowly coming around to more sensible actions. I am treating him like my juveniles & honestly am getting more results with that approach than anything.
>
> ML Criss

For years I had felt David was a hopeless case, one of those rare exceptions who thirty-one rehabs couldn't help. A vicious, endless circle of despair seemed to have engulfed my son's life. The fact that David actually cried on hearing about Poppy—the fact that he rightly or wrongly blamed himself for her death—showed me that maybe down deep he truly possessed feelings that he was finally allowing to come to the surface.

In one of my conversations with David, he finally acknowledged that he needs his family. He told me that he realizes now that he can't live without me. "I have only one mother," he said. "And I'm not going to lose you. I'm not going to let you go."

Little did I know that the worst was yet to come.

CHAPTER FIFTY-EIGHT

The Nightmare!

It was the morning of June 30, 2014. Bobby and I were back in Palm Springs, looking forward to a fabulous summer. I was in a great mood. It was a glorious day and I couldn't wait to breathe it in. Then again, life can turn on a dime.

It was 9:05 when the phone rang. The voice on the other end blurted out nine words that would change my life forever. "This is Ellie. They think David had a stroke."

The words went through me like a knife. I was frozen in time and space. I don't know how long it took for my brain to kick in, but when it did, the questions shot out with machine-gun fire. "What do you mean he had a stroke? Where is he?"

"Rancho Springs Medical Center...in Temecula," said Ellie. "I'm with him now."

"When did this happen?"

"Just after midnight."

"Why didn't you call me?"

"I didn't have your number. I called 911."

Everything was happening so quickly, I didn't have time to piece anything together. I was strictly in reaction mode. I didn't even know who Ellie was. Everything was such a blur that morning, I wasn't even sure that was her name. "It's a long drive, so I don't know when, but I'll be there," I told her.

"He's in intensive care," she said.

I hung up and screamed for Kyle, my assistant at the time. I told him to get Danny, my houseman, to drive us there. "I'm going with you," Bobby said.

"No, you're not," I said. I didn't want Bobby anywhere near a hospital. I didn't want to expose him to any germs. He was upset, but he knew I was right.

I raced to the car with Kyle, and Danny drove us to the hospital.

At the time, David was living in a poolside apartment in Temecula, roughly a two-hour drive from Palm Springs. A few months earlier he had started a new job and said he was the happiest he'd been in a long, long time, maybe in his entire life. He worked as a placement counselor for drug addicts—a job he'd done before and was really good at it. Being an addict himself, he understood the mindset of an addict, something a non-addict can't really comprehend. As far as I knew, David was clean for once in his life.

A few weeks before the phone call, David had told me he'd been placed on temporary leave by the company he worked for, and he was terribly upset at the unexpected turn. "Why is it I'm always under a black cloud?" he asked.

"What happened is really sad and unfortunate," I told him. "But they said it was only temporary—not permanent. David, you have the ability and connections to move forward. You've done it before, you can do it again." I tried hard to stay positive, not showing my sadness that David was uprooted once more.

I found out later that David had been calling Bobby and asking for money. Bobby never told me because he was afraid I would think David was back on drugs. As it turned out, he was.

After two hours on the road, I finally arrived at the hospital. Danny waited in the car and I ran inside with Kyle, where we were directed to ICU. The scene was chaotic. Doctors and nurses were tending to patients separated from each other by plain white curtains. A nurse pointed me to a bed at the far side of the room. I pulled back the curtain and what I saw was bone-chilling.

David was on a breathing apparatus, in a coma, all kinds of tubes sticking out of him. His face was twisted, and I couldn't tell if he was paralyzed or not. It was absolutely horrifying to see my son like that. I tried to comprehend what was happening, but it was all coming at me too fast.

The young girl at David's bedside introduced herself. It was Ellie. I pulled her outside the curtain. I wanted answers.

"Did they give him the shot?" I asked. From what I knew there was a shot they gave stroke victims, but it had to be administered within three hours of the actual stroke for it to do any good. The first three hours are critical.

David before his stroke.

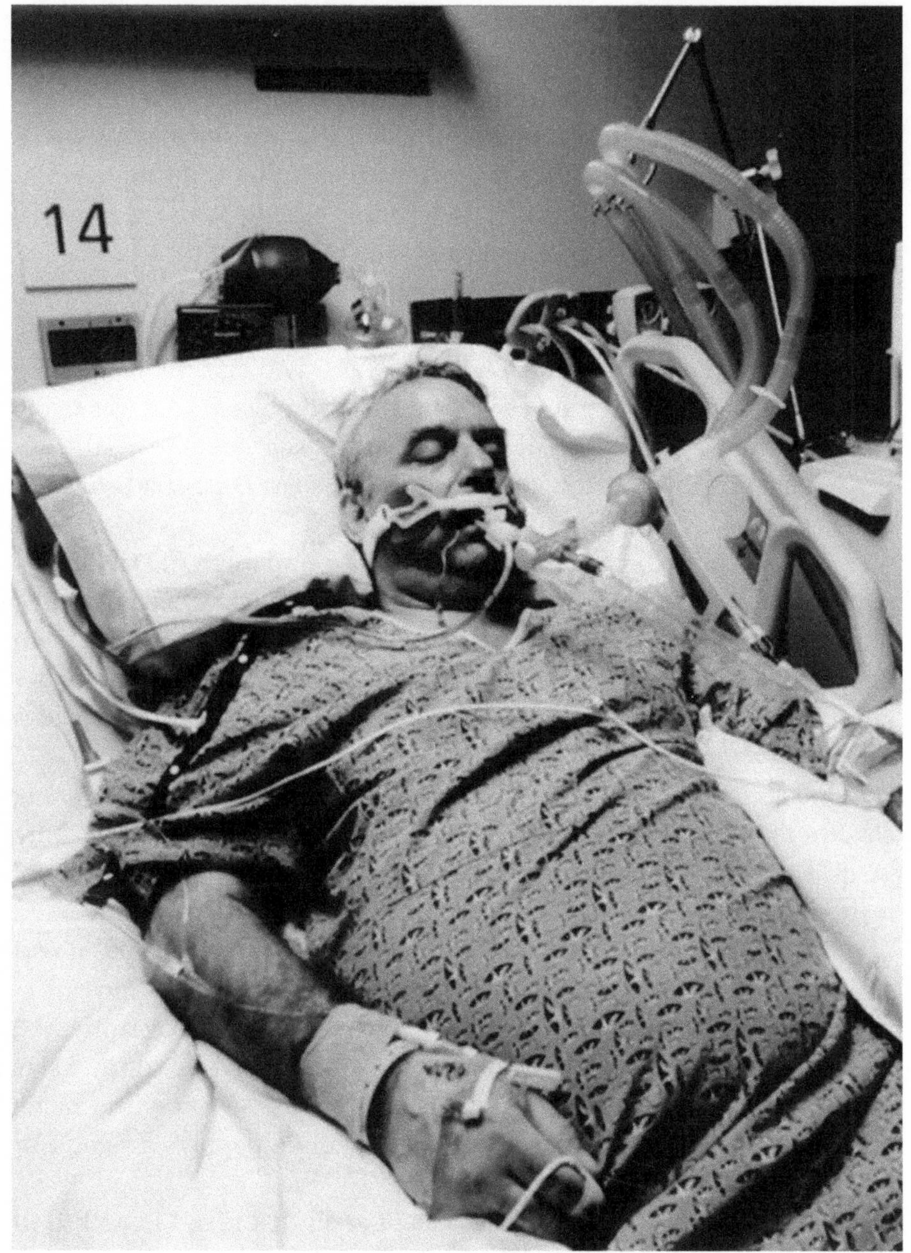

David following his stroke.

"No, they didn't," she said.

A little later the pieces began coming together. When Ellie called 911 she didn't tell them the truth about what happened. She told them David was asleep and just rolled off the bed. He was slurring his words and that's why she called 911. The paramedics didn't want to give him the shot because they couldn't determine exactly when the stroke occurred. As a matter of protocol, they don't give the shot to someone who has suffered what they call a "sleeping" stroke.

The true story, which I soon found out, was that David and Ellie were *both* doing drugs. I learned that Ellie was David's girlfriend and that he had met her at a drug rehab sometime before where she was being treated for substance abuse. It was even more surprising to learn they had been living together for about six months, a fact David had gone out of his way to keep secret from me.

The doctor at the hospital told me they found meth in David's system in addition to cocaine. Ellie finally admitted that she had gotten the drugs from a guy at a gas station in Temecula—and he gave her meth instead of cocaine. Ellie said David didn't know he was taking meth, but I didn't believe that for a second. David was much too savvy about drugs not to know what he was taking.

Weeks later David admitted he was also taking Viagra and drinking alcohol that night. His story goes that he ran out of his blood pressure meds, and the pharmacy wouldn't give him any without a prescription. Is this all true? I really don't know.

After speaking with as many doctors and nurses as I could, it was clear nothing more was going to happen that night. I had found out as much as I could and I was exhausted. The stress and uncertainty had completely drained me. Ellie volunteered to sit by David's side and stay in touch. I left all my phone numbers at the nurse's station and made them promise to call me immediately if anything happened—good or bad. At that point, Danny drove us home.

As tired as I was, I don't think I slept at all that night. I checked in constantly with the hospital and with Ellie, and the answers were always the same: David is still in a coma—no change in his condition. It was now a waiting game.

The next morning the head nurse called to tell me they had to move David to Inland Valley Medical Center in Orange County because

Rancho Springs didn't have the facilities to deal with him. It wasn't an option.

While the move didn't sit well with me at first, it turned out to be a godsend. Dr. Fred Abshire, a renowned brain surgeon, was assigned David's case. For this, I will be eternally grateful. Dr. Abshire brought in Dr. Yung, a pulmonary expert, and together they performed more tests. During this time, I commuted daily to the hospital from Palm Springs.

And no, I still wouldn't let Bobby go. The next day, Steve and Wendy Kramer, Bobby's son and daughter-in-law, came to see David at Inland Valley and spent the day with me.

After more bloodwork, the doctors said David had suffered a severe catastrophic stroke. In fact, it appeared he had probably suffered two strokes. They said they found definite traces of meth in his blood, which may have been the cause of his bleeding among other things. David was still on a ventilator and a feeding tube, but he was showing signs of coming around, despite being completely paralyzed on the left side.

When David finally came out of his coma, he knew who I was and scribbled a question on a piece of paper: "Did cocaine cause this?" His writing trailed off the paper and was barely legible, but I knew what the question was. "We don't know," I said. "It's possible...maybe...I don't have the answer."

It was then the next bolt of lightning hit. Dr. Abshire told us David's brain was swelling and they needed to do surgery to relieve the pressure to save his life. With a grave expression on his face, he added, "If we don't operate, the result could be fatal."

Once again, my world was knocked off its foundation. I knew the situation was grim, but I wasn't prepared to hear that David might die. The doctors wanted to know what David liked to do and what his hobbies were. The questions seemed absurd at the time. What did it matter what he liked to do when his brain was swelling and he could be gone any minute?

But they were the experts, so I did what they asked. I told them David loved to play golf, that he was practically a scratch golfer—that he was a brilliant, self-taught guitarist, wrote much of his own music, and played guitar like Carlos Santana. He had a God-given talent.

Dr. Abshire listened carefully to what I said; then in a kind and gentle way, he said, "The prospects for David having any quality of life are not very good. He's never going to be able to do things he loves. And it won't be a very good life for you either."

It was a surreal moment. I stood there shaking, stunned, overwhelmed by the decision I had to make. I looked at my son-in-law, the raw emotion plainly visible. "Steve, what should I do?"

I could see the tears welling up in Steve's eyes. "Toni, I can't make that decision for you. I don't even know what I would do if he were *my* son."

"I can't make the decision right now," I told Dr. Abshire. "I need some time to think about it. If God wanted to take him, why didn't he already take him? I can't answer whether you should operate or not. I need more time."

Dr. Abshire repeated that time was not our friend. He needed to know, one way or the other. He gave me his cell phone number and told me to call him.

I sobbed all the way home to Palm Springs. I yelled. I screamed. I can't ever remember feeling so much pain. My phone rang in the car and it was my dear friend Ruta Lee, who I call my sister. She was at our favorite Croatian restaurant, Miro's, and she wanted me to come to dinner. Despite not eating for a couple of days, I told her I was in no mood to eat. "I can hardly breathe—how can I eat? Besides, I can't be there for hours."

"You're coming," insisted Ruta. "I'm going to wait here all night for you if I have to."

"Okay, I'll be there."

Before we went to the restaurant, I asked Bobby and Kyle to tell me what to do. They both had the same answer: "It's a decision we can't make for you. You have to make it."

When I walked into Miro's, Ruta was sitting at a table with her husband, Webb. I froze right there in the doorway, and my eyes locked on Ruta. I swear, I saw God in Ruta's eyes. You need to know that Ruta is the most religious person I know. No matter where we are in the world, she finds a church. If Ruta wasn't in show business, I'm sure she would have been Mother Superior.

So there I was, staring at Ruta. Not a word passed between us, yet I clearly saw the answer in her eyes. With that I excused myself and hurried outside. I phoned Dr. Abshire. "I've made my decision. Operate."

"I'm leaving for the hospital now," he said. "Every hour counts. I expect I'll be done before midnight, but Mrs. Kramer, I can't tell you for sure he'll live through it."

"Dr. Abshire, I have complete faith that you will do the very best you can. If it's God's will that he doesn't live through it...believe me, I won't hold you responsible in any way. I want you to know I believe he will live through it. But please don't worry about how I feel. I'll deal with it. I want it to be God's decision."

I walked back into the restaurant as if the weight of the world had suddenly been lifted from my shoulders. For the first time in days, I had a feeling of calm. Everyone asked what I had decided to do. I said to Ruta, "I saw the answer in your eyes." I sat down and ate dinner, even had a martini.

Dr. Abshire called me around 12:30 in the morning. "It's over. And he's alive."

"I knew he would be. Thank you," I said.

What the doctors performed was a craniotomy. A piece of the bone at the top of the skull, called the bone flap, is removed to allow access to the brain and relieve the pressure. The brain flap was implanted in David's stomach to preserve it—and months later, after the swelling healed, it was replaced.

When I saw David the next morning, his head was wrapped in bandages and he was wearing a helmet to protect his skull. Within a day or two, he could speak. His face was slightly twisted and his speech was slurred, but I could still understand him.

Seemingly overnight my great summer had turned into the summer from Hell!

My daily trips to the hospital became a grind. The long drive each way took its toll on me—and on Bobby, even though I still refused to let him go with me. He was frantic, concerned for my health. In truth, we were all basket cases.

In mid-July we transferred David to Desert Regional Hospital in Palm Springs. Our own personal doctor, Dr. Baer, became our advocate at the hospital. Without an advocate, it's impossible to get any credible information. Doctors and nurses don't really want to talk to you—and they definitely don't want to tell you anything.

David claimed that he died in the ambulance on the way to Desert Regional. He said that during the trip his ventilator slipped from his mouth and nobody put it back. He told me he saw my mother—and Poppy—and begged them to please let him go back—that he didn't want to die. "I promised them I would go straight this time. Just give me one more chance."

You know how many times I heard David ask for one more chance? I can't even count them. Do I believe David's story to be true? Probably. And here's why:

My mother was a medium extraordinaire. She could make contact with the dead, and the spirits would visit her in her bedroom or bathroom. David loved my mother passionately—unlike my son Adam, who was indifferent when she became ill. But David was attached to her. He would massage her back and her shoulders, and tell her how much he loved her. There was a definite connection between David and my mother. God only knows how many times she paid off his drug debts and kept him out of trouble. So, yes, I give David the benefit of the doubt on this one.

David was at Desert Regional for close to six weeks, during which time he began rehab. But it was time to move on—time to move David to a long-term facility. Dr. Baer desperately tried to convince us to put him in a nursing home, but we strongly disagreed. He kept repeating over and over that we would get one hundred free days of care. And I said, "And a lifetime of Hell."

I had to remind Dr. Baer that David didn't have a disease—he'd had a stroke. He needed to learn how to function again, not waste away in some nursing home.

In the meantime, I called my friend Janet Levy in Palm Beach. Janet had had a stroke some thirteen years earlier. The doctors told her she'd never walk or talk or be able to use her arm again. Janet proved them all wrong. If you saw her today, you'd never know she had a stroke. She moves like lightning—talks a mile a minute—and dances up a storm. Janet is a dedicated humanitarian in Palm Beach and works tirelessly to help others. She is truly a force.

Janet shared her experience with me, and made it clear that the first six months were critical if David were to recover. If he didn't get the proper care, he could be bedridden the rest of his life. She told me David must receive six hours of rehab a day. "Someone needs to watch him all the time," she said. "If not, they'll give him fifteen minutes of rehab and forty-five minutes of gab. You really have to have a policeman there."

And so, taking Janet's advice, we began the grueling process of finding a rehab facility for David. Over the course of days, Kyle and I made more than a hundred phone calls. Some places offered forty-five minutes of rehab—others an hour—some even three hours, but none would take David to live in, and that's what he needed.

To make matters worse, the doctors at Desert Regional were anxious to move David out. "I'm going as fast as I can!" I told them.

I never gave up. Kyle nicknamed me "the warrior in five-inch heels." We finally found Winways, in Orange Country. Thankfully they agreed to take him in.

August 13, 2014, David was moved to Winways. He had the most wonderful physical therapist, Cheri, as well as an occupational therapist and a speech therapist. And yes, they worked him six hours a day. Slowly but surely we saw some improvement.

Shortly before David left Desert Regional, Dr. Baer informed me David had suffered damage to his eyes, an issue called a field cut. As a result of the stroke, he had lost vision from the center of both eyes—to the areas left of center. To make matters worse, they discovered that David's right optic nerve was severely damaged as well. He couldn't even read the big "E" at the top of the eye chart. They declared him legally blind.

As the days went by, the list of doctors grew: he had a stroke doctor, an internist, an eye doctor, a cardiologist, a specialist for his bladder, and probably some I've forgotten. But I give David credit—he never complained to me about the obvious. Never said, "My God, I can't see—I can't walk."

In September, Janet Levy and her husband, Mark, came to Palm Springs. Looking to see if there was anything she could do to help, Janet came to Winways with me and spoke to David and the therapists. One therapist explained that David had to learn to work the good side of his brain as well as his muscles—that the side of his brain that was working would eventually take over for the side that wasn't. But it was all about repetition, trying to teach the good side to compensate for the bad side. Janet said I had to tell the therapists to constantly remind David to move, move, move and walk, walk, walk. What Janet did for me goes beyond friendship.

David is back in Palm Springs now, working everyday to bring some sense of normalcy to his life, but it's a hard uphill battle. It's unlikely he'll ever be able to live alone. He will never be able to drive or run his own household. But he is now able to walk a little with the aid

David's birthday at the hospital, with his brother Adam (right) and Adam's partner, Douglas.

of a cane and is determined to recover. Ironically, it took a stroke to cure him of his drug addiction. Just recently he told me he finally found real joy in his life.

As for Bobby and me, this whole experience has been one long nightmare. How will it end? When will it end? I don't have a clue. Probably never.

I feel sad when I look at David because I see someone who is exceedingly bright—someone who graduated with honors—someone who could have done anything he wanted with his life. And yet, he threw it all away and wound up like he is.

I know now that we should have cut him out of our lives twenty-five years ago. We enabled him to the point of destroying himself—and us. We should have been tougher on him. Would that have worked? Another question I can't answer.

Sometime before David had his stroke, he said, "Mom, I don't know why you've hung in with me all these years. If the situation was reversed, I don't think I would have hung in with you." I guess I wasn't listening. I know now that the biggest mistake you can make is forgiving an addict. You get pulled into their world. They have you exactly where they want you. And they have no conscience.

It's clear to me now that there are only four ways a drug addict can end up. They can OD (which David did a couple of times), they can wind up in jail (David was there a few times as well), they can wind up sick (David's there now), or they can wind up dead.

So yes, I'm conflicted. I feel sorry for David, and at the same time I'm angry at him for what he did to himself—and what he did to me and my family. He lied to me his entire life.

Do I think I made the wrong decision to keep him alive? Honestly, I don't know. I often wonder if I should have let him meet up with Mommy and Poppy in heaven. I wonder what kind of life I've sentenced him to. When I see his struggle, I wonder who's going to take care of him when I'm gone.

At the same time, I resent him for taking Bobby and me down with him at this time in our lives. How many other lives did David destroy in addition to his own? It's safe to say—everyone who ever liked him or loved him. In truth, there is no good ending to this tragedy. Many times it crossed my mind that the devil I thought I saw in my little boy grew into David.

Fast forward. September 2018. Miracles do happen. The prognosis that David would never be out of a wheelchair was altered by his fierce determination and resolve the past four years. Endless hours of rehabilitation that took him from not being able to stand for more than sixty seconds without falling to where his balance has improved so he can walk short distances with the aid of a cane and a brace. His left arm and hand have not yet recovered, but he works at it with the same gutsy drive he put forth with his leg. Though legally blind, he stubbornly believes he will again play his guitar and write music, as well as be the near-scratch golfer he once was.

The devil may have control of his life, but God had the last word.

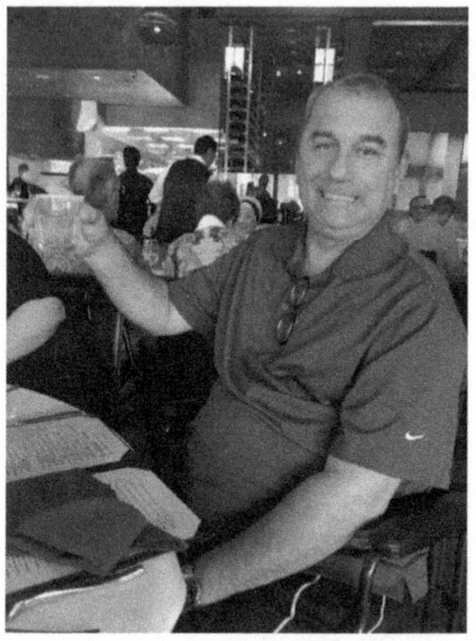

David on the mend. September 2018.

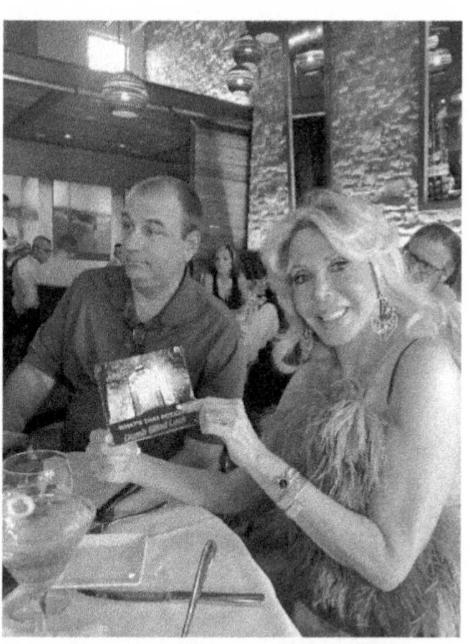

Toni with David at his birthday, July 29, 2018.

Never give up. Never give in. Never say never!

CHAPTER FIFTY-NINE

Martin Short

December 5, 2014. The night I was reborn.

It was Lois Pope's Lady in Red Gala. Lois, a former singer and actress on Broadway, gained fame as the woman in the Taittinger Champagne ads. She was married to the late Generoso Pope Jr., founder of the *National Enquirer*. When her husband died in 1988 at the age of sixty-one, the sale of the *Enquirer* added to her already substantial fortune. A Palm Beach socialite and philanthropist, Lois is the founder of the LIFE Foundation, benefitting disabled veterans.

The setting once again was the opulent Grand Ballroom at Mar-a-Lago. Donald and Melania were at a table toward the center of the room, taking it all in. The theme for the gala was "A Night in Shanghai." The star attraction was Martin Short, who would be the first to admit he doesn't look the least bit Asian. Ha ha.

Martin, an Emmy and Tony Award-winning actor, is best known for the wacky and quirky characters he created for movies and television. Among the quirkiest is the overweight, always-munching-junk-food Jiminy Glick, celebrity interviewer. I was the celebrity he would interview that night. Martin is so adorable you just want to squeeze him. But not too hard.

Lois knew I was in a deep depression because of my son's stroke, and she took it upon herself to see if she could help me find a way out. She had arranged for me to do the skit with Martin the night of the gala, and I went to Mar-a-Lago that Saturday afternoon to rehearse. When Martin saw me, he asked why I was there. "To rehearse," I said.

"No rehearsal." He laughed. "We don't need to rehearse."

"Good," I replied. It reminded me of what Dean Martin once told me. "I never rehearse when I do my TV shows because I feel when you rehearse you leave the best and funniest lines on the rehearsal floor, and boy, you never get 'em back again."

Toni and Bobby with Martin Short, Lady in Red Gala 2015.

So, I went home to get myself ready for the night. People who know me say I'm fearless, but to say I wasn't nervous would be a lie. After all, I would be on full view for all of Palm Beach to judge, and I hadn't been on stage for a few years. In truth, my Palm Beach friends didn't really know me as a performer. They would soon enough.

I arrived at the gala with Bobby that night full of mixed emotions. I had flown my son David, and his two caregivers, to Florida from California, and he sat at our table in a wheelchair. I was worried about David. I was worried about Bobby, who was worried about David. And I was worried about myself. To complicate matters, my heart had been pounding like bongo drums every night for the past month, and my cardiologist had wired me up as a precaution to make sure it was nothing serious. He finally diagnosed the problem as benign arrhythmia. I removed the wires before I went to the gala. I was just hoping I could keep my emotions in check long enough to get through the bit with Martin. I desperately wanted to be on my A game. Being an acute A-type personality, this was a requirement.

My black and red Chinese dress, slit up high on both sides, was perfect for the Asian-themed evening. To top off the dress I wore a humungous black, red, and gold Chinese headdress which Kyle had found online in Australia and had shipped to Palm Beach.

Lois opened the evening with a moving speech about her foundation, then introduced Martin. He did a few minutes of stand-up and appeared as some of his famous characters. The crowd in the ballroom clearly loved him. The laughter made me feel good as I sat at my table waiting for my intro. Nobody in the room knew what was about to happen.

Martin left the stage for a couple of minutes and came back out as the hilarious Jiminy Glick. He gazed out at the audience, wondering if there was a celebrity he could interview, and his eyes settled on me. His introduction went like this: "This young lady is a legend, not only in show business but in the world of charities. She's here tonight because we love her. Please welcome Toni Holt Kramer."

I left my table, practicing under my breath how to say "Good evening, you are very sexy" in Chinese. My Chinese girlfriend, Shalon, had taught me those words earlier in the day.

I joined Jiminy on stage and barely got out my greeting when he said, "I'd love to mount you right here." He smothered me with an embrace, and the audience howled with laughter, as did I. I sat in the chair across from him, and the interview was on. I got into the spirit immediately. Remember, we didn't rehearse, so the questions—each more outrageous than the last—were as new and unexpected to me as they were to those watching.

"Why did God give men nipples if we're not supposed to breast-feed our pets?"

"These toilets that flush automatically, do they see when you're finished or are they just guessing?"

"Where were you when the Queen killed Diana?"

By this time, Jiminy and I were laughing as hard as the audience. As he stuffed a donut into his mouth, the conversation turned to my career in Hollywood, and I was finally able to answer a question.

"Who was the biggest jerk you ever interviewed?" asked Jiminy.

I didn't hesitate. "Richard Dreyfuss." With that, Martin's piano player nearly fell off his bench.

We talked about my career, how I got started in Hollywood, and about my favorite subject—me. I found out later that Martin's Jiminy Glick interviews with the likes of Tom Hanks, Steve Martin, and Ellen DeGeneres usually lasted five or six minutes. *Our* interview lasted over eleven minutes, so I know both Martin and the audience had a good time. I certainly did.

I walked off the stage that night and back into the life I had enjoyed for so many years. I recalled an article I once read about Martin Short. He spoke of the tragedies in his life, and he said you can deal with them in several ways—but the only good choice is to move on. Maybe he sensed a little bit of himself in me that night.

I know comedians well. They are my favorite interviews, much more so than actors. They rely on their quick wit rather than a script someone has written for them. Like the Greek masks of Comedy and Tragedy, they understand happiness and pain. Martin Short, I love you!

By the end of the evening, I was swamped with compliments about the interview, and the stress that had been building up in me was gone.

Martin Short as Jiminy Glick interviews Toni at Lady in Red Gala.

Palm Beach society—and the future president of the United States—caught a glimpse of the Toni Holt Kramer they had never seen before.

The next day, my iPad was filled with emails, and my phone rang off the hook with friends who were either at the gala the night before or who had heard about it. Many were surprised at how well I handled the interview, how at ease I was on stage and in front of the cameras that taped the event.

I wasn't surprised. After all, I had spent the majority of my life on live television. I was comfortable. I was secure. I was really at home.

CHAPTER SIXTY

Superman

Bel Air, California. May 24, 2016. My husband, Bobby, took a terrible fall and broke his hip and femur. The fall was unbelievable, since only the day before we had taken a two-mile walk up a mountain in Palm Springs.

The closest hospital was UCLA Medical Center, but my doctor wanted Bobby to go to St. Johns Hospital in Santa Monica. Lucky for us UCLA was too crowded and they couldn't accept him. Instead, the paramedics took us to St. Johns and we got the doctor we needed, the renowned surgeon Dr. Yun. Two days later Bobby was operated on.

The staff at St. Johns recognized me from my years on television, and we received superstar service. Being a germaphobe, it was almost impossible, but I managed to spend a week in the hospital with my husband. If ever you find yourself in the hospital and want to get out alive, you must have an advocate at your side. In this case, the advocate was me. When Bobby finally arrived home, I arranged for round-the-clock care.

By this point in my life I had switched political allegiance from Hillary to Donald Trump. It was a difficult and emotional decision, but I was extremely unhappy with the direction in which our country was leaning and there was no doubt in my mind that President Obama was spearheading the movement. My greatest fear was that if Hillary became president, she would follow in Obama's footsteps and there would be no turning back. That was something I just couldn't let happen.

Bobby and I had plans to go to the Republican Convention in mid-July, but now that was not going to happen. I was so looking forward to going to Cleveland to watch Trump get the official nod and squeal with delight after working my tail off for him. I didn't say anything to Bobby, but I was clearly disappointed.

After all, I had turned the Trumpettes USA into a real force to assist Trump in any way I could to get him into the White House. I was exhausted but exhilarated from all the TV, newspaper, and online interviews I was doing.

Despite so many people in LA screaming at me as I drove around Beverly Hills and Bel Air with a Trump bumper sticker on my Rolls, I stuck with it. I heard the groundswell of voices threatening me and

French Presse photo shoot with Toni, Linda and Fred Williamson in Palm Springs.

anyone else in the entertainment business if we dared to support Trump. "You'll never work in this town again" was the mantra of the liberals. I didn't care what they said. I believed. I thought and knew he would win.

In June, I received a phone call from a producer for the French Presse, a well-known media outlet. Sebastian wanted to do an interview with me.

I was in Palm Springs at the time and invited Fred Williamson (the former NFL football star turned international action movie hero who played for the Oakland Raiders and the Kansas City Chiefs) to join me for the interview at Villa Paradiso

Fred was the very first man to join my Trumpettes USA, and is officially known as my #1 Trumpster. Linda, Fred's wife, and early Trumpette, sat in on the interview as well.

Villa Paradiso was christened by Cary Grant. Grant adored the splendor and serene setting of the estate, similar in style to Mar-a-Lago, only on a smaller scale. Mar-a-Lago means from "the sea to the lake," while my desert paradise is "mountain to mountain."

The interview went just as I hoped it would. I told Sebastian about the Trumpettes, and repeated my firm belief that Donald Trump would be our next president.

"How can you be so sure?" he asked.

"He has to be," I said simply. "There is no other choice. 'Why' doesn't exist in my vocabulary."

I didn't know it at the time, but that interview would be the beginning of great things to come for the Trumpettes. The floodgates were definitely opening.

Into July, Bobby was feeling better and he insisted I go to the convention. He wasn't well enough to go with me, but he didn't want me to miss out on my dream. "If you don't go for the entire four days, at least go for two."

"A deal," I said.

Bobby chartered a private plane for me and off I went. It was a thrilling experience to see the thousands and thousands of people who were there with the same diehard dedication as mine: to see Trump as president.

Like Coney Island, there were vendors on the street selling T-shirts, sunglasses, buttons, pens, and pins of all kinds, anything that echoed the name Trump. The vendors yelled like carnival barkers. "Step right up and get your Trump T-shirt! Get your Trump hat!" It was crazy but wonderful.

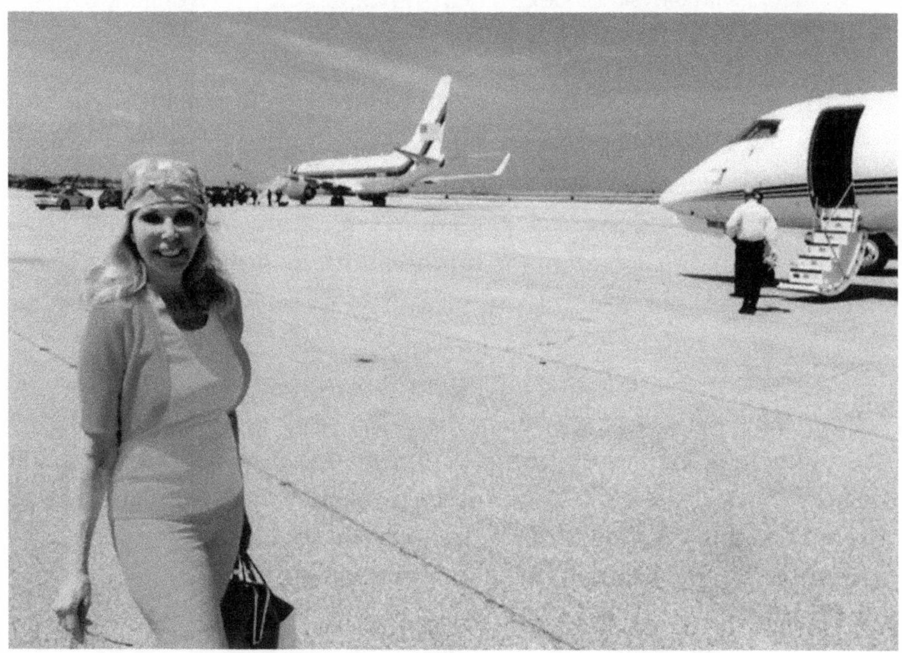

Toni heads off to the Republican Convention 2016.

Toni with Governor Rick Perry at the Republican Convention.

The perimeter of the Convention Center was lined with barricades to stop any would-be terrorists. Getting inside the center itself wasn't easy either. I needed a badge to go everywhere. Badges of all kinds hung from ribbons around my neck, but I didn't mind one bit. I loved it. I had the time of my life. I even made it to the Rock 'n' Roll Hall of Fame for an event where I got an admiring eye from Governor Rick Perry, now our Secretary of Energy.

I was interviewed constantly by the media outlets, including the *London Telegraph* newspaper and various freelance reporters. I didn't say no to anyone. The convention staff treated me royally, and I received access to the private club at the top of the center. Television sets spread around the club allowed me to watch everything that was going on. Or I could observe the proceedings "live" from my seat overlooking the floor of delegates.

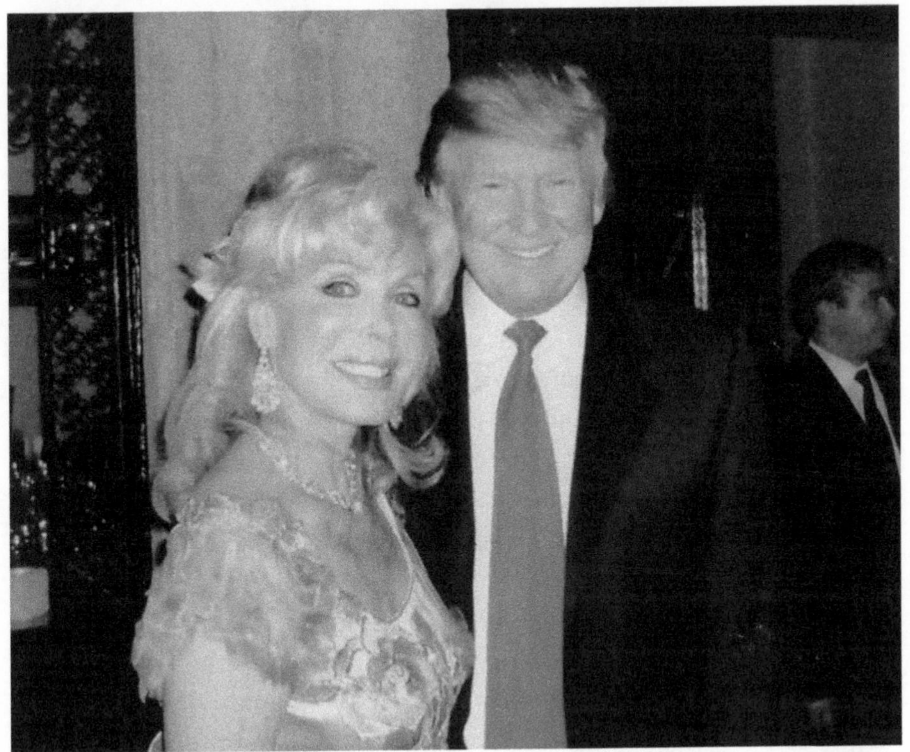

Toni and Donald Trump, without his Superman suit.

To me, this was a job. My job. I was on a mission. I wasn't there only as Toni Holt Kramer, I was there as founder and president of the Trumpettes USA.

On the plane back to California, I imagined Donald Trump, blond hair waving, blue eyes sparkling, wearing a Superman suit, hovering above the White House, waiting for we the people to elect him president of the United States. The image was complete with Trump sliding into a chair behind his desk in the Oval Office. This vision repeated often in my head and helped me to keep my eye on the ball.

A few months later, Bobby and I were back in Palm Beach. I knew Florida was a must-win state for Trump, and I was determined to do all I could to help get out the vote for him. Especially the women.

I came up with an idea: "Adopt a Trumpette." I booked one of the two dining rooms at Café L'Europe, a most exclusive and luxurious restaurant on the island. I set the luncheon for October 29, approximately two weeks before the national election. The idea was for all my invited Trumpettes to bring a friend or even two. The purpose was to increase our base, spread the word, and make those who were undecided decide in our favor.

A few days before the luncheon, I received a frantic phone call from Bruce, the maître d' at Café L'Europe. "Toni, we need a wall-stretcher. We can't get another person in here. We already used the second room. We're completely sold out!" That was music to my ears.

On the day of the luncheon, a diverse group of women from all walks of life joined with a surprising number of men to show their support and spread the word. The energy in the room was electric. The lunch was great, the speakers were even better. We revved up the crowd with the truth about Donald Trump and why he had to be our next president.

I thanked everyone for coming and told them emphatically, "You don't have to love Trump. You just need to love America."

By the end of the afternoon, two TV companies were waiting to interview me. ITN from Great Britain, and a local Palm Beach TV show hosted by Richard Peritz that reached forty-four million people across the country.

As Election Day neared, I spoke to everyone who would speak to me. Even *Palm Beach Today* magazine gave us a full page. I did everything I could think of to get people to vote for Trump. I worked long into the night to mobilize the Trumpettes from coast to coast.

The four founders of the Trumpettes—Terry Ebert Mendozza, Janet Levy, Suzi Goldsmith, and yours truly—even rented a van with a neon sign going around it, urging people to vote for Trump. I'm not sure what the residents of Palm Beach thought about a funky van driving up and down the tree-lined streets and past the polling places, but we loved it. The truck circled from Palm Beach to Miami Beach and back, spreading the word.

Without a doubt, Florida held the key to the White House, and I was determined to do everything in my power to help Trump unlock the door to the Oval Office.

Unstoppable me never gave up.

Rhonda Shear

The Trumpettes luncheon at Café L'Europe.

Palm Beach Today International
Glossy Social Events Magazine $4.25
December 12, 201

Adopt a Trumpette Luncheon

at Café L'Europe, October 29th, 2016

The Trumpettes' mission was simple: "To recruit more people to vote for the Palm Beach candidate and to keep supporting Donald J. Trump", said Toni Holt Kramer.

She is the founder of the Trumpettes, a women's group based in Palm Beach, FL that supports President-elect Donald J. Trump, and now has members Nationwide, and also interest worldwide.

"They don't have to love Trump," Toni Holt Kramer said. **"They just need to love America. We have the most diversified group of women."**

Toni Holt Kramer, Founder of The Trumpettes

Toni Holt Kramer added, "The Adopt a Trumpette Luncheon was conceived [illegible] Trump supporters the opportunity to take someone to the lunch that was potentially undecided on how they would vote. We had wonderful speakers and were entertained by Doug Verge at Café L'Europe. I must give special praise and many thanks to my Founding Trumpettes, **Janet Levy, Suzy Goldsmith, Terry Ebert Mendozza, and myself,** who donated the money that enabled the Trump Mobile to visit numerous polling stations from Miami to Palm Beach. Also, tremendous thanks go to **Robin Bernstein and Annie Marie Delgado** as well as **Rhonda Shear Fagan** who flew to California to take the TV interview for the **Trumpettes USA** with **me** and **Nightline.**"

She also added, "Another highlight of our lunch was **the Trump sunglasses adorned with Swarovski crystals** that were available for purchase and designed by my longtime friend **Sandy Martindale**. During the lunch, **Robin Bernstein** and I were interviewed by **Richard Peritz**, where we shared the spotlight with **Rudy Giuliani** for The Shalom Show. Also, ITN flew a film crew over from the UK who covered the lunch and aired it on their major network in Great Britain."

PBTI would like to commend both Donald Trump on his victory in the 2016 Presidential election, as well as Toni Holt Kramer and The Trumpettes for their work and support in the days leading to the election. Donald Trump's Victory is the Victory for all of us and the Victory for America.

Lorrie [illegible], Robin Bernstein, Janet Levy, Terry Ebert Mendozza, Toni Holt Kramer, Suzi Goldsmith

My name is Rosa Castillo Olivas.

As an immigrant who was sold and trafficked into the USA, I embraced Donald J. Trump during his campaign because I firmly believe America needs to take action in the prevention and fight against human trafficking in the area around the USA/Mexico border. My friends and I feel passionate about our support for Donald J. Trump for President because he has openly addressed problems that affect the USA and Mexico.

We love America, and we support and respect our constitution.

Rosa Castillo with friends, [illegible], Janet Levy, and Don Ray

Palm Beach Today Magazine

The Trumpettes hit the road.

CHAPTER SIXTY-ONE

"You're Hired!"

So, here it was, the morning of November 8, 2016. Election Day was finally here, the moment of truth for my candidate, my choice from four years earlier, Donald J. Trump. And in many ways, it was a moment of truth for me too.

As I brushed my teeth and tried to decide what I was going to wear that evening to Mar-a-Lago, I thought back to when I first met Donald Trump. I recalled how I would send over articles about politics and the economy to his dinner table at the club, along with a note: "Dear Mr. President. Thought you might like to read this." Yes, I called him Mr. President even then.

One memorable night Bobby and I were at Mar-a-Lago when Donald came walking across the patio where I was standing. As he passed he whispered in my ear, "I'm running." That's all he said, and kept on walking. That was April 2015, nearly two months before he officially announced he was running. I was exuberant, but not surprised. I knew it was going to happen. My gut had been telling me that all along. Fiercely loyal, I vowed not to repeat what he told me to anyone.

As I looked through my closet for the right dress, my mind wandered back over the journey that had brought me to this day. I remembered the exact moment Trump announced he was running. Terry Ebert Mendozza and I—aboard a cruise ship in the middle of the Med to celebrate my birthday—decided to form a women's group in support of Donald Trump. I also remembered the day in Beverly Hills that Terry and I, along with Janet Levy and Suzi Goldsmith, became the founders of the group we called the Trumpettes USA.

All that seemed like twenty minutes ago. Yet, I had lived years since that time. Years working, thinking, and following every political show I could watch. I was obsessed. No matter who I watched or who I listened to, I needed more information—more political analysis. I decided who I

More Trumpettes, from left to right: Lorrie Winnerman, Robin Bernstein, Ambassador to the Dominican Republic, Janet Levy, Terry Ebert Mendozza, Toni and Suzi Goldsmith.

liked and who should be fired. I could tell who was a true Trump supporter and who, in their heart, was not.

I liked Sean Hannity and Monica Crowley. I felt they honestly liked and supported Trump. I adored and respected the late Charles Krauthammer, but he didn't seem as devoted to Trump as I hoped he would, although eventually he came around. In my mind, if you were going to be in Trump's corner, you had to understand him. The one thing nobody spoke about was that Trump didn't need to run for president.

Was he crazy? What was he on? What was he eating? What was he breathing? Why would a man who was so incredibly successful and beyond wealthy want to be president of the United States, a thankless, messy job at best?

There was only one reason that made sense. He saw where our country was headed and was determined to stop it from going over the cliff. Whether you think he's a narcissist, an egomaniac, or whatever your call may be, somewhere down deep in his heart and soul, there lives a conviction that he can and will make a difference in our country. Think about it. Only a man with his audacity—a non-politician, someone who doesn't know the ropes of Washington, someone who not only did battle with the Democrats but fought people of his own party—could possibly persevere. There wasn't anybody or anything that could stop him. His determination would surely win out.

All of these things flashed through my brain. And I knew the answer to all the questions. I believed he knew he could win because—in some strange way—he was chosen, maybe even anointed, to be the savior of America.

Donald Trump shows off Toni's Graff diamond.

I finally decided to wear white. Red was just more than I could handle, and sometimes red wears you. When I tried on the perfect white dress, I chastised myself for a tiny potbelly that had mysteriously appeared. But I quickly excused myself because I had been under such enormous stress that I hadn't kept up my workout regimen. After all, I was fighting for my country, which was a lot more important than my figure (well, for a few months anyway).

The plan for the evening was simple. Terry, Janet, Suzi, and I, and our husbands, would meet at Mar-a-Lago for dinner. Then later, celebrate our victory. We knew that the future president and his wife, Melania, were gathered with their family in New York. We didn't pack an overnight case, but Bobby and I were determined to stay till the wee small hours of the morning until the verdict was in.

During dinner, I couldn't help but think about Hillary and our friendship. I thought about her run against Obama eight years earlier, the total support I had given her, and my disappointment when she dropped out. I felt badly that I hadn't written her a letter to explain why I had chosen to support Trump and not her.

In my heart she was not the same Hillary Clinton I used to know and support, not the same warm and caring Hillary who called me following the death of my mother. Her personality and temperament in the last few years leading up to and during her latest run for the Oval Office seemed so much harsher and colder than the woman I first met and admired. In some ways, I barely recognized her. To me, the election became Hillary versus Hillary.

I found her arrogant and out of touch with the people, blinded by what she felt was rightfully hers: the presidency. Sure, time and circumstances often tend to change who we are, but I didn't agree with a number of things she had done or the alliances she had made. I didn't like the scandals, the accusations, and how she seemingly dodged the truth.

Hillary had become the leader of a Democratic Party I no longer knew or understood. I was convinced if she won, it would be the end of the United States as I knew it and wanted it.

After Hillary's loss to Trump, I was deeply disappointed in how she handled the defeat. She came across as a sore loser, blaming everyone and everything she could for her failure to win. Even today, she seems to

Election night at Mar a Lago. Toni and the Trumpettes have dinner.

live in a world of total denial. Remember, she lost to a political unknown.

While Hillary has always been nice to me, my bottom line was simple: I loved my country more than I loved Hillary, and I didn't think she could save our country. As it turned out, it didn't matter that I never wrote the letter. I'm sure Hillary has already figured out why I changed camps.

My mind was buzzing with all sorts of things as we ate dinner. We were seated at a large table on the Mar-a-Lago patio, pretending to be calm while our insides were churning like an egg beater. Between drinks and uneasy laughter, we would make a run to the bar where a large TV broadcast the results of each state. The bar was jammed, wall-to-wall people. Every time a result came in that favored Trump, a loud cheer would fill the room.

The bar had a lifetime of history, and the portrait of Marjorie Merriweather Post, the original owner of Mar-a-Lago, looked across the room at the portrait of a young Donald Trump. When I looked up at Mrs. Post, I thought I saw a tiny smile on her lips as if she knew her dream that her home would someday become the winter White House for the president of the United States was about to come true.

Back at the dinner table, we held each other's hands, squeezing each other's fingers, and hanging onto our husbands' arms. While the early returns didn't look great for Trump, we all stayed positive. "It's going to be okay," I said. "He's going to win. He's got to win. He will win! He won't let us down! He doesn't know how to lose!"

Those words made me think back to the Lady in Red Gala on December 5, 2015. It was there I was introduced to a former ambassador, an older, elegant-looking white haired man. We began talking about the upcoming election, and he asked me, "Who are you going to vote for?"

"Well, if Donald Trump gets the nomination, I'm voting for him."

He looked at me as though I had lost my mind. "He's not going to be president. He's won't even get the nomination."

My antennae went up. How could he say those things with such confidence? What did he know that I didn't? Then he said something that I've never told anyone until now.

"From what I heard, there was a meeting a short time ago in Bel Air, California—a meeting of very important Republicans." My informant continued, not stopping for another breath. It was supposedly decided that in the event Trump does get the nomination—all the money and support from these Republicans would go to Hillary."

I was stunned. How could that be? Why and how could these Republicans already have a plan mapped out to defeat the possible nominee of their own party? It didn't make any sense.

I wondered if Hillary knew this. It was hard to imagine that she didn't. But who knows? Game on, I thought. I wrestled with whether I should write Trump a note, telling him what I had just heard. But I decided not to. I couldn't verify if what the man had told me was true or not, and passing it on would just stir the pot of doubt. Besides, Trump was smarter than all of us. He knew who his friends were as well as those who were not.

As the election night results poured in at Mar-a-Lago, I couldn't help but smile. I wondered what that man was thinking now.

Toward the end of dinner, my three Trumpettes and I did a "live" iPad interview with *Good Morning Great Britain*. We enthusiastically told all the Queen's men and women how excited we were and how we knew our man would win.

Our dinner conversation turned to why we were so confident that Trump would be victorious. "The last few weeks were the key," I said. "He obviously figured out which states he needed and went there. He rallied his base. People couldn't get enough of him. If they couldn't get into the rally, they waited outside and cheered for him anyway. Sure, he was a billionaire with a lifestyle people could only dream about—but they could understand his simple, straightforward way of talking. He wasn't a snob. He came across as a man who values two things more than anything else: country and loyalty."

Everyone at our table agreed. The people who went to his rallies got that. They could feel it. Despite everything else, he was one of them.

Being a former TV personality, I understood what that familiarity meant. When you let someone into your home for over ten years, whether you're watching him on TV from your bedroom, living room, even your bathroom, that person becomes part of your family. No matter what others might say, you trust him or you wouldn't have let him in for all those years.

It was my unwavering belief that people across America had grown tired of politicians lying to them year after year after year. They wanted someone honest, strong, and genuine, someone with guts. To me, that was Donald Trump.

We finished dinner around 11:30 and headed to the bar. This was serious time now. The returns were coming down to the wire. We kept our eyes glued to the TV screen, and made a "T" with our fingers for the Trumpettes to anyone who was looking at us.

About this time, it started looking better and better for Trump. There was lots of screaming and laughing as the results dribbled in. We were all exhausted, but we were just as determined to hang in for the long haul. It looked like we were headed for the White House.

Around 1:45 in the morning, John Podesta, the chairman of Hillary's campaign, announced that they were calling it a night and things would resume in the morning. This was not a concession; it wasn't anything. Why tomorrow? I got hysterical. "They're going to do something terrible! They're going to do something dishonest! They're going to steal this election from Trump!"

Bobby grabbed my arm and told me to simmer down. He pulled me toward the door. "C'mon, we'll be home in ten minutes. We can watch from the bedroom."

We got home by 2:00 a.m. and turned on the TV, just in time to hear them announce that Donald Trump was elected president of the United States. I cried. And laughed. And cried some more. What an enormous victory for our country.

I ran to the phone and called my girls, Terry and Suzi and Janet. We screamed; we cried some more and shared our joy. We helped do it!

After I hung up Bobby turned to me. "Thank God this is over. I couldn't take another year of this."

We hugged. "Yes, it's over, darling. But only for that moment. Our work is just beginning."

The next morning the phone calls and emails and texts started bright and early.

From Basia Hamilton in England: "...proud of you. Lots of love, Basia."

From Anneliese Langner in Germany: "...great result for your hard work. Much love, Anneliese."

From Dr. Borko Djordjevic in Montenegro: "We won I am so happy. "

From Lorrie Winnerman in Aspen: "Let's party and pray for President Trump. Love, Lorrie."

From Cesare Piperno in Italy: "Toni…you did it! Lechaim."

From Suzy Dion in Indian Hills, California: "…so proud of our Trumpettes leader Toni Holt!"

Toni, the Trumpettes and President Elect Donald Trump.

From Holly Elizabeth Hall: "...how inspirational you are to me. Thank you for being a wonderful role model."

The calls kept coming in. CBS called. *Vanity Fair* contacted us to do a two-page center spread in the Inauguration issue of the magazine. Within days, the requests for interviews poured in from press outlets all over the world. And more Trumpettes and Trumpsters joined our movement with each passing day.

This told me that people from all over the world were watching us. I think they believed if Trump could get the United States straightened out, he could save their country as well.

Yes, the hard-fought battle had been won, but the war still rages on. The Trumpettes USA—started by four concerned and dedicated women—had indeed become a movement.

Guess what, folks? We've only just begun. Join us at TrumpettesUSA.com. You're welcome from any part of the world because we truly are one world. With Donald Trump at the helm, it will be a better world for us—our children—and our grandchildren.

We made history and the victories will continue.

Trumpette to Trump the Winter White House

Toni and President Elect Donald Trump at the Winter White House.

CHAPTER SIXTY-TWO

"What Really Happened!"

So, what really happened? I will tell you what my thoughts are.

Blame it on my gut. I've learned over time to trust that knot in the pit of my stomach when something just isn't right. And something was definitely wrong. It became clear to me years before Hillary decided to run for the second time that she was a different woman than the one I had grown to know. I was no longer comfortable supporting her and the idea that she might actually become president gave me many sleepless nights.

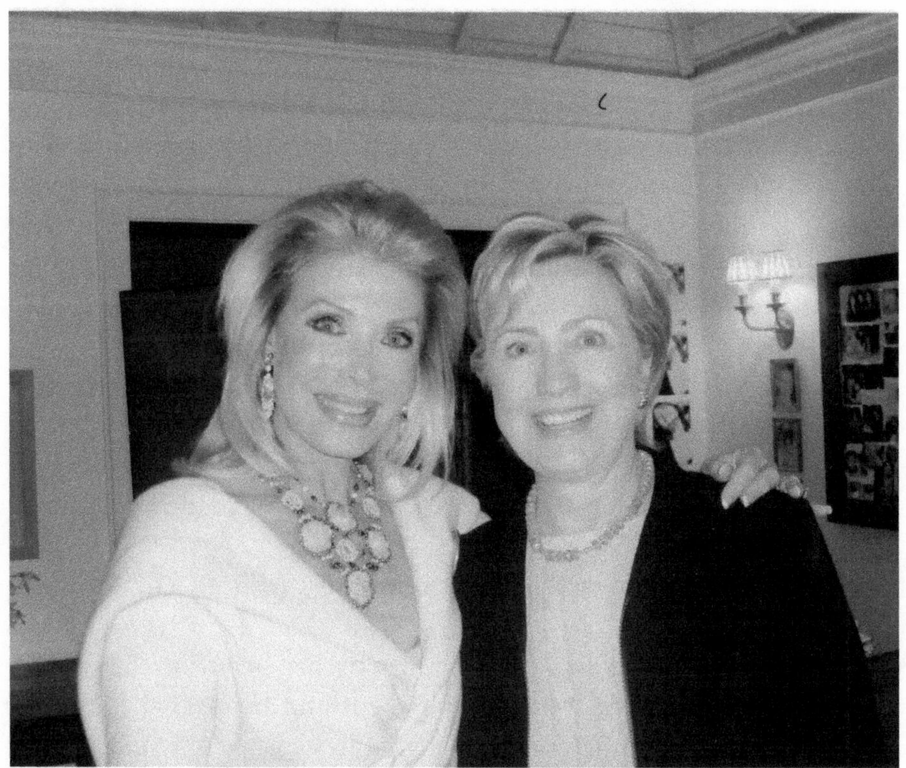

Toni and Hillary, in happier times.

Although it broke my heart for our friendship to go in this direction, to me Hillary had become a totally different person. She even looked different. There was a hardness in her face, an anger to her tone. Her eyes didn't twinkle like they once did. From my point of view it seemed the passion that made her so special to me was gone. She had no new thoughts. Her stump speeches were predictable. Everything she said was a rehash of everything she had always said. She moved like her feet and her thoughts were grounded in cement.

I became convinced that her drive to become president had less to do with serving the American people and more about Hillary. It was all about making a comeback. Like General Custer, this was Hillary's last stand to regain her dignity and belief in herself.

The list of poor decisions she made became longer and longer, and the safety net provided by the Democratic Party was stretched wider and wider. Only a Clinton could have survived that mess.

I was thoroughly disappointed in her handling of the Benghazi tragedy. I was disgusted by the stories of pay-for-play and the scandal-ridden Clinton Foundation. How does someone destroy 33,000 emails requested by the Justice Department and not suffer the consequences? What about her unprotected server in Colorado and multiple devices that got wiped clean? How did Bill get away with meeting the Attorney General on the turmac only days before Hillary was to be questioned by the FBI? And not under oath, I might add. Too many questions and no good answers for me.

"Where there's smoke, there's fire," my mother always said.

Adding to my disenchantment was her relationship with George Soros, a man whose vision for America was as far away from mine as humanly possible. And Hillary's 'fake' love affair with Obama after he destroyed her first attempt to become president only made my stomach churn even more.

So my choice was easy. My love of country, without a doubt, came first.

I've thought long and hard about why her behavior changed so much. In my mind, all the embarrassment and betrayal she suffered with Bill, without publicly acknowledging it, had taken its toll. Think about it: Bill's girlfriends were popping up everywhere coupled with his long term relationship with Gennifer Flowers, (who joined the Trumpettes at its inception). How much can a woman take? What woman do you know who would put up with that kind of humiliation and choose to remain silent? And worse, choose to remain married. To pour salt in the wound, a new documentary is about to be released that details Bill's sexual relationship with Monica Lewinsky.

I believe Hillary's desire to become the world's most important woman fueled her insatiable need to be president, president under any circumstances, under any conditions. Hillary was obviously willing to say or do anything to achieve her goal. What would it take, what did she need to soothe the pain of her bitterness? I can think of only one thing: Power.

And now she doesn't even have that. Sometimes life does terrible things to a person, and that hurt is so deep there is no coming back from it.

In her unexpected and mortifying defeat, Hillary proved to be a sore loser. Simple grace and the acceptance of reality were tossed out the window along with the truth. I expected so much more from the Hillary I knew. Whatever dignity she had left was lost in the pages of her new book, *What Happened?* There, she blamed everyone but herself for her defeat.

Sad to say, Hillary, *What Really Happened,* was you.

CHAPTER SIXTY-THREE

January 18, 2018

I had a flourishing career in reality TV long before reality TV was in fashion. During my thirty years in Hollywood, I did over three thousand interviews and never once used a script. I understand the power of television, and I am certain Donald Trump's exposure on *The Apprentice* is what carried him straight into the White House. Every week millions of Americans invited him into their homes. He joined them in their living rooms, bedrooms, even their bathrooms. That connection with the audience, that intimate meet and greet, made people feel as if they really knew him.

We shouldn't, therefore, be too surprised that President Trump turned the White House into a reality show. *As the White House Turns* has become a daily soap opera not to be missed, with a cast of colorful characters you just can't make up. Real-life people with real-life squabbles laid out daily for all to see. Unlike most TV stars who play characters created for them by writers, Trump is authentic. What people saw on television is what he is: a tough leader, someone who knows what he wants and takes no prisoners. They saw someone who would fight for them no matter the odds.

Our President is a master at manipulating public perception of himself. The best press agent in the world couldn't do a better job. He's a complicated, multifaceted man who doesn't fit any particular mold. As a negotiator, there's no one better. He asks for the moon and settles for a star.

As a former builder and contractor, he understands budgets and timelines and has the ability to see the big picture in ways others don't or can't. His bold moves and statements, often criticized and unpopular, are designed to achieve a certain goal. While he appears to shoot from the hip on many occasions, I believe everything he does is well thought out with the end game in mind.

Because of his tweets, we know how Trump feels and what he's thinking even before we've had our morning coffee. No matter how bad the news is against him, no matter how much the mainstream media tries to destroy him, he never seems publicly upset. He appears to thrive on criticism that would make most of us hide under our covers.

Yes, of course, there are times when we are surprised or woefully disappointed at things Trump says or does, but to his credit, he accomplished a great deal in a very short time. He is a polarizing figure, no doubt. You either love him or hate him, and sometimes both, but nobody is neutral. I'm convinced that the passion people have for and about the man—pro or con—is why it was easy to fill both ballrooms at Mar-a-Lago, the winter White House in Palm Beach, for my first Red, White and Blue blowout to celebrate his first anniversary as President of the United States.

* * * * *

The idea for the event was conceived in September of 2017. The baby was delivered January 18, 2018.

It was the beginning of the charity gala season in Palm Beach. Every year since Donald Trump owned Mar-a-Lago and turned it into a private club, the magnificent venue played host to many of the major charities, but not in 2017. It was Trump's first year in office, and for a myriad of reasons, most of which were political in nature, the powerful women and men who run the charities decided instead to run as far away from Mar-a-Lago as possible. More than twenty charities pulled out at the last minute, and they scrambled like crazy to find new venues for their events. Many wound up at the Breakers Hotel, aboard cruise ships, and in any other venue that could hold a guest list.

It's important to note that many of these were the same women and men who treasured their membership at Mar-a-Lago and couldn't wait to see and shake hands with The Donald when they went there for dinner or some special event. To say they were two-faced to turn their backs on him and his club would be putting it mildly. So much for loyalty, hmm?

Palm Beach was abuzz with all the talk about charities pulling out, and negativity about Trump was rampant. But he was my guy. I had worked hard to help get him elected and I was not about to desert him like so many others. In fact, all the negativity inspired me. I saw it as an opportunity to do something Palm Beach had never seen before.

I met with my main Trumpettes and told them my idea: Put on the party of the year to honor Donald Trump's first year in office. "I'll get

Trumpettes from all over the country—all over the globe—to rise up and join us for a red, white, and blue extravaganza. We'll hold it at Mar-a-Lago. Where else? And I want to do it in January, to coincide with the anniversary of his inauguration. That'll give us a jump on the new year with fresh publicity."

My friends thought I was crazy, and they fired questions at me. "How can you make such a monumental decision on the spur of the moment? It takes a full year to put an event like this together, and you want to do it in three and a half months? Without a full-time committee? Without a team? How can you possibly pull it off? How can you possibly win?"

My answer to them was simple. "How can I possibly lose?"

Remember, I'm a warrior in five-inch heels. That's the way I think. That's the way I do things. As my mother often told me, "If you think it, you can do it!" There wasn't a doubt in my mind.

While my friends remained skeptical, they did agree to go on the journey with me. They soon saw a side of me they hadn't seen before. Toni from Hollywood was about to take a run at Palm Beach.

The idea for the evening was firmly implanted in my brain, but there were still a few things I needed—like money, talent, and people. Crossing my fingers and holding my breath, I hired an event planner,

The Red, White & Blue underwriters: (L to R) Denise Rizzuto, Bradley Hillstrom Jr., Dr. Bradley & Tina Hillstrom, Linda Adelson, Fred Assini, Angela & Gary Travato.

Carol Brophy, and boldly guaranteed Mar-a-Lago that at least two hundred people would attend the event. Did I know that for sure? In a way I did, but even I was surprised at the incredible response.

We pegged the ticket price at $300 a person, less than half of what the big charity galas charge. Even luncheons in Palm Beach can cost $350 a ticket. Carol drafted a save-the-date invitation encouraging everyone to wear red, white, and blue. Meanwhile, I made phone calls to talent, rounded up speakers, and sent out a blast to all my Trumpettes around the world.

Things were moving quickly when I received a phone call from Alexandra Clough, a columnist for The Palm Beach Post. "I hear you're planning a party," she said. "Want to talk about it?"

Alexandra and I spoke at length, and I told her all I could about the party. A few days later her article appeared in The Post, and we were off and running. Eleven days later we had sold out not only one ballroom, but two! For the first time in history, Mar-a-Lago had sold out both ballrooms for the same event. And we hadn't even sent out a single invitation.

A few nights later I saw President Trump at Mar-a-Lago, and he inquired about the event. "Is there any chance you could build another ballroom?" I joked. He laughed. "I promise. I'll fill it," I said.

Through the generosity of a couple of Trumpette supporters, I was able to engage the bombastic Judge Jeanine Pirro to be our keynote speaker. Jeanine and Donald have been friends for years, and she is a major supporter of his presidency. Her commitment became a major drawing card. People from all over the country, and many from other countries, made reservations to come. We sold eight tables from California alone. In just a few days we had over seven hundred guests for the main ballroom, and another hundred for the second, smaller ballroom. By the time the event took place, we had another seven hundred people on the waiting list. Something magical was happening. Trump supporters were coming from everywhere, and the Trumpettes were coming out in force.

On the day of the event, my set designer, Cameron Neth, made my vision a reality. With the help of Trumpettes Janet Levy, Suzi Goldsmith, and Denise Rizzuto, Cameron worked tirelessly from early in the morning to get the ballroom ready for the big bash. Huge TV screens were set up throughout both ballrooms so everyone would have a great view of the entertainment. By the time they finished working, the room was a sea of red, white, and blue. And not a minute too soon. The event was scheduled to begin at 6:30 around the pool, but people began arriving as early as 4:30. Excitement was definitely in the air.

That wasn't all that was in the air. Rain and cold were in the forecast, but luckily the rain held off. The cold didn't. It was the coldest night of the year, but the eighty heaters we placed around the pool kept everyone warm and their spirits high.

Speaking of spirits, I'm convinced my mother was looking down on me that evening. I could almost hear her voice. "You did it, honey. Good job!"

Dressed in the colors of the flag, Doug Verga and his Dixieland Band entertained the crowd poolside with their lively New Orleans sound. Cocktails flowed freely while servers passed around food that carried out my traditional Americana theme: cheeseburgers, hot dogs, French fries in a cone, and the hugely popular mac & cheese.

By 7:30 everyone was ushered into the two ballrooms. Once again, America was displayed in all its red, white, and blue glory. It was the most patriotic theme you could imagine. I could feel it all the way down to my white Casadei shoes. This was going to be a night to remember. Once everyone was seated, we kicked off the evening with a vintage video starring John Wayne, called God Bless America. The legendary actor was assisted with the inspirational musical message about America by other

L-R Janet Levy, Fred Williamson, Terry Lee Ebert Mendozza, Suzi Goldsmith

greats from that era, including Bing Crosby, Bob Hope, Lucille Ball, Red Skelton, Phyllis Diller, Dean Martin, Ann-Margret, Johnny Cash, and many, many others. By the end of the video, the crowd was standing and cheering. Check out the video on YouTube. It will give you goosebumps!

After the video the live show began. Christine Rona delivered a stirring rendition of the National Anthem, followed by the President's son Eric Trump and his wife, Lara, a former TV anchor, who took the stage and welcomed the crowd. "There are friends…and there are friends," said Eric, "but Toni is one of a kind."

He related how I had called him three months earlier and said, "Eric, I want to do a great party!"

Toni with Eric and Lara Trump

"Well, here we are!" Eric smiled, and everyone erupted with applause. He went on to say that he was amazed at how many people he had met who had come from so many different states around the country. They ended by saying how much his family loves me. It made me very proud.

Known as the Frank Sinatra of the desert (Palm Springs), Frank DiSalvo belted out the powerful song that he and Ed Gerney had written especially for the President, "Make America Great Again!" You can hear it anytime on our website: TrumpettesUSA.com.

L-R Kendra Reeves, Mike Lindell, and Toni

L-R Frank DiSalvo, Judge Jeanine Pirro, Addy DiSalvo

Roberta Linn

Toni and Robert Davi

Niger Innis, the national spokesperson for CORE, the Congress of Racial Equality, gave a rousing speech in support of President Trump. Mike Lindell, the My Pillow guy who many of us go to bed with every night, followed with his own heartfelt words of support. Mike is now in the Guinness Book of Records as the most watched man on television due to his My Pillow commercials.

After a long, laborious speech from one of our contributors who never met a microphone she didn't fall in love with, Judge Jeanine stepped onto the stage to enthusiastic applause. Jeanine greeted the crowd and commented on how happy she was to be at beautiful Mar-a-Lago. She paused, looked around the Grand Ballroom, then said with a knowing smile, "This sure ain't no shithole!" The crowd roared.

The Philippe Harari Orchestra, especially Philippe himself, kept the magical evening swinging. He worked tirelessly with the talent and provided the accompaniment for Las Vegas legend and former Champagne Lady with Lawrence Welk, Roberta Linn, who also arrived from Palm Springs, where she resides.

The closing act was actor and singer Robert Davi, easily recognizable as the villain in over one hundred movies. But that night, Davi, a staunch supporter of President Trump (not an easy position to take in ultra-liberal Hollywood), shed his tough-guy image and turned on the charm, reminding everyone of Ol' Blue Eyes as he weaved his way through the crowd, mesmerizing the audience with his talent and charm.

By the end of the night, I must have taken five hundred selfies with people from every corner of our great country. I asked them all to share their dedication to the Trumpettes and the President with all their friends and family.

To immortalize the evening, the BBC had been following me around with a camera crew for two weeks prior to the event. Ed Balls, a former UK politician and the host of the one-hour documentary, even moved into the guest suite at my home. I had learned of the BBC's interest around Thanksgiving of 2017. When I saw President Trump at Mar-a-Lago, I told him the BBC wanted to come to the event. Always a quick decision-maker, he okayed it on the spot.

L-R Lara and Eric Trump, Toni and Ed Balls

L-R Toni, Robert Davi, and Ed Balls

At Renato's Restaurant in Palm Beach. Seated L-R: Suebelle Robbins, Sher Kasun, Janet Levy, Terry Ebert Mendozza. Standing L-R: Denise Rizzuto, Toni, Herme de Wyman Miro, Ed Balls

Being on a roll, I quickly added that Japan TV wanted to come as well, ASHAI Television. I got the same response. It was a done deal. ASHAI Television shot the entire evening, and we aired in Japan the next night.

Author Laurence Leamer and his effervescent and glamorous wife, Vesna, were also at the party. Vesna is from Slovenia, the same as Melania. Laurence's 2009 book, Madness Under the Royal Palms, was a best seller. I couldn't put it down. I read it twice. His latest book, soon to be available, is called, *Mar-a-Lago: Inside the Gates of Donald Trump's Presidential Palace.*

Even the Washington Post, certainly not a fan of Trump, was represented by journalist David Fahrenthold. A political analyst, David won a Pulitzer Prize for his coverage of Trump and his campaign. Being an instinctive gambler, I decided to seat him at my table. The gamble paid off as David and I liked each other immediately, and he had nothing but positive things to say about the event.

TOWN AND COUNTRY

Meet the Trumpettes: Inside the World of Donald Trump's Most Adoring Fans

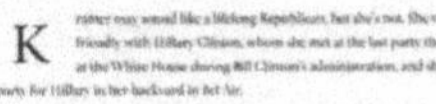

Town and Country Magazine

Other journalists were there as well, including Sam Dangremond from Town and Country Magazine, and Arnelle Vincent from Le Figaro, the oldest daily newspaper in France.

All in all, it was a night to remember, and I couldn't have been happier. Everyone had a great time. Well, almost everyone.

* * * * *

It's been said there are only four emotions: anger, fear, sadness, and happiness. I'd like to add a fifth to that list: jealousy.

People don't gossip about those who fail, so I know my event was a major hit. Unfortunately, my success brought out the jealousy monster in a handful of people. It took me back to my days in Hollywood, where envy and jealousy tend to thrive. But the back-stabbing in Hollywood is like kindergarten compared to some of the sharper knives in Palm Beach. Over the years, I've learned to be strong in the face of adversity. If not, it's easy to fade into oblivion or be devoured by the monsters who find gratification in burying you.

In truth, it was terribly painful trying to comprehend why some people derived such pleasure in wanting to cast a shadow on me, but after dealing with it for a few weeks, I got back on track. I had made up my mind two years earlier to plant my five-inch heels firmly in the footsteps of Donald Trump, and I was damned if I was going to let a few barracudas shove me out of the way.

Throughout my life I have stuck to my guns about what I believed, and I was not about to switch gears. I came to the conclusion that if Trump can get by every day with a target on his forehead, then so can I. After wading through all the gossip, I could only dismiss the pathetic mentality of those who think the whole world revolves around them and the four-square-mile island of hubris known as Palm Beach.

President Trump is Unstoppable…and so am I.

On the positive side, the aftermath of the event stirred even more interest in The Trumpettes. Coverage of my event hit the front pages of The London Times and The Daily Mail. New Trumpettes and Trumpsters have been joining daily, and many from outside the United States.

One of my newest Trumpettes is Gina Rinehart, said to be the richest woman in Australia, a mining magnate and the chairperson of Hancock Prospecting. Another is Her Royal Highness Princess Camilla of Bourbon-Two Sicilies, Duchess of Castro. Both women are incredibly supportive and have offered to work in any way possible for the mission of the Trumpettes.

THE TIMES

A step too far? Ed Balls celebrates with Trump

Henry Zeffman, Political Reporter

January 23 2018, 12:01am, The Times

Ed Balls with Tina Hillstrom and Toni Holt Kramer at President Trump's party

Toni Holt Kramer is a socialite and self-professed "Trumpette"

Mr Balls, the former shadow chancellor who lost his seat at the 2015 general election, spent Saturday night at Mar-a-Lago, Donald Trump's Florida residence, for a party celebrating the first anniversary of his presidency. Rather than demonstrating a dramatic ideological turn to the right, Mr Balls, 50, was filming a BBC travelogue entitled *Ed Balls: My Deep South Road Trip.*

The former *Strictly Come Dancing* contestant's presence in Florida was revealed after he posed with Tina Hillstrom, a member of the "Real Women 4 Trump" campaign, and Toni Holt Kramer, a socialite and self-professed "Trumpette". Few of the pair's fans seemed to recognise Mr Balls, however. After Ms Hillstrom posted the photo on Instagram, one commented: "I can't believe you know Toni Holt."

Mr Cameron, meanwhile, was spotted keeping a low-profile at a damp Disneyland Paris.

Former Prime Minister David Cameron

They tried out Star Tours: The Adventures Continue, a simulator that is based in the Star Wars universe.

Unfortunately for Mr Balls, his visit to Florida meant that he missed Norwich City, the Championship football club of which he is chairman, lose 2-1 at home to Sheffield United. It is not known whether Mr Cameron managed to fit in a visit to Villa Park to watch Aston Villa beat Barnsley 3-1. But then again he did also say that he supported West Ham.

The London Times

Feedback | Like 14.1M | Wednesday, Jan 31st 2018 | 5-Day Forecast

Home | U.K. | News | Sports | U.S. Showbiz | Australia | Femail | Health | Science | Money | Video | Travel | Columnists | DailyMailTV

Ed Balls parties with the 'Trumpettes' at the President's Mar-A-Lago resort as he films a documentary for the BBC

- **Former Shadow Chancellor Ed Balls was snapped at a Trump party**
- **The Strictly star was there as part of his new documentary on the US south**
- **The event was held at Trump's Mar-a-Lago resort in Palm Beach, Florida**

By AMANDA CASHMORE FOR MAILONLINE
PUBLISHED: 14:43 EST, 22 January 2018 | **UPDATED:** 16:28 EST, 22 January 2018

130
View comments

Ed Balls was snapped partying at a **Trump** anniversary event with two staunch supporters of the President.

The previous Shadow Chancellor of the Exchequer was at the exclusive event at the Mar-a-Lago resort filming for his new documentary Ed Balls: My Deep South Road Trip.

Tickets for one couple to attend the event in Palm Beach, **Florida**, cost $1,000 (£716), reports **The Mirror**.

In an Instagram post, Trump supporter Tina Hillstrom (left) said: 'BBC interview Ed Balls. Tina & Toni Holt Kramer changing the way women talk politics'

President Trump himself was unable to attend his own party due to the budget crisis.

Balls had been interviewing two trump fans Tina Hillstrom and Toni Holt Kramer, founder of the Trumpettes USA.

In an Instagram post, Hillstrom uploaded a picture of the three of them with the caption: 'BBC interview Ed Balls. Tina & Toni Holt Kramer changing the way women talk politics'.

Confused people took to Twitter to air their puzzlement over what was going on. One said: 'I assume this isn't Ed Balls living it up at Mar-a-Lago but whoever it is looks worryingly like him'.

The former Shadow Chancellor photographed with Trumpette Sher Kason. Tickets for one couple to attend the event in Palm Beach, Florida, cost $1,000 (£716)

Ed Balls with Toni Holt Kramer (centre) who he was interviewing for his documentary My Deep South Road Trip

Another added: 'I thought this was photoshopped. What is Ed Balls doing at Mar-a-Lago? How to lose any remaining credibility you may have once had'.

Speaking about his show, Ed Balls said: 'It's one thing to swap being a politician for reality TV and embarrass your family in the process. It's quite another thing to swap reality TV for the US Presidency and turn the world upside down.

'I've always loved visiting the American south - the food and the music are fabulous and there's so much to learn from its history. But I was as shocked as anyone else by the way the south helped sweep Trump to victory.

'So I'm looking forward to visiting the communities at the heart of the Trump revolution, getting to know the voters who elected him and finding out what they think of him one year on.'

The Daily Mail

I've continued to do interviews both in print and on television, including a "live from Palm Beach" segment for Good Morning Australia, where I have been a frequent guest along with other Trumpettes. Every week I receive another request from another show or publication somewhere in the world.

Underwriters and guests are already lining up for my next Trump event. I'm beginning to believe that the Trumpettes are a new kind of "we the people" political force.

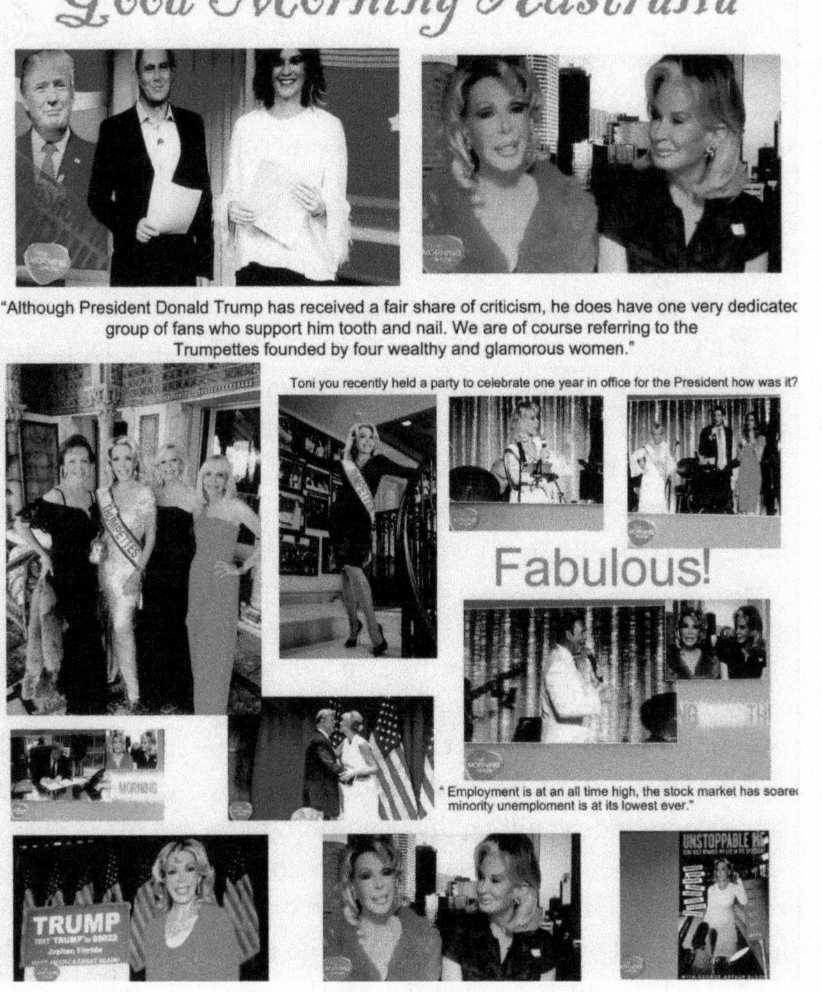

Good Morning Australia

CHAPTER SIXTY-FOUR

Reflections

I give a lot of credit for my success to Peggy Clarke, who probably wouldn't know who I am today, assuming she's even still alive. Peggy, I wish I could find you. Or maybe, if you're out there, you'll find me. Facebook me. Find me on my website, TrumpettesUSA.com. Or, ToniHoltKramer.com. Or, UnstoppableMe.com.

Peggy was my fellow model at the Huntington Hartford Modeling Agency who had taken me to lunch at the exclusive 21 Club in New York when I was sixteen and offered me the most valuable advice of my life. "Don't take your beauty for granted. Do other things. Learn languages, educate yourself, read. Read everything you can get your hands on. Become aware of what's going on around you. Turn yourself into an interesting woman. And never rely on your beauty alone because someday that will fade. This way, you'll have something to fall back on."

I don't know if I took it to heart at exactly that moment, but her advice made a tremendous impression on me. I never forgot it—and somewhere along the line, I did take it seriously. I'm fairly certain it's what drove me to be who I am today.

For example, I never asked myself if I could be a Copa Girl or questioned whether I could be a model—I just went for it. Regardless of the fact that I had no experience, I never second-guessed myself when I chose to become a Hollywood reporter—I just made it happen. I never asked myself if I could get involved in politics—I just did. I learned French because I wanted to speak another language. I jumped headfirst into the stock market because I wanted to increase and protect what I had. That in turn taught me a lot about politics. You can't do the stock market without understanding the conditions of the world.

As I think about Peggy Clarke's words to me all those years ago, I realize that I have so much advice of my own that I want to share, so many lessons I've learned from the struggles and successes in my life that I think could be of help to others. Most important is to never fear failure.

While I acknowledge I've had angels pop into my life who have helped me beyond measure in times of need, I feel I've worked hard to earn everything I've achieved and I owe a lot of that to my unwillingness to fail. I never start something thinking, *What if I don't succeed? What if something goes wrong?* If I did, I'd never get out of bed in the morning.

I believe you need drive and ambition to be successful. You have to constantly test yourself and stretch your limitations. Learn, learn, learn! It's all too easy to back your car into your garage, close the door, and cry about everything that's wrong in your life. Life is way too short and much too precious to waste. Don't put up unnecessary roadblocks for yourself. As for me, I never let the fact that I didn't have a formal education stop me from reaching for the brass ring, just like I did on that merry-go-round at Coney Island when I was a child. Like my mother said, "If you believe in something and you think it…you can do it."

In a slightly different way, this was the simple advice I tried to pass on to Poppy and her friends that night on the street corner in Palm Springs. It's this same advice I want to pass on now. Nothing is more important than curiosity and the desire to learn something new every single day. I believe these are the first steps in finding the secret to happiness.

Sometimes I'm sorry I'm only one person. I often feel there isn't enough of me to go around because I want to live so many different lives and be in so many different places and meet so many different people all at once. I'm constantly hungry for knowledge and experiences.

I recently came across the traits of a Gemini: socially outgoing, curious, prone to banter, creative and quick to task, emotionally unreachable and difficult to pin down. And finally, there is a huge discrepancy between how a Gemini would like to be perceived and how she or he really is. I guess you can call me a true Gemini. Just like our president, Donald J. Trump.

Looking back on my marriages—the ones I've chosen to share with you—I firmly believe that some of my husbands have given me the college education I never had. Thanks to them, I went to the College of Life. Or maybe it was the University of Survival.

Tony Murray tutored me on how to run a business and exposed me to jet-set society. John Yantis taught me about finances and the stock market and, in an ironic lesson learned, made it abundantly clear that you need to be careful about whom you trust. Arthur Crowley provided guidance to me through the intricacies of our legal system and, by example, showed me the importance of the proper work ethic. He also taught me that you should never sign anything you don't read and fully understand. Girls, are you paying attention?

The Universe and God blessed me when I married my darling Bobby. He has given me the freedom to be who I am and has encouraged me to express myself without limitations or conditions. He's my best friend, the love of my life, and the dearest, most considerate person I've ever known. Not once have I sneezed in the middle of the night that Bobby—still fast asleep—hasn't reached into his pajama pocket to give me a Kleenex. Never once do I leave the house without Bobby telling me to be careful, to watch where I'm going, and to drive carefully. He worries about every single thing I do. And the icing on the cake is that every year he sends me a love letter. The following is an excerpt from the very first one he wrote:

> My Darling Toni:
>
> I have always wanted to write you of my feelings and thoughts but somehow I never have. But now on this special day of your birth I feel I must tell you just how grateful I am to be married to you.
>
> I am not so good as a writer but I must tell you the feeling I get when you walk into the room, the relief I feel when I know you're home safe—the thrill of holding your hand—just knowing we're together is my Blessing from God.
>
> Never a day or night apart…no words could say more. I pray God will grant us many, many more years to love and cherish each other.
>
> I always close with "I love you." Please always remember no matter how often I say it—it means I love and cherish you with my heart and soul…always & always.
>
> May God bless us both. Bobby

Without question I am a far, far better person than I was before I married Bobby. Growing up an only child—and abandoned by my father at an early age—I was very fortunate to inherit an extended family when Bobby and I were married. Up until then, my life was very full but not enriched with family other than my mother. All of that has changed now. Even David and Adam call Bobby their dad.

Bobby's son Steve, an attorney, lives in LA with his wife, Wendy, and we love spending time with them. They have three wonderful grown children, Jennifer, Jordan, and Jonathan. Richard, Bobby's other son from his second wife, lives in Montana with his wife, Beth, and their two children, Marina and Nevada.

Someone recently asked me what my mother would think of my book. I think she would be very proud. So much of her life was built around doing everything in her power to give me the chances I would need to succeed. I don't think I let her down. Somehow I've managed to survive this roller-coaster ride of my life and make the most of my opportunities. Through it all, my mother's faith in me was unwavering, and for that I have no words to express the love I have in my heart for her.

After Mother's death, my cousin Enid told me she had a visit from my mother, a psychic vision. Enid had never had an experience like that in all her years of meditating, so it really shook her up. All of a sudden, she told me, my mother was there with her. To me, that vision was a sign that my move to Florida was the right thing to do. I'm convinced Mother wanted Enid and me to be together after all those years of being apart. My relationship with Enid is one of complete trust, and I'm convinced—as is she—that we share one brain. We know we have each other's backs and can rely on one another. Enid is like my sister, and to have her and her husband, Louis, in my life now is an unbelievable gift.

In many ways, Mother was an artist—she created the canvas that became my life. I know she's around me this very minute, watching every move I make. I really believe that. If I had only one word to describe how my mother would feel right now, I'd say...victorious.

Yes, victorious. To be victorious is not only to win but to survive.

But then she would add, "Honey, what are you going to do tomorrow? And don't forget to plan for next year...and never give up. Move forward with passion and the belief you can do anything you want to."

So, with that in mind, my friends, I'll see you all around the country as I plan to hit every talk show that will have me. Wherever we might be, if we cross paths, please don't forget to come up and tell me you read my book. I really want to meet you. As I said, curiosity and the desire to learn something new every day are what drive me.

I can't believe how many past friends have found me on Facebook, and I them. For years I rejected social media as a fad. I thought, *Who needs it?* Now, not only do I believe in it, I understand it. Sure, it's addictive—but in a good way.

Social media is good for people's lives—and not only the younger generation. Too many people are lonely and many feel they're too old to make new friends. Or they're shy or they think they don't look as good as they used to, so they don't want to go out and do things. In essence, they feel socially abandoned. Truth be told, older folks become isolated—they can't help themselves. Isolation is the road to the cemetery.

Facebook, on the other hand, has given everyone an outlet and the ability to find old friends and make new ones, all from the comfort of their iPad.

For me, Facebook has pushed back the horizon line and given me something else to look forward to each and every day. It's a portal into knowledge. I can ask questions and share opinions, trade photographs of the past and present, and connect with people all over the world. Anyone and everyone can do Facebook.

Thank you, Mark Zuckerberg. In your own way, you've helped to save humanity. Social media is so totally relevant today, I wonder what took me so long to embrace it. No matter, I'm there now. And I know in my heart, if Mother were alive, she'd be on Facebook too.

Never give up, never give in, and above all, never look back!

Love to all, Toni

Toni and co-author George Arthur Bloom.

FINAL CHAPTER 2019

Yet to be Written

"WE SHALL SEE…!"